A TALE OF TWO LIVES

THE SUSAN LEFEVRE
FUGITIVE STORY

by

Marie S. Walsh

aka

Susan LeFevre

A TALE OF TWO LIVES

Copyright © 2011 by
Marie S. Walsh

ISBN: 978-0-6154468-8-2

A TALE OF TWO LIVES

With special thanks to my friends whose help and encouragement in writing this book was invaluable;

Christopher Keil, Tracy Burr, Steve South, Terri and Alan Wise, Judy & Dr Paul Bernstein, Albert & Flo LeFevre, Dr Chris & Patti Gorman

Website: http://www.SusanLeFevre.com
by
Cats at Keyboards, Ltd.

A TALE OF TWO LIVES

*This book is dedicated to my husband and children
whose love and support gave me strength throughout
this difficult journey.*

Chapter 1

Saginaw, Michigan, May 2004

The sun's first dim rays light up the fluorescent pink walls—the eye-popping color I chose to have them painted when I was 16.

I am nearly 50 now. My husband, Alan, is sound asleep beside me, my children are safe back home in California, and my parents are in their bedroom downstairs. We are visiting my parents in what I know will be the last time I see my mother. I am certain she will die today.

The last 12 hours have been hectic and harried. My sister's phone call, announcing that the priest has just given Mom last rites, set in motion a chain of events I seem to have walked through like a zombie. Somehow, Alan arranged the last-minute tickets. Somehow, I packed a bag and attended to the myriad details of dispatching the kids to friends' houses, leaving instructions for the housecleaner, changing the message on the answering machine, and firing up the alarm system.

But all I could think of during the frantic drive to the San Diego airport was that if we missed the plane, I would never see my mother alive again. At the terminal, I handed my driver's license to the TSA screener and held my breath. He checked the name—Marie Walsh—looked at the picture, looked back up at me, then handed me the license. I

1

exhaled a sigh of relief. I wondered how many more years I would have to worry whenever I handed someone my ID. A moment later Alan and I were waved through the metal detector and we ran to our gate.

Later, in my mother's room, time is frozen at 30 years ago, the last time I was here. The green shag carpet feels the same under my bare feet. I run my hand over the country wallpaper embossed with baskets of peonies, as I used to. The familiar bedside table is crowded now with pill bottles, but I recognize the scratch in the table-leg nearest the bed. Only the sickroom smell—of plastic bottles and multicolored medications, of illness and decay—betrays the passage of time.

On the dresser top, under the crucifix, is the wedding photo of my parents. With the arched entry of the church behind them, they look like a glamorous, updated version of *American Gothic*. My father is tall and dark and jaunty, my mother smiling and spirited, her shoulder-length blond hair seeming to bob animatedly in the still photo.

Today, my mother is prostrate with disease and groaning in pain, and I sit down carefully on the edge of her mattress. My father, standing on the opposite side of the bed from me, hovers over us. A veil of silence and duty hangs between my mother and me, but I reach through it and caress her shoulder gently. Her low groaning sounds like someone else's voice.

My father reaches over and places a pill in my mother's mouth. She begins to choke; he tries to give her water, but she coughs it back. She can't swallow.

"It's stuck!" she manages to say. "Use a knife, anything. Push it down!"

A TALE OF TWO LIVES

My heart rate soars and my fists clench. "Why are you giving her a pill?" I demand. "She needs morphine."

My father is suddenly abashed, as crestfallen as a scolded little boy. His long, serious face looks weary and defeated. Resolute in his loyalty to my mother, he has taken care of her for decades, as rheumatoid arthritis limited her movements, deformed her limbs, and wracked her with pain—her own body at war with itself, the white cells attacking the red, the body tearing itself apart. Even now as cancer consumes her, he has rarely left her side, and perhaps he senses, as I do, that these are her last moments.

"She doesn't like the idea of *hard* drugs," he says, "so they give her Vicodine for the pain."

Hard drugs, *hard* drugs. His emphasis is clear, and the words open wounds from the time when hard drugs tore my family apart. Even on her deathbed, even in this agony, my mother won't allow *hard* drugs to soothe her pain. Her screams of agony are past bearing.

"She's dying of cancer, not a toothache! She needs something stronger!" I tell my father. "You need to call the hospice nurse and get her some morphine right away."

My father doesn't argue with me. "I will," he says, and heads for the kitchen to place the call. I realize that if the nurse comes to deliver morphine, I will have to hide in another room.

I stroke my mother's back. I can feel her still fighting tenaciously against her failing body. I've seen this before. I've been trained to work in hospice care, and I recognize the phenomenon. It's quite common: People hang on through great pain because of unresolved issues. I reach through the veil again.

"Listen to me, Mom. You've been a wonderful mother and grandmother. We all love you very much and we'll all be all right. It's okay for you to leave us now. You were a good mom, a good woman."

She looks up at me. She can't answer, but I see she understands. I think I see relief on her face, so I go on. "We all had so many good times together. You don't need to suffer any longer. It's okay to say good-bye."

This is all I can do. I am helpless before this kind of suffering, helpless in the face of this terrible illness. *Please God*, I pray. *Let her let go.*

Her frightened look fades and her eyes glisten with tears. She struggles to speak. I can feel her mustering the last grains of her strength. Finally, in a whisper, my mother says, "I'm sorry. I should have been there for you...I shouldn't have told them. I'm so sorry."

A sharp pain shoots through my chest. And I realize that it isn't just the illness my mother is dying from; it is also the guilt—still burning, perhaps even more fiercely these last weeks. "I don't care what you did, Mom. There is nothing for you to feel sorry about. You've suffered enough. We all have. It was a long time ago and we all made mistakes back then. All that matters is that we pulled through. We've had so many happy years together!"

I have been fleeing my past for most of my life. But now again it seems that what happened when I was 19 will never let us go. My dying mother is still a victim of it. My husband and children, though they are not aware of it, are victims as well. How many innocent generations will be touched by this?

My mother opens her eyes and I stroke her forehead. Her skin is thin and papery. "Turn me to the window," she says haltingly. "I want to see the light."

A TALE OF TWO LIVES

It is not hard to shift her frail body. Her limbs flop lifelessly and she moans again.

I sit down again at her side and watch her face. Her skin seems to be growing darker. Then her features—nose, chin, ears—seem to change shape. My mind freezes and I stare when, just as suddenly as the transformation had begun, it stops. The strange distortions disappear and are replaced by her familiar features. As I am trying to collect my thoughts, I see a shadowy image rise from her body and float upward, as if on a draft of warm air.

I lean down close to my mother's barely breathing body and hold her in my arms. I don't believe in the supernatural, so I reason that the stress and emotion of the morning must be affecting my imagination. Her head lies cradled in my lap and her face is no longer distorted by pain; her groaning has ceased. She releases a long sigh and as I gently stroke her head, her exhalation ends, and she is still. Her pain is over.

I sit for a moment holding her, then call out to my father. "Dad... she's gone."

My father runs into the room and releases a primal cry, like that of a wounded animal. He has lost his life's partner.

The two of us cradle her until her skin begins to cool under our hands.

Throughout the day, the family gathers. We congregate in the living room. Funeral arrangements must be made, questions answered. It is afternoon before Alan and I have a chance to sit down alone together. I bring him a cup of tea, let him take his first sip, then tell him that I want us to leave Michigan tomorrow and fly back home. "I don't want to stay for the memorial," I say. "I came here to see my mother alive, to be with her at the last. That's what's important. Her spirit has moved on." I pause. "And this way, you can get back to work."

Alan is shocked and bewildered. "It's your mother, and all of your family will be here. They'll need you. What kind of person doesn't go to her own mother's funeral?"

The kind of person who has never told you the secret of her past. The kind of person who still sometimes wakes screaming in the night and cannot explain to you why—not without revealing everything she has kept from you for the 18 years you've been married. Since I can't voice this, I continue to speak of my dislike of funerals, my abhorrence of their morbid character, my eagerness to go home to our children. The rest of my family remains silent as well, and we prepare to leave Michigan.

As I put down my suitcase by the front door, Alan begins loading the car. My father reaches out to embrace me, his eyes filled with sympathy as well as sadness. He understands how much I would have wanted to attend my mother's funeral with the rest of the family. He had no illusion about how difficult it was for me, once again, to come up with excuses to my husband in order to hide my "special circumstances." "You're a remarkable daughter," he says, "You've accomplished so much—out of nothing."

I hug his tall aging frame firmly and whisper, "We've both had a long, winding road to travel over the years, Dad, but we've survived it." I take his hand and squeeze it in mine, adding, "I know how much you're going to miss Mom, we all are, but you're going to be all right. You're remarkable too."

Our flight back to California is fraught with tension and disquiet. Alan is stunned, distraught, wondering what kind of person he married—a woman who won't attend her own mother's funeral. I am mired in grief and am haunted by the extent of the guilt my mother carried all these years despite my assertions that she was not to blame.

But there is another feeling coursing through my body as well. Today, as I sit in silence beside my angry and confused husband in the plane, I feel the first glimmers of hope.

It was for my mother's sake that I have kept my secret for 30 years. It was to honor her wish that I not "dredge up the past." Mom had been confined to a motorized wheelchair for many years. "All I have left is my dignity; please don't take that away," she would say.

In the new identity I have created, in the new and "proper" life I have forged, I have built a set of unbreakable rules that prevent me from sharing my story even with my husband, certainly with my children. Like me, my mother had been branded forever by what happened when I was 19. While she lived, the least I could do was lessen her suffering. So I did.

But now she is dead. As I fly west toward California, toward our children waiting for our return, I see an opportunity. Under a new law, the crime of which I was convicted in Michigan 30 years ago is no longer grounds for imprisonment. The cast of characters has changed. The world has changed. I have changed. Maybe I really can clear my name. Maybe I can finally live a completely normal life. Maybe I can actually be free. Flying into the setting sun, I try to imagine a day when I can tell my children and my husband the truth about my past, and once again live as a free human being.

Chapter 2

Back in Carmel Valley, I settle again into my usual routine of shuttling kids to sports and friends' homes, working in their classrooms, and indulging in my own activities and various volunteer projects. Many of my evenings are spent attending my husband's business functions and fund-raisers.

My mother's death has jarred events of the past to the forefront of my mind. The knowledge that I am a fugitive is always with me, hanging over me like a dark cloud but I work hard not let it undermine the life I've built. I long to forget about my troubling circumstances and move forward, yet I know that it would be a dangerous move to become complacent. I have to constantly remind myself that I don't have a normal life. The smallest mistake, such as driving over the speed limit, could be fateful. I also have to stay diligent in order to get evidence to fill in the missing pieces in my unusual conviction. I've never lost hope that some day I'd be able to vindicate myself. I know I can't go on much longer, living outside the law like this.

When the kids were small, I took a break from trying to resolve things since I had no one to care for them in the event my efforts backfired and I was again torn away from my life. Instead, during those years, I wrote almost every day about the circumstances of my arrest and the so-called due process. It was as if I felt writing it down enough times would give me the answers I needed. Over the years I contacted a number of attorneys. Even they were baffled about my case. The attorneys I consulted didn't believe what I was saying could be true. They had never heard of a drug offense involving a teaspoon of drugs, resulting in a 10-to-20-year prison sentence, especially for a teenager who'd never been in trouble before. A couple of the attorneys said they could help me, but all they did was take my money and then quit taking my calls.

No matter how many times I went over the details of my conviction, the same questions arose. Why was my sentence so out of line with others when I was only accompanying a boy who sold the drugs? It was my friend Ritchie who took two and a half grams of heroin, about a teaspoon, to a guy in a parking lot. The under cover agent, posing as a druggie, offered him $300 for an amount of drugs worth less than $50. Ritchie wasn't a drug dealer either, but he also received a 10-to-20-year sentence. And there were other questions that persisted. Why had I been told in the presence of my attorney and my father that I would get probation if I agreed to plead guilty? Why had my uncle, a prominent attorney in town who said he knew the prosecutor on my case personally, advised me to take the plea deal, knowing, as I found out later, that it was a ruse?

I did learn in the years after my conviction that the 26-year-old drug agent who set up the arrest, a guy named Reno Greely, rose up the ladder quickly within the force and was now the state police chief in Michigan. He was also part of a small but powerful network in the state working toward pushing for new laws that would expand the prison industry.

It was difficult to find out what was occurring in Michigan after I'd left, but from time to time I made a point to check an absconder website on the Internet that listed people with outstanding warrants in Michigan. There were more than 100,000 names on the list and many had violent histories, which seemed to explain why no one had ever looked for me after the day I escaped. My name was mentioned, but mine was the only entry that didn't have a photo attached. I was relieved that my picture wasn't on there, and I wondered if Greely's being police chief was responsible for keeping it off the site. I knew the details of my case were not ones he would have wanted exposed.

It had been more than 20 years since my escape, and my parents said no one had ever come to their home in Saginaw or questioned any members of the family. It seemed obvious my benign case was not a high priority. By now I was aware of the new changes in drug laws that occurred a few years after my conviction that made it mandatory to have more evidence to ensure someone was actually a drug dealer, as opposed to relying on the word of a drug agent who had much to gain by stretching the facts. First-time offenders found with 55 grams of drugs or less were given probation. (The flip side of the new laws was that someone possessing over 55 grams received the equivalent of a life sentence.) The laws were enacted specifically to prevent abuses that had occurred in cases like mine.

So far I knew I'd been lucky, but my luck was about to change in an instant.

One day not long after my mother's death, a relative contacts me to alert me that my picture has appeared on the website. I also learn that Greely is no longer state police chief. All those years my picture stayed off this site, but now he has hurriedly left office—the result of a scandal over racial profiling—and my picture is up. I feel Greely has kept me out of the public eye because he doesn't want

questions asked. But now, my photo is there for all to see—
or rather, the mug shot of Susan LeFevre, 19 years old.

I know this isn't good news, and not long after
hearing about the addition of my picture to the site, I hear
from another relative that a parole officer in Saginaw is
calling family members and banging on their doors to ask if
I am still alive and living in the country. I have no idea why
this officer chose me from the lengthy list.

This is stressful news, but I continue to try not to
give in to fear. I keep busy while trying to decide what I
should do. I remind myself of my many blessings and
during the day I'm able to stay upbeat, but nighttime is a
different story. Sometimes I awake from disturbing
nightmares that involve my being chased. I jolt awake just
as I am being grabbed, and a couple of times I screamed
out. Other nights I lie in the darkness, gripped by a sense of
dread and fear. I feel vulnerable as the full realization of my
plight engulfs me. It terrifies me to know that I was facing
many years in the notoriously brutal Michigan prison
system. I already know the kind of horrific place these
prisons are after being in one for almost a year before I
escaped. Panic and anxiety flood my mind. I want to wake
my husband sleeping beside me and tell him what happened
to me as a teenager and the struggle I was faced with trying
to turn things around. I want to have someone understand
what I went through, but I know I can't. I don't want him to
have to share in the nightmare, nor do I want to allow the
past to contaminate any more of my present life. I know I
have to suffer this alone.

I renew my effort to contact someone to give me
legal advice. I find that all of the attorneys I call are anxious
to talk to me when I tell them I was arrested on a drug
charge and need representation, but when I go on to explain

that I wasn't involved in selling drugs and was innocent of the charges for which I was convicted, I can feel a sudden drop in the excitement on the other end of the line. Defending a moneyed drug trafficker is one thing; defending someone who was railroaded and doesn't have a lot of money is another.

Finding private moments in which to call attorneys and conjure up the grim details of what happened to me at 19 is a grueling experience I never get used to. The first few attempts I make end with me hanging up abruptly because I am overcome by emotion in the middle of the conversation. When an attorney asks about my sentence I find it impossible to say the words "ten to twenty" or "prison," and I break down.

On the surface I have the life I had always wanted: loving family, close friends, and the respect of the community around us. No one would have suspected that privately I am dealing with such a dark secret. Only a few family members and friends know about my circumstances, and they live far away; when I do see them, my past is a topic we rarely discuss.

So for the next year, the parole/absconder/probation agent, whatever he is, continues to telephone and visit anyone with the last name of LeFevre in Michigan. In other states, he sends police to bang on doors of family members, still asking whether I am alive and if they know my whereabouts. Some have an idea of where I am and some do not, but all say they have no information. No one knows anything more than possibly my phone number.

Still, I begin to feel the first pinch of a tightening noose.

I begin to prepare my children for the possibility that I may be gone for a while. I try to train them to do more around the house. It's another secret for me to keep, as I encourage the kids to take on more domestic responsibilities.

I finally reach an attorney in Detroit named Margaret who sounds honest and informed. She advises me against turning myself in no matter how difficult it gets. "Michigan is rated worse than most third world countries for the way they treat prisoners and the excessive length of sentences handed out. The human rights group Amnesty International lists Michigan as having some of the most brutal and corrupt prisons in the world," Margaret says solemnly. "And I can't imagine why they would go after you thirty years later for a small nonviolent offense. The state is broke and prisons are already overcrowded. The agent is probably doing a few routine calls and he'll go away soon. I wouldn't worry about it."

"It's hard not to worry," I tell her. "Week after week he keeps harassing my family members and it only seems to be getting worse."

I continue to talk to more than a dozen Michigan attorneys from all over the state, trying to find someone to help me. With each phone call, the portrait they paint of the state's justice system is bleak. Again, a few lawyers say, "Sure, send us a retainer and we'll see what we can do." I've been down that road before. Others speak frankly. Over and over I hear the same message. "Few people have any idea how aggressive the prison industry has become," says one. "They're the most powerful lobbying group in the state. The prison industry strong-arms the government into giving them more money while teachers and police officers are being laid off and roads are crumbling. It's a very lucrative business for many. They don't let anyone go; it would set a dangerous precedent."

When I tell lawyers that the case is from Saginaw, the response is even more cynical. It seems the majority of defense attorneys are familiar with Barney Duncan, the prosecutor in Saginaw and the person who held sway over my case.

"I'll take your money if you want to give it to me," says a well-known Lansing attorney, "but I'll tell you right now you're just wasting it. Duncan is known as the most perverse prosecutor in the state. A lot of attorneys see him as being in the pocket of the prison industry."

"But I am not guilty," I counter, "I have evidence now that I was set up. I don't want to uproot my family and make them suffer for something that happened to me."

"It doesn't matter. Keeping innocent people in prison is like a notch on Duncan's belt," says the lawyer. "It shows the industry he's really tough and will deliver. They seem to support anyone they believe will help expand the industry."

I tell him, "I can prove how corrupt my conviction was. I have evidence to prove the drug agent lied about information against me and apparently against many other innocent people as well. I was told that cases were overturned because the defendants were able to prove Greely falsified evidence. These guys set kids up just to boost their career."

"I had guys with wagonloads of evidence proving their innocence, but Duncan fought their release all the way," the lawyer says. "He couldn't have cared less whether they were innocent or not." I can hear him wince as he says this.

The guy at least cares, but when I try to hire him, he says he can't take my case for at least a month because he has a trial coming up that will take all his time and energy. I want someone to get on this right away. And while most of the lawyers I talk to tell me to keep running at any cost—whether I am innocent or not—I don't see how I can live much longer with people threatening my family.

The information I've been receiving is depressing. What kind of strange coincidence was it that the drug agent who lied about evidence against me was later made a police chief and the prosecutor in charge of deciding on my case now has a reputation as a sociopath? I'd never met Duncan, but a couple of years ago I'd seen him on a TV show, *Dateline*, that featured a controversial case he handled. The segment was about Duncan doggedly pursuing a man for a murder that it seemed highly unlikely the man committed. Though there were no witnesses, and all evidence pointed to another man who had left the country, Duncan pushed for a life sentence, and in a Saginaw courtroom he got it. The show was overwhelmingly critical of Duncan and featured legal experts from the Michigan Innocence Project who pointed to his history of prosecutorial misconduct. The eeriest thing was the smug way Duncan looked at the camera, as if knowing he looked good to the prison industry. The critical tone aimed at Duncan seemed to have as much effect as accusing a Klu Klux Klan member of being a racist—in front of the clan.

It is hard to describe my sense of urgency. A fugitive is never free. In your head, you are always on the run. Hovering always on the fringe of your brain is the knowledge that everything you have can be taken away in a split second if you are found out. So I keep calling, and finally I reach an attorney in Grand Rapids who sounds optimistic and says he can file what in Michigan law is called a 6500 motion as well as a commutation request to the governor. The 6500 motion is a claim that something fundamentally wrong took place in the original trial or during the conviction process, and that the convicted person is thus entitled to relief from the conviction or the sentence. As for the commutation request, the lawyer feels my chances should be good since my charge was nonviolent and so long ago.

The governor is looking for cases of nonviolent offenders to release. She has come under a lot of pressure from the state's chamber of commerce, which is collecting signatures from Michigan businesses that are fuming about the recent tax hike, the money from which is going straight to the prison industry.

The lawyer also feels that the politics may be turning my way. The prison industry has grown 400 percent in the last 15 years, and in his assessment, the state has gone wild arresting people "just to fill the prisons and create jobs." For these reasons, he thinks the time may be ripe for the governor to look favorably on my petition for a review of my sentence.

"Can you start proceedings while I remain free?" I ask.

"I can file the motion and commutation request without your being present. I've done it before. If things go well and we can negotiate something, you could fly back here to Michigan later." He assures me that he will start working on the case as soon as he receives my retainer.

"Are you sure you will be able to start working on this right away? This parole officer is really starting to alarm people in my family, and I don't want them to come to my house and throw me in jail."

16

"I'll get right on it," he says.

Once again, my hopes rise, and I send the retainer.

I feel nervous for the first time in my home and spend a lot of time traveling up to Orange County to be with a longtime friend, who is dying of cancer. I trained as a hospice worker a few months earlier and the education proves invaluable in helping me deal with her impending death, and seeing what she is going through helps me put my own situation in perspective. My friend is younger than I and very much in denial about dying and having to leave her children and husband behind. It is a wrenching time.

My prolonged absences to be with her put a strain on my marriage and family. Much of the time, my son now comes home from high school to an empty house. I think I may be in my own kind of denial. I still have never told my family about my past. The thought of doing so is difficult to deal with, and I manage to persuade myself that maybe they never have to know.

I keep calling the Grand Rapids lawyer, but he is always in the midst of a new case and says he is still waiting to get my records—the essential first step. "It's such an old case, it must be hard for them to find," he says. This seems odd, since records are usually available right away. Every few days I call and he promises he'll start on my case the following Monday.

Meanwhile, I'm still getting phone calls from family members who continue to receive calls from the parole officer. He continues to initiate that police bang on the doors of relatives' homes. His search for me has been going on for almost a year and a half. He is still not sure if I am in the country or even alive, but at one point he tells family members that if I am alive I should turn myself in, because since laws were changed and the amount of drugs involved is minuscule—it is only probationary now—there is a good probability that I would be released right away. His reassurance to my relatives is of course absurd: I've been trying to turn myself in for years.

Over the years I had two attorneys try to negotiate terms for me to turn myself in. They contacted the Saginaw prosecutor to ask him if he would reconsider my unusually long sentence and the fact that I would agree to surrender. It would save the state money, and hopefully I could get this resolved one way or the other. The first attorney I approached was my own uncle. I had contacted him about talking to the prosecutor in Saginaw before anyone began looking for me. My uncle was a prominent attorney in Saginaw and just happened to be a close personal friend of Duncan's for more than two decades. He not only socialized frequently with Duncan, but his daughter, whom I had known as little Ruthie, a cousin I hadn't seen since she was in grade school, worked for several years for Duncan as an assistant prosecutor. I asked only that Duncan agree to reconsider the long sentence I had received and the bizarre circumstances of my conviction. My uncle was well aware that I had been told that I'd been promised probation at the time and he knew I had never touched drugs again after I left Michigan more than two decades earlier. The response I got was shocking. He said, "Duncan says that under no conditions are you to come back to Michigan. If you do, he says he'll make sure you get more years on top of the ten to twenty years you already have."

This was upsetting news but not the end of it. My uncle went on: "Duncan really hates your guts. He said if you surface, he'll make sure you regret it."

I was dumfounded. I asked my uncle, "Why would he hate my guts? I've never met him. He wasn't even in office till ten years after I left the state. I don't know how he could legally give me more time for a charge for which I had already received the maximum penalty possible. He couldn't have been referring to the escape because it occurred in Detroit, where he had no jurisdiction. What is he talking about? Why wouldn't he want to try to resolve this?"

"Beats me, but the good news is, Michigan is so broke they wouldn't be able to afford extraditing you back if anything did happen."

"Uncle Jim, you can't imagine how hard it is to live like this, worrying about my children and my husband finding out. Not knowing from moment to moment when this could explode in my face. Did you tell Duncan I was told I would get probation? Did you tell him the amount of drugs involved, that people get probation for amounts ten times that amount now?"

He didn't bother to answer. He handed the phone to my father, and that was the last I heard from him. To be sure my uncle wasn't making this up for personal reasons, I asked another local attorney to talk to Duncan. He got the same threatening response: if I turned myself in I'd be sorry—he would increase my sentence a lot more. If I knew what was good for me, I would stay away. The attorney had never heard anything like it. Why would a prosecutor tell a fugitive not to turn herself in? The attorney reiterated the same thing my uncle told me—that Duncan was hostile just hearing my name.

It was a complete mystery. How could someone whom I had never met hate my guts? All I know—and all I can learn from family members and friends in Michigan with whom I keep in touch—is that my uncle is a personal friend of the person preventing me from gaining my freedom, and that this man, Duncan, who is president of the state prosecutors association headquartered in Lansing, works closely with Greely. It is a tight network: Greely, the drug agent turned state police chief who arrested me; Duncan, the prosecutors' prosecutor; and my uncle, the high-profile attorney. The first two even work in close physical proximity and have worked together in Lansing for 20 years. That is also, of course, where the prison industry lobby lives and works.

I have been Marie Walsh for more than 30 years now. My other "identities" are Alan's wife and Maureen's or Katie's or Alan Junior's mom, but I haven't been Susan LeFevre for three decades. Although I live as a fugitive, and am careful to avoid being photographed when my community activism generates a mention in newspapers, the majority of the time I am Marie Walsh, mother, volunteer, avid tennis player, bridge aficionado. But the persistent drumbeat of phone calls alerting me that someone is out there searching is like a recurring cancer. Susan is being resurrected; the girl I buried so long ago while driving across the Midwest is coming back from the past—a corpse raised from the grave. I face the grim task of knowing I will have to tell my family the facts about my past. At the very least, I will need to explain it to my husband before it all blows up in my face.

It's a decision I have dreaded for many years. How do you tell someone something like this? I continue putting it off waiting for the right moment, but it never seems to be the right time.

Then, one evening during dinner I receive a call. The voice on the other end is an extended family member.

She screams as I quickly take the phone into the hall, "The police are back at your brother's again! There's a bunch of them this time and they're banging on his door threatening to break it down if he doesn't answer it! You have to do something. We can't live like this. They're thinking of going to an attorney if the police keep threatening them!"

I answer in a low voice to prevent my family from overhearing, "I have an attorney in Michigan working on it. They'll go away if you just tell them you don't know anything. No one knows my address anyway. Just tell them that. Every attorney I've talked to says it's unlikely they'll keep this up, and one of them is working on an appeal."

The call is upsetting. No one had heard from the agent in a while and we'd hoped he'd moved on, but obviously that wasn't true. I feel too anxious staying in my home. I know that if they are still banging on my brother's door in Arizona, they don't know I'm in California, but the frantic call unnerves me and I don't feel like being logical anymore. I can't just sit here until another SWAT team breaks down the door. I had automatic weapons pointed at me when I was arrested at 19. I don't want to deal with that again or expose my family to such a traumatic event. I run upstairs and begin packing a bag. I don't know where I am going, but I don't want to stay home. I'll go somewhere for awhile until the attorney has gotten further with my paperwork. But what can I tell Alan and the kids?

Alan is aware that I had gone through a turbulent time with my parents as a teenager. That much I had explained before we got married. I told him when I was young, a boyfriend and I had gotten into using drugs and my parents went nuts and...he had never let me finish after that. He especially didn't want to hear about problems I had with my parents. He liked calling them Mom and Dad and they thought of him like a son. Whenever I spoke about the past and the details got a little gritty he cut me off, saying, "It doesn't matter now; everyone did drugs as a teenager and had problems with their parents." I didn't argue with him then, but I would have to tell him something soon.

Alan comes into the bedroom as I am stuffing some things hurriedly into my suitcase. "Marie, what's happening? Who was that on the phone? What are you doing?"

"I hoped I'd never have to tell you this. I tried to tell you before but you didn't want to know."

"It's all right, just tell me now. There's something serious going on. I need to know what it is."

I take a deep breath and look at him standing there.

I hate all the lying and times I've had to make excuses to him to explain complications that came up. I want more than anything to tell him, I'm so tired of holding everything in side all these years, but I know that telling him would be the worst thing now that they are looking for me and they could come to the house at anytime.

I try to explain to him, "I can't tell you the details now. All I can say is that something that happened to me long before we met has been hanging over me and I need time to work it out."

"What are you talking about? Why is this happening now?"

"If I tell you, it could get you in trouble. It's better that you don't know. I'd give anything if I could tell you and the kids –but I can't. I have to get out of here, that's all I can think of at this point. You're safe as long as you don't know anything. All you need to know is that I love and appreciate you and the kids, and I don't want to mess up your lives. I have to figure things out. You know I'll do everything I can to keep the family together but I have to leave now."

I throw the last of some cosmetics into my purse. It is hard to know what to pack. What do you wear to disappear into the night and fight an invisible force that has been your enemy for more than half your life? Did I need earrings? Workout clothes? What was I going to be doing when I left?

Alan is still standing there, stunned. "Just tell me what's going on. I need to know. I can help you." He pleads.

"It'll be better if you don't know anything or where I am." I tell him again.

The next moment I hear the kids at the door. "Mom, are you all right?" My son, Alan Jr. who is 15, says looking at the suitcase. Katie, his older sister is right behind him. I realize I need to reassure them that I'm not leaving them. I feel torn that I can't reveal the real reason I'm rushing out of the house so abruptly, so late in the evening. I try to decide if I can think of a lie that will comfort them when I see the worried look on their faces. I feel tempted to use this as the moment to finally tell them about my experience as a near casualty in the drug war but I catch myself knowing they could be charged as accomplices if I did.

"I need to talk to you and Katie soon. I just want you know that this has nothing to do with your dad and I." I reach up and hug my husband again, kissing his cheek. I don't want to let go. "I love your dad and you kids very much and wouldn't let anything ruin that but I'm dealing with something I can't tell you about this minute. I'm sorry to sound so mysterious. I'm trying to take care of a problem and I'll be able to tell you all about it soon enough. Promise me you'll help Dad around the house and I'll be back home before you know it. Someone will have to feed Bailey every morning and take him outside. Can you promise me you'll do that?"

"Mom, what is it? Please tell us. We should know what's happening to you? Why can't you tell us?" Katie cries out.

"Yeah, mom, why are you taking a suitcase?" Alan Jr. asks.

"I'll contact you soon." I say as I hurry out the room suspecting I've only made things worse for them.

I leave that night and go to the house of a friend who lives nearby. She is someone I know through playing bridge, and she doesn't know most of my other friends. She has a six-bedroom house and lives alone. I ask her if I can spend the night, though I don't know what excuse to give her. She is nice about letting me stay in her guest room, and the next day she says, "I know what you're going through. My ex-husband..." She curls her hand into a fist and hits it against her head as if someone is hitting her.

It becomes obvious everyone will think I'm running from my husband because he's been beating me. What can I give as the reason I'm not going home? That the police are looking for me? I'm an escaped convict. I can't tell her the truth, but I also can't go on letting her think I was being physically abused by my husband. He doesn't deserve that.

"No, it's not what you think. My husband would never hit me. We're just having an argument," I offer, giving her the best excuse I can come up with.

The next morning I thank her and check into a hotel. I want to be close to home, to be there for the kids, and although I am usually frugal I feel this is a necessary expense.

The next couple of weeks are a stressful time. I do a lot of thinking and decide that uprooting the family isn't right. My husband had taken a position with a new company that he really enjoys and the kids have all their friends nearby. And I am tired of running. I always told myself that I would do whatever I could to avoid letting the dominoes keep falling and affecting other areas of my life. I was no longer a confused teenager. I had evidence on my side now. I had people who cared about me who would fight for me. If I tore my life apart and ran away again, I would be letting them wreak havoc on my life after all.

Over the years I had written letters to people or organizations who I felt might be sympathetic to my plight. I knew the odds of their helping me were absurdly low, but I was desperate and my options were limited. I wrote a 20-page letter to the legal writer at the *L.A. Times* who wrote articles about people unjustly treated in the court system. I wrote to a couple of law professors and even to the TV talk show host Oprah Winfrey. I fully envisioned my 25-page letter ending up in the waste basket for wacko mail, but Oprah's show with its message of compassion was a strong reassurance that helped me keep my head above water through some of my harder days. There were times when I questioned whether I wasn't indeed what my parents' generation would have described as "damaged goods." The philosophy on the show was that people could not only overcome being "damaged" but if they embraced the right values, their tragedy could make them even stronger than before. It was the message of unconditional love and faith that religions used to talk about before the dialogue got hung up on gay and reproduction rights.

I wished I had my mother around to talk to, but at the same time I was relieved she wasn't here to be exposed to what was happening to the family. Knowing that neighbors and friends could see police officers banging on the doors of family members would have hurt her terribly. She had lived through decades of a painful illness and stayed remarkably upbeat, but she would have felt humiliated by what was going on now. My mother and I had had a tumultuous past; there was a time when I felt she wanted to destroy me. It is my opinion that she went mad for a couple of years, but it was also my mother who showed me no matter how far off track a person had gone, she could turn her life around and not only rebound but become someone remarkable. She found herself and lived many years as a shining example of strength, kindness, and acceptance—the tools I needed more than anything else to overcome my own obstacles.

Another person I wrote to was my second cousin, Collette, who lives in the Southern California foothills. Despite having a large family she invited me to join them on many holidays a couple years after my arrival in California. I assumed since she lived this far from Michigan that she didn't know my secret, but even if she did, I knew she would not judge me harshly. That was the kind of person she was. She was very involved with helping people and she and her best friend, a nun from her church, spent many weekends at a garbage dump feeding poor people who came there to pilfer through trash for food. Knowing people like this who I considered saints gave me strength. Collette truly cared about people who were "the least among us."

The only letter I ended up mailing out was the one I sent anonymously to the *L.A. Times*. When I contacted the legal writer he said he had fifty cases as compelling as mine and they were still suffering in jail despite just as much evidence that they were innocent too. The other letters I stalled on and kept embellishing, making sure they were hidden on my computer with a password.

While at the hotel, I worry about my son returning home to an empty house every day after school. Since the Michigan attorney had seemed optimistic about my chances, I decide to return home. I am sick of running. I've been trying to turn my self in for years through lawyers I've hired to talk to the prosecutor in Saginaw. It seems absurd that he rejected my offer and threatened to give me more time if I surfaced and now the same bureaucracy was spending all this time and effort to bring me in. I decide to put my faith in the fact that the circumstances of my case will make it obvious that I never should have been sent to prison in the first place. I decide to say a lot of prayers and hope for the best. Other than uprooting the family, I don't see any other options.

Of course, my family asks me more questions and I tell them that I will fill them in when I can. To prepare for the worse I attend to incidental matters like getting a dental checkup, having read horror stories about health care in the prison system. I avoid having dinner parties or the bridge club to the house, envisioning a SWAT team pointing guns at my guests as agents apprehend me. The memory of a group of armed, uniformed men pointing rifles at my face when I was 19 still flourishes in my head all these years later. I don't want my kids traumatized like I was. I worry about what could happen to them? What if they suddenly emerge from their rooms as a SWAT team breaks down the door and a nervous agent fire at them in panic? Every day I pray the attorney is making some headway and this tense waiting game will end.

I call the lawyer again, and he still hasn't begun my case more than a year later. An Internet article reveals that he is about to leave his practice to become a judge. When I call to confront him, he says his partner will take over my case and will talk to me the following Friday. I remind him he said he would address my case immediately more than thirteen months earlier when the calls to my relatives first began. He evades my comment and I have little choice but to wait on pins and needles till I can speak to his partner who hopefully will be able to help me out. When I finally talk to his partner, I'm unhappy with his negative attitude and tell the original attorney I want my money back. He says he suddenly has to take a call but he'll get back to me in a few days. I realize he will probably not give the retainer back and that yet another attorney has taken advantage of me. I'll have to start over again. There is nothing else I can do.

Chapter 3

The phone rings as I am out in the courtyard in the morning planting succulents, the one plant I know my husband can't kill in the event I'm not there to care for them.

"Mrs. Walsh? I'm working next door at the Greenberg's' doing some tree trimming and I'm afraid I accidentally cut a palm frond that fell on one of your plants out front. I think it may be damaged. Would you meet me outside to look at it?"

I go out front, and the guy shows up. He talks fast and sounds more aggressive than most landscapers. My heart stops dead when he pulls out a badge and asks me if I am Susan LeFevre.

"I am Marie Walsh," I manage to say. "I am Marie Walsh." Then he shows me a mug shot from 33 years ago, and I know that my parallel universes have finally collided.

"I'm taking you in," the tree-trimming marshal says, "but let's go into the house first." As we walk up the front steps, I feel like my legs could buckle beneath me. My mind is quiet and calm as part of me knows that the alternative is screaming voices that won't help me in any way. I have to stay clear headed I tell myself. I can deal with the emotion later. My first thought is breaking it to my family that the police are taking me away. Within moments, another man joins the first agent, and I lead them to my room. "Leave all your jewelry," one of them tells me. "You don't need anything. Don't bring a purse." I slip off my wedding band and the diamond engagement ring I've worn for the last 23 years and put them on my dresser. My daughter Katie who

29

was in the next room getting ready for school rushes in to see what is going on.

She's startled to see two armed men in my bedroom. "It's all right, sweetheart. We're going to be all right." I try to reassure her, "This is about something that happened a long time ago and we'll take care of it now. We're going to be alright. I need you to be strong. I need you to be here for your dad and brother," I say as she begins to sob. "It'll be okay, don't worry." She cries harder, wrapping her arms around me. "As long as we have each other, it'll be okay," I repeat. It hits me that the nightmare that my family would be hurt by this has come true and the protected life I tried to build for them has been shattered.

"I have to call your dad." I say finally as I quit hugging her.

The marshals tell me I am going to Las Colinas, the women's lockup in Santee, a San Diego suburb a half hour away, and I phone Alan to say I love him and am sorry, and that's where I'll be.

I leave empty-handed, not thinking to bring reading glasses or money, and the marshals walk me to their black BMW, waiting until I'm in the back seat to slap on handcuffs. I'm relieved that they didn't do it in the street, in front of my neighbors. There was no sign out there that anything was amiss.

The second cop leaves us, and the tree trimmer starts driving. Before long he is on the phone to a friend, gloating, laughing.

"Do you really have to do this?" I plead from the back seat. "It was so long ago. I've led a good life. Thirty years ago was a crazy time. I have a different life now—I have children at home. Do you realize what you're doing to me? My children, my husband ... everything I have could be destroyed."

"All I know is, I'm going home tonight," he retorts with a laugh. Emphasis on the *I'm.*

At Las Colinas he hands me off to police officers, who lead me to a hallway with a large cell on one side with a half wall of Plexiglas. It's the holding tank, a secure waiting area with dull painted-concrete walls, harsh neon light, and a narrow slat of scarred wood along one side that serves as a bench. For a while, I'm the only one in it. I sit there for several hours with my hands cuffed in front of me as officers going in and out of the building pause to look. I feel like an insect in a specimen jar. My case is unusual, and I'm an object of curiosity. On the other side of the hall is an office, also half-walled in Plexiglas. An officer sits at a computer behind a small opening, the processing window.

Eventually the door to the cell opens and an officer leads me across to the window, where I'm asked for my name and address. *My name.* I stutter over "Susan" and begin to cry as I say "LeFevre." I hadn't cried before, but now I'm sobbing. It takes me several tries to get my address out, and finally the officer gives his best guess at the name of my street and sends me back to the tank. A couple of hours later, I'm led to an adjacent room, strip searched, and given bright green coveralls with large black numbers on the back, then returned once more to the tank. It's another hour before they take me to the fifth floor, which holds thousands of parole violators and absconders—the term used to describe my situation.

The floor has several wings, all identical: a central room filled with metal chairs and tables surrounded by iron doors, each opening onto a cinder-block cell with three narrow bunks, one above the other, bolted to one wall. A small tabletop hangs from the opposite wall, and a metal toilet/sink stands in the corner. The space is perhaps 6 feet wide and 10 feet long.

The top bunk of my cell is occupied by a woman in her 20s with long dreadlocks, who scarcely gets up during the time I'm here. She doesn't speak, but she alternates between intense crying and hysterical laughing all day long. I learn that the court proceedings she's involved in could go on for two to three years, but I never find out what charges she's facing.

In the middle bunk when I arrive is a short, stout woman who's part Native American Indian and part black. She's talkative, and except for her crossed eyes, she seems pretty normal and kind. She seems irritated, though, that the officers have asked her to move to the bottom bunk and give me her space.

I'm able to keep the door slightly ajar, and I sit close to it on the floor, looking through the crack that leads to the common area just beyond. The size of the cell makes me anxious and the walls seem to sway inward. My body fills up with the same terror of my first stay in prison, all those years ago. The cell is so tiny that I feel that I've been locked in a coffin.

It's a relief that the Indian woman keeps talking, and after awhile I talk back.

She notices that I flinch every time the toilet flushes, the noise echoing off the concrete walls. It reminds me of past moments I would rather not remember. "You can flush a whole toilet roll down one of these things," she says. Then she starts throwing small bits of lint and paper into it, and she keeps it flushing all night long.

I press my hands to my ears but I can't block out the noise. It sounds like the plumbing is trying to suck everything in the room to another place—hell or a madhouse. The same twisted emotions I felt years ago hit me like a tidal wave and make me want to give up.

As despair racks through my body, the blood seems to drain from my arms and legs and I feel lightheaded. Before I know it, I've crumpled to the floor and my heart is pounding so hard I think it's going to give out. The Indian woman hits the buzzer and guards come running, and I'm taken to a room nearby to have equipment check me out for a heart attack. When the male guard finds that my heart is beating normally—it is obviously just severe anxiety that caused me to collapse—he becomes cruel. He comments that I'm going to wish I hadn't evaded them for so long. I can't understand why a stranger would feel so vindictive. I feel almost lifeless as I lie there. My head is throbbing when they push me back into the cell.

Small concerns fill my head. I'm supposed to meet with friends tomorrow to play bridge and with the girls for tennis the next day. What excuse can my husband give for my sudden absence? I'm thankful that at least my situation wasn't made public. This will make it easier on the family. I decide to tell my husband to explain that I had to go to Michigan to help out with a family issue. I've been swallowed up in the murky underworld again, but this time I welcome being anonymous.

But the next day, I learn that an article about me appears in the papers. The cop who brought me in had gone directly to the press to boast that he'd captured someone who had been a fugitive for more than 30 years. The story refers to my house and black Lexus SUV as if we have a staff of servants and an estate. The truth is that we live in nice suburb in a close-knit family community. My husband worked six days a week and we clipped coupons, bought second-hand cars, and pinched pennies for years so we could finally move to an area with good schools and have a home large enough for three growing children.

The article is being passed around the common room as we eat breakfast from Styrofoam trays. I've been in California long enough that I quickly calculate that thousands of prisoners eating from a different Styrofoam tray three times a day should fill a landfill for about 50,000 years. I wish this were my biggest concern. As the article circulates from table to table the women are reading it aloud and discussing it, though they won't hand it over so I can see until it's my turn. The faces in this sea of green jumpsuits are young and older, many of them Latino and black, all of them weary. "Did you see where the prosecutor in Michigan says she was a high-level syndicate member and had a whole crew of dealers working for her when she was nineteen?" one woman says. A syndicate member? I don't know what they are talking about. This is the first but not the last time I will hear this allegation. "Soccer mom," another inmate adds. "And she didn't tell no one about her past, not even her husband, for thirty years. Well, its Alice's turn next." I figure that's me. Alice. Alice in Wonderland. Alice in chains. I see that the person making the syndicate member claims is my uncle's friend, the Saginaw prosecutor. My uncle warned me that Duncan hated my guts, as he put it, but to tell the media I was a high-level syndicate member seems over the top even for him. Another comment he makes is that I'll have to serve five to nine years before I'm eligible for parole. I can't even touch my food.

Alan and the kids come to visit that night. The kids stand out in this place like shiny pearls with their innocent eyes and smooth skin that's never been tattooed or dehydrated by substance abuse. The visiting area has a long wooden counter that's divided into "phone booths," each with a window that faces an identical setup on the prisoners' side. They crowd around the window and pass the receiver around. Alan is a rock. He's been in touch with lawyers, and he promises that he'll find a way to get me out. "We're not going to let them tear our family apart," he tells me. He looks as if he'd cry if we were alone.

The following day the guards call me out from the cell for another visit. As I lean against the Plexiglas wall of the unit so they can fasten chains on my ankles, waist, and wrists, I can see into a unit across the hall. Forty or fifty women sit in the same green outfits at identical-looking metal tables. One of the women looks at me and suddenly stands up, clapping her hands. In the next moment, every woman in the room stands and claps. My heart lightens when I realize they are clapping to show support for me, but the guard securing the chain on my ankles gives it a painful yank in angry response to the attempt at camaraderie the women have made. I cry, but this time because I am touched by the message the women have sent. The guard shortens the chain between my feet so that it is almost impossible for me to walk to the visiting room and I have to move inch by inch down the long hallway.

I expect to see Alan there, but instead the room is packed with cameras and reporters. After being closed in a cell for days, I am stunned to be out and looking at a room full of familiar faces I've seen only on television before. I reflect back on my teenage appearance in the courtroom, when the judge and prosecutor and my own attorney manipulated to have my sentencing held in a closed room so no one else could know what they were up to. Since my secret was out anyway, I think I should at least give the details as I know them. I have little faith that I might get a fair hearing in Michigan after what I'd experienced there before. I tell the local reporters about my ordinary life, the promises that I'd get probation if I agreed to plead guilty to a drug charge, the fact that I was 19 but reporters were told that I was 28. I explain that the laws have changed so much in recent years that today, I'd have gotten probation. Ironically, in the 1970s sentencing was usually more lenient than it is now, but circumstances in Saginaw were unusual.

"You're like the girl next door," one reporter tells me. "You're like anyone in this room." I hope somehow the court system will see it that way, sees what I've made of my life. Another reporter mentions that he's heard I'll be sent back to Michigan on some kind of bus or truck.

I am again returned to the dark, cramped cell and the iron door is closed. I'll remain locked in with the other two women for the next 30 hours except for meals, which are eaten outside the cells on metal tables. The following day when we are finally let out again, I call the lawyer in Grand Rapids and tell him what the reporter said about my being transported by truck. He scoffs. He's never heard of a truck transporting prisoners cross country. "They'll be flying you back if you go, that's for sure," he says confidently, adding, "There's nothing I can do till you get to Michigan. Just call me when you get here." He hasn't gotten around to getting my file; he's done nothing on my case. My husband says that we received a bill already for more money. I have this terrible feeling that the feeding frenzy has only just begun.

My family comes to see me again. Maureen tells me that she has started a website called savemymom.com, on which she states that she and the family were devastated by my sudden apprehension. Almost immediately she was contacted by Leon Coward, the absconder agent in Michigan who spent more than a year looking for me. Coward wrote to her site saying that it was her mother's fault for lying to you all those years that the family was suffering, not his. "You're mother is the one who has done this to you." His words and tone upset her even more.

Maureen then went to Coward's website, where he explained that he picked my case over all the others on the list because he thought it would be "quirky." Finding someone who had been a fugitive that long intrigued him. With a little more investigation, we learn that Michigan legislators funded a special task force to focus on rounding up absconders from all over the country and bringing them back to Michigan prisons. At a time when Michigan was laying off teachers and pieces of the ceilings in school classrooms were falling in on students, it seems that the crooked system the lawyers had warned me about was accurate.

After a few days, I begin to receive an outpouring of mail from family, friends, and many people I've never met who write heartfelt letters empathizing with my plight. Alan tells me that the owners and CEO at work have started a foundation and generously funded it to help with my legal defense. I receive a letter from Tracy Burr, one of the owners, who writes eloquently that although she can imagine how much I am suffering after being torn from my family like this, the exposure of the secret that I've had to live with all these years and my strength in overcoming such adversity gives her and others inspiration. "Everyone has secrets," she says, "and my courage and determination not to let my problems interfere with trying to raise a good family and lead a respectable life has given encouragement to others."

The letters from well-wishers continue, and the following day I receive a large envelope filled with almost 100 cards from my neighbors and friends in Carmel Valley. Some of my neighbors, upon hearing of my tragedy on the news, piled into several carloads and caravanned 30 miles to visit me at the prison, only to be turned away because of visiting restrictions. Many of their letters divulge that they, too, had gotten mixed up in drugs when they were young and felt it could easily have been them who got sucked into the system. I'd known many of the women for years, yet details of our pasts had never come up until now. Each compassionate letter is like a hug at a time when I feel I'm being ripped apart limb by limb.

The only letters to affect me more than those from my friends are the ones I receive from my children. Alan Junior writes that he admires my courage and that millions of people "love me intensely". Maureen and Katie write equally loving letters, saying how much I truly mean to them and how much they looked up to me and appreciated my being there for them all those years. While Maureen tends to her new website on my behalf, Katie says she will arrange her work schedule to drive Alan to school every day and help cook meals. She writes that I am the core of the family and the whole family will diligently work for my release. I feel fortunate to be able to hear loved ones and friends express their feelings so intimately. Such expressions of emotion are seldom made until funerals, when they're too late to be appreciated by the loved one.

Despite the outpouring of support, I spend most of the next 14 days in my cell, too anxious to eat, biting my nails until my fingers bleed. I had never done this before. The Indian woman reads spiritual literature most of the day in the murky light, and our dreadlocked bunkmate continues her frightening cycle of laughing and weeping.

Chapter 4

Finally, something seems to be happening. The guards wake me at 3 in the morning and tell me to grab my personal belongings. They cuff and shackle me, snapping heavy chains around my bare ankles, then lead me to the first-floor intake area. This time, they chain me to a bench in the hall outside the holding tank. There's a steady stream of new arrivals in the waning hours of the night, mostly streetwalkers in tight, low-cut clothes who'll be here until someone pays a thousand dollars to get them out. No one will tell me why I've been moved, and as the hours go by, I begin to think I'm about to be released. When I ask the officers in the window what's happening, they yell, "Shut up," or, "You'll find out when it happens."

Several hours later, a large woman stands in front of me putting on rubber yellow gloves. She orders me to an area to get searched. I have no idea what to expect, but she doesn't end up touching me and I'm given an orange jumpsuit to change into. The guard who shackles me when I emerge is a large man whose wide buckled belt is almost hidden under a huge stomach. He has a gruff presence and looks ominous in his black uniform and heavy boots, but his eyes are unexpectedly warm and he puts the cuffs around my wrists loosely so they don't cut into my skin. It's an unnecessary kindness.

He leads me outside, where a large white bus has pulled up. The lettering on the side says "TransCor." A man standing a few feet away holds a rifle pointed slightly above my head. The guard makes me stop next to the TransCor sign, and someone takes my picture.

TransCor advertises its services with photos of clean white buses that, but for the sheets of diamond-hole metal grating over the windows and dividing the interior into neat compartments, could belong to some small-town transit system. The bus I climb onto, though, is nothing of the sort.

With the heavy chains rubbing against my bare ankles, I struggle up steep stairs into a makeshift jail that looks as though it was put together in someone's garage in one afternoon. Chain-link fencing has been bolted to the trailer of a transport truck to divide it into three compartments. The first is big enough to hold seats and cots for the four guards who will take turns driving and supervising us. Next to that, the women's area consists of a small section of six or eight seats stretching back to another chain-link partition. The final compartment, a larger version of the women's area, is for male prisoners. A crudely constructed commode area with sheet-metal walls stands in the farthest corner.

Each of the compartments has its own entrance, a roughly soldered gate hanging in the middle of the woven wire, and each gate is secured with a padlock. When the bus begins to move, the noise is earsplitting, sheet metal clanging against sheet metal and padlocks rattling against chain link with every turn of the big vehicle's wheels.

The guard at the top of the stairs unlocks the women's compartment and when we're inside, he fastens on the "black box," a rectangular piece of metal that covers the chain and locks of my handcuffs and holds them rigidly together so I can't move my hands more than a few inches from my waist. There's one other woman in a seat. She's young, perhaps in her 20s, with long straight hair and a face

41

that looks as though it's seen more than its share of harsh times. The guard motions for her to stand up and hooks our chains together. Now I notice that she smells of stale alcohol, and that she has frequent gas. We'll sit in adjoining seats until one of us gets off. Being joined to someone else makes the chains scrape harder against my skin, which is already raw from friction. I'll be in this seat almost 24 hours a day for more than a week, though no one tells me that, or anything about where we're going or how long the trip will take.

The addition of the black box makes every minute uncomfortable, and my arms and back ache constantly. My shoulders are in spasm within the first hour. I had been in physical therapy for rotator cuff injury from tennis; having my arm pulled forward in one position for a week and a half was intensely painful and I knew would damage my shoulder, probably permanently. But things only get worse. The first time I'm allowed to use the sheet-metal outhouse, the guard jerks my handcuffs as he unlocks them and says, "Who put these on this loose?"

"Please," I say. "My skin is going to start bleeding. It's so sore already."

"Just get your wrists up here," he barks, and then he tightens the cuffs almost to the breaking point.

"I'm fifty-three, officer. I assure you I'm not going anywhere," I tell him. I gesture toward the locked chain-link fence secured with a padlock and the three other armed guards between me and the outside door.

"Just put your wrist up here," he barks as he yanks the metal cuff around my wrists as tight as possible. "We had an eighty-three-year-old on here last week and he made it." He pushes away my wrist in a hostile way.

A TALE OF TWO LIVES

There are six men chained to seats when we set out. Most of them are black or Latino, mostly in their 20s or early 30s. We talk through the barrier, and most of the guys say the state of Michigan has come after them because they've missed alimony payments. Terrence, a large, friendly-looking black man in his 30s, gives me an ominous sense of what's in store for me on this trip. He'd been picked up at his job a week ago in Texas and has spent the days since on the truck as it made its way up to Las Vegas, where it waited with the engine running for 14 hours in a parking lot to pick up another passenger, and then sat, still handcuffed in a chair, to where they'd picked me up in San Diego. Now we were back in the same Vegas parking lot, and heading who knows where else before we hit Michigan.

"They came for me at work and my boss said he'd hold my job open if I wasn't gone too long," Terrence says, "but it's been a week already." He has a wife and kids back in Texas, and the air goes right out of him when he starts worrying about how they'll get by while he's gone, especially now, with the cost of paying his way back home. Whenever that will be.

From what I can tell, that's the most common story—couldn't manage the alimony. There's just one person whose story we don't know—he's sitting in the back, and he doesn't seem to speak English.

I begin to think of the bus as a slave ship, full of people snatched out of lives that, on some level, had been working. What I've seen so far is frightening—people chained to chairs in passageways and forgotten in cave like cells. Dozens of prisoners in rooms meant for a handful, left for six or eight hours with no place to sit and hardly room to stand. People shackled with tortuous black boxes in privately owned transport trucks on mysterious routes. If

43

animals were treated like this, someone would be arrested. But the bus, the jail—they're full of invisible people.

The sound is deafening as we make our stop-and-go route east, and with every small ridge in the road, the metal clashes anew. At one point a guard gets up and wraps a piece of cloth around one of the padlocks to stop the incessant banging that rises above the rest of the racket. The stink builds. We can't bathe, or even wash our face, and the sheet-metal shed can't contain the smell of the toilet. I want to itch my head or forehead and can't reach that far to relief the irritation. My fingernails are ragged and red, my wrists raw red from the constant rubbing. I'm scarecrow thin from being unable to eat and my shoulders burn with pain. I can understand how a person could lose her mind under circumstances like this. She could just retreat to some internal cave, disconnecting the circuits that explain the world to us—anything to avoid dealing with a reality this obscene. I haven't used drugs in 30 years, haven't even thought of them—but if I had them now, I think I'd take them.

I'd often wondered how I'd ever gotten into drugs as a teenager. I knew that I'd faced more than a few traumas before I turned 20, but as I got older what I couldn't understand was why my brain hadn't told me drugs weren't the answer. Now, chained up in a bus and heading back to face years in a prison that's been labeled one of the worst in the world, I can suddenly empathize with my younger self. Common sense loses its power when you are in such agony that the only thing that makes sense is making the pain go away.

As the trip wears on, the anxiety is excruciating. I know I have a good chance of winning an appeal and that my family is waiting for me and that I love them more than anything, but it gets harder to hold onto the thought of them, and sometimes I wish for death. A few weeks before I was picked up, knowing the hunt for me was on again, I got a prescription for Zoloft. But someone in Las Colinas told me you couldn't kill yourself with pills like that, not on psychotropics—she'd tried it herself after spending two months in jail.

Terrence has been sitting on this bus for a week already and I know he has at least another week or two to go. His handcuffs are much tighter than mine since his wrists are much wider, and he's miserable. But he doesn't look like a man who's hunting for a permanent exit. I tell myself I have to be strong. My prayers will be answered, and I'll be able to block out the clamor and clear my mind. I pray again for strength. Every minute of the screaming in my head and the clanging outside seems like an eternity.

One guard covertly tries to give me a few breaks— an extra one of the scratchy little wool blanket we cover ourselves with, or a small water bottle that I can keep after lunch to sip on if the uninsulated truck is sweltering that day instead of cold. But another guard makes a point of checking my handcuffs and chains and tightening them. He scrutinizes what I have around me and confiscates anything he decides I shouldn't have. When he sees my extra blanket, he snatches it away, accusing me of taking it from a pile across the aisle even though I've been chained to my seat. I look out the window at the lines of field crops spinning by. My mind wanders to the past, and I question how my life changed and I ended up here…

Chapter 5

Grafton, Ohio 1964

Until the night a tornado slammed into our house when I was 12, I thought we were an ordinary family. Midwestern. Catholic. Happy. Perfect, even.

My parents met in Saginaw, Michigan, through friends they met at Saginaw High. My mother, Gerry Doerr, was blond, green-eyed, and the prettiest girl in town according to my dad. "Your mother's picture was in the front window of Schmit's photography studio in the middle of town," he would say more than once. They courted while he was in the navy and then in college at the University of Detroit. They moved to Ohio not long after they got married, to live near his new job as a store manager for the Kresge Company, the parent company of K-mart. Starting out, they moved every three or four years as he opened new stores in Indiana, Detroit, and small towns in Ohio, and we kids—five, eventually—were born along the way.

The first home I remember clearly was in an area outside Youngstown, surrounded by woods and meadows, where the houses had long backyards bordering a creek. There were no girls in the neighborhood, so I was the lone Indian when the boys played cowboys—and I happily spent much of my time alone. I could wander for hours, lost in a world without words—a swamp full of cattails and wildlife, velvety black birds with brilliant red patches on their wings and little crowns on their heads, or a field with tightly rolled bales of hay. I built small dams along the creek and sailed leaves or twigs along the current, and on hot days I'd lie on

46

a soft bed of pine needles and be lulled to sleep by the breeze shuddering mildly through the branches above me. Climbing trees and exploring meadows, I was rarely bored.

When I was 10, my father went to work for a company called Pitman-Moore, selling pharmaceuticals to doctors. Our new home base was a little town called Grafton, 30 minutes from Cleveland.

This was our Mayberry. We could walk to school and church, there were kids in most every house, and all of us traveled around on bikes, zooming out to the woods just beyond the neighborhood to hike around and hunt for evidence of what we knew were Indian villages. It was also a short ride down to the town's main street, a one-stoplight stretch of businesses. Some of the older stores, like Dunham's Dairy Bar, had wooden sidewalks and tall false fronts that made them look as though they had two stories rather than one, and there was a Laundromat, as well as a modern pharmacy.

On Hickory Street I became close friends with several girls my age and we played with Barbies, got the little kids to compete to prove who was the best younger brother or sister that week, and organized neighborhood kickball games and water balloon fights. It was a given that we'd keep an eye on our siblings.

If there were stresses involved with adapting to another new town, my parents didn't show it. Though money was tight, they hired a babysitter for us every weekend so they could go play bridge and socialize with other members of the newcomers' group in town, and both of them took pride in fixing up the first house they'd ever owned. My father planted petunias along the front walk, and my mom decorated our little three-bedroom, one-bath home with the rich colors that were all the rage (avocado green, harvest gold) and filled vases with stylish arrangements of artificial flowers.

In the service of keeping chaos at a minimum, all of us had chores to do. Jerry, in the privileged position of eldest son and football star, polished shoes once a week and was supposed to mow the lawn. (Buff and 6 feet 2, he wore his burgundy and white letter jacket even in the summer.) Little Kathy set the table for dinner, and David would clear it. Much more fell to me as the oldest girl in the family. After school, there were baskets of laundry to iron, including my father's white shirts and the family bed sheets, which my mother would dampen and keep rolled up in the freezer, a tip from one of the household hints columns we liked to read. Then there was cleaning—Mom and I would dust the furniture and sweep the wooden floors daily—and cooking. Dinner was served farmhouse style at our house, promptly at 6, and each day I'd peel a dozen or so potatoes, put frozen meat to thaw in an electric frying pan, wash and cut up head lettuce and vegetables for a salad, and turn the preparations over to my mother, returning to help dish up what she'd made. Afterward, I'd tend to the cleanup, and there were times when I'd watch as everyone else left the house to enjoy a long summer evening while I stayed behind in the kitchen, putting away the food and washing serving bowls, pans, and dessert dishes. Sometimes I'd still be scrubbing pans when my brothers wandered in an hour later to get a snack. But I felt that my role as "good helper" made me a valuable member of the family, and though my mom was more stern than effusive, I was confident that I had her respect, as distant as she stayed. Being friendly to your children during these years was considered inadvisable. It was more important to remain an authority figure than a friend. My parents took this to heart. They were raising five kids in a small house in the suburbs with one bathroom, one phone, one TV, and one car. The pressure of having good kids was tantamount. A wayward kid would disgrace the family and subject them to vicious whispers behind their back.

I don't think my mother was alone in using phrases like "If you don't mind me, I'll break every bone in your body or I'll beat you to a pulp." My hyperactive brother David was a constant target, his actions interpreted as pure defiance, and there was only one answer in the early 1960s for defiance: the yardstick. But as long as you did as you were told, life was smooth. I couldn't understand why kids would act up. Kids who misbehaved in church or in classrooms baffled me. I didn't judge harshly, but I failed to understand why they just didn't get it. My only run-in with trouble was one day at dusk, when I was on my way home from a particularly good wander and became fixated on a scene of changing colors. The sky was on fire, contrasting with the golden bales of hay, and as a V formation of geese flew over the bright autumn foliage, I was mesmerized. I stayed until suddenly the light was gone, and making my way home in the dark I could see my mother's face—red, furious. I was only a half hour late, but she had already called the police and was livid that I could have been so insolent. I remember thinking I was too old for her to physically punish me but she did. I felt that my helping with the younger kids and the housework should have given me some slack. But my mother lived in constant fear that a drop of defiance ignored could bring on a tidal wave of ruination around the corner.

I'll always remember feeling more degraded and humiliated than corrected, but I knew my mother was doing what she thought best and I was confident that our family was exceptional. Every night when we said our prayers and thanked God for our blessings, I felt lucky to have such a good family.

What's striking to me now is how much work it was to keep our household going, and how peaceful our first years in Grafton seemed to be. Life hummed along, and only the backdrop seemed to change. Summer's greens faded into orange, then blurred to a somber gray, but just as the bleakness seemed unending I'd awaken to a glistening white backdrop and blue skies. We'd skate on ponds, searching for patches of smooth ice that looked like a clear pane of glass standing between us and a murky but lively world of other life forms as we watched fish swimming below.

My girlfriends and I began to pay attention to boys, if only from a distance. We'd watch for a cool older guy— we called him Cutie—who rode a motorcycle and hung around outside the Laundromat. We were also big fans of the sexy blond secret agent Illya Kuryakin on *The Man from U.N.C.L.E.*, squealing as he chased after Russian spies. And when *Dark Shadows* debuted, we'd get together right after school to enter the gothic world of Barnabas, the vampire, and Collinwood Manor. I got a glimpse of adolescence about that time when I took my mother's dark red lipstick from her purse and passed it around before a church dance. When my parents saw their bright-lipped daughter and her inexpertly made-up 12-year-old friends, there was hell to pay—part of my punishment was being marched over to my girlfriends' parents and made to apologize. For a kid who was shy around adults, it was the kind of torture that a yardstick couldn't begin to inflict.

Later that year, Mom found out she was pregnant again. She'd been talking about getting a real estate license and fantasizing about vacations like the ones Judy and Karen's parents took to Europe or the Bahamas. But my father had resisted the idea of her going to work, and now it seemed out of the question. If she was moody, and a little more irritable that usual, I was almost too busy to notice. On top of the usual homework and chores, I was inhaling spy novels to earn reading prizes at school and also going to catechism class so I could make my confirmation and participate in confession. I'd learned a lot about sin at home—anytime my mother talked to her friends or got on the phone to chat with her mother in Saginaw, there was plenty of conversation about good girls going bad, getting pregnant and ruining their families' reputations. Since I still thought the route to pregnancy involved God's putting a baby in a woman's stomach, I couldn't really understand why there was so much jaw dropping and so many exclamations of "How could she do that to her family!" when "she" seemed to have so little control over the process. But I knew I would never destroy my family's good name by getting pregnant before I was married. The lipstick had caused more than enough trouble. I'd stay on the path my mom and grandmother had laid out by example. *Know your place. Follow the rules. Don't question what you're told. Only cheap girls try to grow up too fast.* My mother loved to see adolescent girls still playing with dolls and dressing the way they did as children. My mother wrote letters to her mother almost every day to save on the expense of a telephone call.

The same basic themes came up in catechism class, but it took some mental gymnastics to go along with the program when I started going to confession. Like most kids,

I would tell the priest that I'd had bad thoughts about my siblings or called my brothers pig face, which my mother had strictly forbidden. But if I *hadn't* been fighting, I'd have to lie when I got into the confessional. That was the irony. "Bless me father for I have sinned" was mandatory — and you couldn't just say "but not this week," even if you thought it was true.

Since asking questions about such nuances was a sign of a lack of faith, as I understood it, I knew I was on my own to sort things out. In my classes and at home, much was made of heretics and women who lost their virtue. But the main point seemed to be that Jesus loved all of us, no matter what our background, color, or creed. He forgave even a prostitute and people who had turned against him. I believed in that, but I didn't plan to need that kind of forgiveness.

At catechism one day, the lecture was about Jesus riding into Jerusalem on a donkey while palm fronds waved. The day was already turning hot as we walked home, girls in pastel dresses and patent leather Mary Janes, boys in short-sleeved white shirts and clip-on ties. Summer had blazed in early, and long past dark my parents and the neighbors were still on the front lawns chatting, kids turned loose. It was too late for traffic, and I raced my Schwinn down Hickory Street, a few feet ahead of my girlfriends who were struggling to keep up. "What a night!" I remember thinking as the warm rush of air streamed past my face. "It won't be long before I'm old enough to be out like this whenever I want."

By the time we got to bed it was after 10, and it was still dark when a loud booming noise and the sound of screaming woke me. I was startled to see a huge hole where one of my bedroom walls had been. My mother was panicked, almost crying, yelling, "Susan, wake up!" My sister Kathy and I scrambled to the doorway to join the rest of the family. The boys ran down from their upstairs bedroom a moment later and we stood together, shaken up, seeing if we were all okay.

There was just one injury—Dad had stepped on some glass and his foot was gashed and bleeding, though he didn't seem to notice. Our power was out, but in the dim moonlight beyond the house we could see piles of debris marking the path of the funnel cloud—a category 4, they'd say later—that had just roared by. Dad wanted to stay put, but Mom had felt the house move and thought the gas main might have opened, so she insisted that we get out. We hunted for shoes, then picked our way across the backyard toward the closest house with lights on. As we approached, we could see it belonged to our friends the Coles. The debris in some places was several feet high as we walked. Washing machines, davenports, and kitchen tables were mixed with clothing and toys and broken dishes, whole houses shaken up and emptied on the ground.

The Coles pulled out a sleeper couch in their basement rec room and we spent the night wrapped in borrowed blankets and sleeping bags.

At daybreak, we pulled on borrowed clothes and took a look outside. The Coles' street seemed fairly normal, with just a few uprooted trees and a scattering of broken bits, but from the backyard we could see that on our street, few houses had been left untouched, and many had been demolished. All that remained of the house on one side of ours was a remnant of the fireplace, which stood several feet high in the middle of piles of splintered wood and fragments of what had been an ordinary life just a day before. Those neighbors had taken refuge under a bed and stayed there all night. The house on the other side of us was missing a few rooms. And down the street, the wind had lifted a large two-story house and set it down intact in the front yard of the neighbors across the street. The joke for a long time was that they'd been invited to "stop over sometime" a few days earlier.

Our house looked better than most, but the whole thing had been shifted off the foundation, and it wouldn't be livable for quite some time. Miraculously, no one we knew had been seriously hurt, though my brother David heard that an older man had been killed on the far side of town.

As we looked around, someone called out the time and said that mass would be starting shortly. We pulled together our clothing as best we could and a large group of us, led by our parents, began to walk through a pathway in the rubble toward church. We kids all held each other's hands. Part of the excitement was that we had lived through such an event, and part of it was that something had actually happened to us that was out of the norm.

Kathy and I stayed with our friends who lived farther out of town for a few weeks, my brothers stayed with other friends, and our parents checked into a Ramada Inn, waiting for the insurance company to give us a check so we could rent a place until repairs were completed. We found a large house in a more rural area, far from our friends, and I spent the next few months entertaining myself by watching the wildlife near the river and chasing the cat when she caught baby chipmunks by the tail. My mom seemed fine most of the time—perhaps a little more distracted than usual—but all summer she fretted about the weather, and every time a storm came up, she rushed us to the basement and made us stand in a tight cluster in the northwest corner, which she said was the safest part of the house. She seemed to be reliving the night of the tornado again and again, and after the thunder and lightning of each passing squall she'd be agitated, sometimes for days. I would later realize that she was traumatized far more by the tornado than anyone knew. Later, I would look back and realize this was the moment she began to decline.

By fall we were back in school, and my parents announced that we'd be moving again. This time we were headed for Saginaw, the place they'd grown up, and left behind 17 years before. Since the tornado, Mom had talked constantly about wanting to be closer to her mother; Dad lined up a new job in marketing with the textbook publisher Holt, Rinehart & Winston, and would be traveling to schools and colleges all over Michigan. We kids would find out what it was like to live in a city 30 times larger than the tiny towns where we'd spent our whole lives. And I'd soon begin to see that the whirling storm that had pushed our home off its foundation that spring had undone the moorings of our family—and my place in it, too.

Chapter 6

M_y parents found that Saginaw had changed significantly in their absence, and our transition to the new house was not an easy one. Our two-story brick house sat back from the road at the end of a long, straight driveway, isolated from other houses. It wasn't long before I realized how inconvenient it is to be 14 years old and live so far from town. The nearest business area consisted of a double-lane highway lined with fast-food restaurants, strip malls, and gas stations. The older downtown urban center on the east side of town, with its diverse population, was off limits as far as my parents were concerned.

The east side was where my mother grew up and my grandmother still lived there. It was the same area my great grandparents had lived their entire lives. My mother had urged my grandmother to move to the west side, but my grandmother was adamant: this was where she was born and she would die there, too.

When we drove through the city to visit my grandmother, my mother would wince and make negative comments about the decaying mansions lining the Saginaw River, that were now government projects. It was evident the large stone houses had once had velvety lawns and had stood as symbols of prominence. I could understand my mother's disillusionment, but it wasn't like her to be outspoken. I remember seeing this as another sign that she wasn't herself. She had always told us, "A well-bred person doesn't talk about controversial issues." She felt women especially had to be careful not to discuss issues like politics, religion, or race.

"What else is there to talk about?" I asked once.

"Discussing the weather is always acceptable."

My mother especially abhorred women who climbed up on a soap box or expressed strong opinions.

Like most 14-year-olds, I didn't pay much attention to adults—especially their social lives. My radar was fixed on more important things like boy watching and analyzing the social hierarchy at junior high, but I couldn't help noticing the changes in both my parents since our move to Saginaw. The sudden pressure of being around extended family members seemed to be having a negative effect.

There had long been rumors about the competitive rivalry between my father and his younger brother, Jim, who lived closer to town with his wife, Anita, and their seven children. Apparently my father, as the eldest in the family, had been my grandmother's favorite, and the two brothers struggled in a constant challenge to outdo each other.

My father told of the harsh conditions he and his brother endured growing up. The LeFevres had once been a prominent, long-established family in Michigan, and my great-great-grandfather was well known for his association with Henry Ford. A life-size replica of my great-great-grandfather's shop, which sold grandfather clocks in downtown Detroit, was featured in the Greenfield Village Henry Ford Museum. His son (my grandfather's father) was postmaster general in New Baltimore, a town 30 miles outside Detroit, and ran a prosperous dairy business until the depression, when the operation floundered. The family lost most of their wealth, and all that remained was the big house on Lake Huron that my great-grandfather had built.

My father and his three younger siblings grew up in a tiny cottage that stood in the shadow of the tall gate of his grandfather's house. The cottage had been built to house temporary summer workers for the dairy business and was poorly insulated. My father recounted how he and his brother scoured nearby railroad tracks to scavenge fallen lumps of coal that fell from the rail cars as the train rounded a bend. The coal was used in the stove as the only source of heat during the long winter months.

Every summer my grandfather, who eventually moved back into his childhood home in New Baltimore, held a reunion that attracted some 200 members of the family. My dad's brother's family of nine and our family of seven stayed at my grandfather's, camped out in spare bedrooms, sunrooms, and hallways. I remember how other relatives circled around my uncle at the reunions as he talked about the people he knew in Saginaw and the politics there. He was an attorney, and seemed to know a lot of important people.

Shortly after our move to Saginaw, my uncle invited us to his house for dinner. I was surprised to find that he and his family lived in a neighborhood where most of the houses needed painting and the lawns were full of weeds. My cousins, as usual, were exceptionally nice and I enjoyed seeing them, but my uncle seemed anxious during the dinner. He complained bitterly about social issues and the changing demographics in Saginaw. Smoking a strong-smelling cigar, he discussed how jobs were being taken by "people on the east side." He said factory workers were making more money than professionals like him. The evening was filled with conversation about welfare cheats, boys with long hair, rebellious college students protesting the war, and women who wanted to be treated like men at their job. He seemed to feel these people were destroying the country. I'd never heard these subjects discussed before.

Later that evening as the adults lingered at the table, I went into the other room with my cousins. The noise level apparently got too high, and I looked up to see my uncle enter the room and angrily grab the nearest of my cousins. He pulled down his pants and beat his bare bottom with a wooden spoon. Everyone else in the room stood frozen, looking on in horror as my uncle grabbed another cousin and repeated the same shocking display. It was an uncomfortable night that has stuck in my mind for many years.

About a month later, we were again invited to my aunt and uncle's, and this time we pulled into the driveway of a brand-new house in an upscale neighborhood. The front room looked pristine with white carpeting, white furniture, and a large, ornate silver tea setting.

Apparently, my uncle had sold a parcel of land on the west side to a housing developer and made a large profit, which he used to buy the new home and other businesses. He also bought a bowling alley, a country club and golf course, and half ownership in the Saginaw Gears, the city's hockey team. The country club was located near our house, and with the exception of the hockey team, all the new businesses were re-branded with the LeFevre family name.

At dinner, my uncle again voiced his opinions on the topics of the day. I assumed that my parents saw that my uncle was extreme in his narrow view of the issues, but before long I began to hear my father talk about wrong-doers in the same harsh tone as his brother. I had never before heard him speak about the need to crack down on what he now perceived as subversiveness. He seemed to assume his brother's hard views that the country was changing as a result of a government that tolerated dissention. This was a period when I first began to see footage on TV of riot police clubbing unarmed demonstrators at the Democratic Convention in Chicago and protest marches against the draft and the war in Viet Nam, and hear about the shooting deaths by campus police of four students attending an anti-war rally at a college in Ohio. I found it hard to agree. I saw the rebellion as a response to the rigid and repressive trends in the country, but I kept my opinions to myself. Looking back, I realize this was the first time I felt the distance growing between my parents and me.

We began to feel the tension in small ways. The following Sunday morning I offered to mow the lawn to get some sun. By Wednesday, word got back to my parents that my Uncle Jim heard about the lawn being mowed on what he considered the Sabbath, a day of rest. His disapproval became an issue around the house for weeks. This was the first time our status as good Catholics had ever been in question. I was surprised at my parents' strong reaction and the fact that my uncle's opinion could send waves of tension through our home.

The LeFevre name had been unknown in Ohio and we'd effortlessly blended in with the community around us. The importance of a family's reputation and good image had been a major topic of my mother's and my grandmother's while I was growing up, but it had been a value, not an issue, until now.

Over the following months, concern over hippie types, invading minorities, and feminists—referred to collectively as the counterculture—grew to become an increasingly disturbing subject that my parents discussed frequently. They were avid readers of the local newspaper, which printed articles that often blurred the distinction between rebellious teenagers and people like Charles Manson. Long hair and bell-bottom jeans were seen as a step toward joining a cult. I remember flinching when I read articles about hippie types and minorities who were portrayed in a dismal light. It seemed as if the backyard bomb shelters and Red Scare of the last decade were being replaced by the country's own dissident youth and minority residents. They were the latest threat du jour.

Although, I credit being raised in a staunchly Catholic environment as giving me many wonderful values, and the early lessons about compassion and unconditional love were reassuring, as I got older, certain things didn't make sense and I had questions. When I learned that Catholic churches weren't located in every country (yes, I was 14 before I realized this), I excitedly asked my father, "How can it be fair that babies who die without being baptized in the Catholic Church are sent to limbo instead of heaven if they lived in a country that didn't have a Catholic church?"

My dad's eyes widened in alarm and he said, "We don't ask questions, we just believe!" I'd never seen him look so disturbed, and decided that thinking things through could get me in trouble.

As the months unfolded, my uncle's name continued to come up frequently around the house although we rarely saw him, and one afternoon as I entered the living room my mother threw the newspaper featuring an article about an event at my uncle's country club onto the chair. She commented bitterly, "It's your aunt who doesn't want to invite us to anything. That's the way the Polish are—they stick to their own."

I was surprised to hear my mom say this, "You and Aunt Anita were never close," I pointed out. "Mom, she probably doesn't realize you would want to be invited to anything." My mother didn't look up, and I got the feeling she was unhappy and wanted to find something to blame. The day before, she had walked into the family room and turned off the TV in the middle of the movie *Love Story*. She said it was not a movie young people should watch because it showed Ryan O'Neal and Ali MacGraw's characters living in sin.

Not long afterwards, when my father learned that my Uncle Jim had become a board member of St. Stephen's, an elite Catholic school in town, he and my mother asked my brother and me to transfer there. We were both good students, but I was just starting to feel comfortable at the local school in the few months I'd been there. Also, St. Stephen's had a reputation for being extremely snobbish. I dreaded having to meet all new kids, but I agreed to change schools so that I wouldn't disappoint my parents.

I started ninth grade at St. Stephen's and it lived up to its unfriendly reputation at first. Everyone there, including most of the nuns, was on a last-name basis. Although we wore uniforms, all the students wore navy-blue pea coats, finely knit sweaters, and the latest fad: penny loafers. After much persuading, my parents finally caved in and bought me the navy pea coat, but the shoes would have to wait. At first I found fitting in at St. Stephen's a challenge. All the girls wore their hair either in a flip or a pageboy, and I could never get my hair to go the same direction. I worried that I would never get accepted if I didn't fit in.

But not long afterward I met a girl named Ann, and we hit it off immediately. Ann was a straight-A student and as straight-arrow as I was. She also liked to laugh, and she called me Susan instead of LeFevre. We went to all the school events together and screamed so loud cheering for our victorious Class C basketball team that we were both hoarse the next day. We became very close, and I began to love St. Stephen's.

But then one day, the first domino would fall.

Ann and I were in our all-girls religion class with Sister Madonna Therese, a nun who seemed older than God. Although we were good students who kept quiet during class and turned our homework in on time. Sometimes we would play innocent pranks to break the monotony of Sister Therese's lectures; a few giggles were worth the possible wrath we faced if caught. One afternoon as she droned on, I began to hum under my breath. Slowly, a chorus of humming schoolgirls, punctuated by little giggles, joined me. Sister Therese looked up sharply, demanding we stop. "Mum's the word! Mum's the word!" she shouted, but couldn't control the buzz that had taken over the classroom

From then on, the students nickname her Sister Mum, and as a result, Ann and I earned a moment of notoriety and an invitation to a party that weekend with a group of popular kids. The party was at the home of a family that was well known in town, so my parents gave me permission to attend. Ann and I were beside ourselves with excitement, but when we got to the party, we found a lot of drunk and sloppy boys, and one of them tried to grab at Ann as she passed. We couldn't believe it when we saw them smoking cigarettes as well as drinking. I called my father to pick us up early.

As we waited on the front lawn for my father to come pick us up, we talked about our disenchantment with the so-called popular crowd and vowed that we'd never like boys like that or try drugs. It felt good to have someone who felt the same way I did about things.

Yet now that I was finally settling in at he new school and enjoying a close relationship with one of my classmates, life as I knew it was about to change forever. The following Monday, Sister Ferrier, who taught Latin and was referred to as Sister Fury by the students behind her back, appeared in the doorway of my religion class. "LeFevre, come with me," she said sternly.

I left the classroom and without saying a word, we walked to the office. I suspected I was being busted for the humming prank. I was then directed to an inner office to see "Father."

"Come stand over here," he said, and I walked around the desk as he looked down at my legs. "I think you know our rule is to wear your uniform to the center of your knee," he said sternly, and I realized my hiked-up skirt was at issue.

Then, just as Sister Ferrier stepped out of the room, Father leaned forward and extended his hand toward my leg and brushed against the inside of my knee. As Sister suddenly reentered Father quickly pulled back his hand in shock. Sister Ferrier's eyes burned into us like lasers.

"Follow me back to the classroom," Sister Ferrier snapped, and I quickly obeyed.

The walk back to the classroom seemed the longest walk of my life. While I was disturbed that the priest touched me in a way that I knew he shouldn't have, Sister Ferrier's harsh attitude toward me bothered and confused me even more. Knowing that the priest hadn't been allowed to touch another human being his entire adult life made it almost understandable what he did. But why did Sister give me such an icy glare? What had *I* done wrong? I could tell she was seething behind her large headpiece. As an unsure 15-year-old, I began to wonder if I was to blame for the priest touching me. Was I a bad person, I wondered. Had I been wrong all these years to think of myself as a good girl? My mind was filled with self-doubt.

When I returned to the classroom, I was anxious to talk to Ann. Surely she'd help me figure it out. Maybe we'd find a way to laugh about the situation later.

When class ended and everyone rushed toward the door, Ann yelled out to me to call her when I got home. I hurried to the bus, not suspecting that this would be the last time I would talk to her for many years.

At home, my mother distracted me from using the phone by handing me a basket of shirts to be ironed, and as I headed to the phone after dinner my father stopped me abruptly. He said he needed to talk to me right away. I remember thinking how unusual it was for him to single me out. With three younger siblings to attend to, he'd never taken me aside like this.

He walked me up to my bedroom and as I sat down on my bed, he said, "Your mother told me the school called today and they said they were concerned that Ann was a bad influence on you. They said you girls appeared to embolden each other and that your mother and I should break the two of you up."

I was stunned. "Who said this? What have we done wrong?"

"Your gym teacher said that you and Ann didn't participate in gym class last week."

I was in disbelief. How could any parent not like studious, polite Ann, with her Coke-bottle glasses and pleasant smile? She came from a respectable family that had been in Saginaw for generations, the kind my mother obsessed about.

"Dad, Ann's my best friend. She's the only real friend I have at St. Stephen's. We do everything together," I pleaded.

My father responded, "Well, the teacher said you and Ann have a bad effect on each other and we need to separate you."

"Dad, the only reason we didn't participate in gym class was so we didn't have to shower and get our hair frizzy. We haven't done anything wrong."

"Your parents and teachers will be the judge of that," he snapped, and after a short pause he said, "I've already called Ann's parents and told them Ann is not to talk to you at school or contact you at home again."

I ran downstairs and called out to my mother. I suspected this was her doing, just like everything else. "Why are you doing this to me?" I cried.

My mother responded, "Parents don't have to explain themselves to their kids." She then grounded me indefinitely for talking back.

I knew my parents' worst fear was having a wayward teenager. I'd heard them talk to people at church about families who'd been disgraced by a rebellious child. Eyes rolled, heads shook, and the attitude was, "How *could* the parents have allowed their child to get out of control?" But I still couldn't figure out what I had done to warrant such drastic actions. I felt I had followed my parents' authority religiously. Having their approval was important to me. I worked hard and was unswervingly straight. It took me a long time to realize that my parents had isolated me from my best friend and taken me out of school to help cover up what they perceived as a potential scandal at the church because of the priests action.

I had little idea at the time that my entire family was heading into a tailspin that would last for many years to come. In my opinion, this would be the fall of the second domino.

The next day at school I saw Ann and she looked as sad as I was, but we both knew that if we talked to each other it would get back to our parents, so, obediently, she looked the other way. I spent my morning classes in dread, wondering if I might have to sit alone at lunch time. When I got home, I attempted to sneak a call to Ann, but my mother caught me and extended the time I was to be grounded, citing my intentional defiance. Naturally, I felt disillusioned and confused.

Though I continued to go to classes and keep my grades up, a few weeks later my parents took me out of school. No explanation was offered. I had never missed a class or been tardy. I asked my mother again, "What have I done wrong?"

Her response was the same: "We don't have to explain ourselves to you."

It was early May, and the weather had already begun to get warm. I figured that at least I could work on getting a tan. Trying to get dark from the sun was a perennial quest for everyone I knew. I sat in the backyard with a silver-foil-covered cardboard, hoping to strengthen the effects of the faint sun rays. Otherwise, I stayed in my room a lot and listened to music, week after week. I discovered soul music on a Detroit station I could tune in only during certain hours, and I listened to artists like Bobby Womack and Al Green. Soul and rock music became my life.

In my depressed state I began to think about my aunt Rosie, my father's youngest sister. Year after year she had stayed upstairs in her bedroom at the big house in New Baltimore. I saw a newspaper clipping of her when she was a girl; she was beautiful, flashing a radiant smile as she received an award at a piano recital.

When I was about 10, we went to visit my grandparents and noticed that Rose Marie was gone. Not long after she began talking to herself and was diagnosed with schizophrenia she was taken to an institution. When she reappeared a couple of years later, her long hair was prematurely ash white and stringy, some of her teeth were missing, and the look in her eyes was vacant and filled with terror as if she'd seen hell. There were rumors that my grandmother had kept Rosie in the house when she was a teenager when it was discovered that she had fallen in love with the gardener's young helper. My grandfather had fought against sending Rosie away and spent most of the family's remaining fortune trying to keep Rosie in private homes, but when the money ran low and the pressure remained, he didn't have much choice since it was felt that the family's reputation was at stake. It later became known that Rosie had been raped and subjected to high-voltage shock treatment while institutionalized. My grandfather never got over the tragedy.

Was this what happened to people who didn't seem right to others? Would I end up like Rosie too? I could feel the air seeping out of my life.

I kept asking what had I done that I was being punished like this? Even a prostitute, Mary Magdalene, was forgiven by Jesus. I felt as though the tornado had come back and stayed, trapped violently within the walls of our house. I felt connected only by a string to my past and the girl who sought constant approval from her elders. The string was being pulled very tight now.

During the months I was restricted to the house, I noticed how much my mother stayed in bed during the day. When she got up, she was irritated about small things that she would never have noticed in the past. I did my best to keep out of her way.

From my bedroom window I could hear the sound of cars and the rumbling of lawn mowers droning in the distance, the sound of people living their lives. My life seemed stagnant and rotting, but I had no idea what I could do to change it.

One day near the end of the long summer, I heard a knock on the door and a girl's shrill voice. "My family moved in on Thunderbird Drive and someone told us a girl my age lives here." I peered at the visitor from the landing. She had overly bleached hair and a skimpy tube top, a look I would have distained a couple of months earlier, but now I was anxious to see someone—anyone—my own age. Before my mother could shoo her away, I bolted down the steps and invited her in.

The girl's name was Candy. We went to my room to talk, and in the course of our conversation I mentioned that I was grounded that summer for skipping a gym class at school.

"My parents are crazy too," she said.

I cringed, knowing that my mother was surely outside my door listening, and now she'd have an excuse to forbid me from seeing this girl as well as Ann.

Moments after Candy left, my mother said, "I don't want you to see her again. She's not our type."

The next day, I slipped out the back door after lunch and headed straight for Candy's house. I knew it is a brazen move to defy my parents, but I felt betrayed by them and I didn't care.

When I returned home a few hours later it was still daylight, but I knew my parents would have noticed my absence and would be angry. Still, I didn't expect what happened next. As I walked through the door, my mother rushed at me screaming and grabbed at my hair, pulling my head down toward the floor and finally pulling out a small tuft of hair by the roots.

I tried to protect myself by covering my head and screamed for her to leave me alone. After a few moments she stopped, but the feeling that I had been violated would remain with me. I had felt worse physical pain before, tumbling out of trees as a kid and falling off sleds, but this type of pain was very different.

I knew my mom was depressed and not herself during this time. The power she once held over us kids was slipping away and she didn't know how to cope. I was not the docile kid I had once been. I wasn't aggressive, but my attitude had grown more cynical after the incident at St. Stephen's.

My father had stood by helplessly as my mother had attacked me. I couldn't figure out why he didn't do more to stop her.

I began to feel like a caboose without an engine to anchor me. I had detached myself from a train that was going over a cliff, but I had no other direction to head. Candy was self-centered and irritating, but I didn't want to be alone.

My mother's condition was worsening, but emotional disorders were not subjects we discussed openly. She stayed in bed much of the day, and attacked me on a regular basis for no reason. There was no defense against her rage. I tried not to annoy her, but she always managed to find something to rail about.

My youngest sister, still just a toddler, looked up to me as if I were her mother as my mother's condition worsened but I felt a distance grow between me and my other siblings because of my mother's critical attitude toward me.

My older brother was on the football team and my sister, who was four years younger, was on the homecoming court and dating a quarterback. When my brother had the rest of the football team over for a party while my parents were gone, everyone got very drunk, and a couple of the guys talked about going out and beating up potheads; but instead they vomited all over our new living-room shag carpet and passed out. I thought that for once the wrath was going to be pointed elsewhere, but the incident hardly caused a stir. Boys will be boys, was my parents' attitude.

It was around this same time period that Candy arranged a ride for us to an area of town that had boutiques and other trendy shops. I hid my faded blue jeans and chandelier earrings in a large purse and sneaked out the back door again. The first boutique had a strong smell of fresh-cut suede and incense. Jackets with fringed sleeves hung on racks alongside suede purses with long shoulder straps, fringe, and beads. I had money from the many weekends I'd spent babysitting but I needed to save it for a car, so I couldn't buy anything, but the boutique was still a cool place to be.

The shop was run by hippie types in their early to mid 20s. They wore granny glasses and tie-dyed shirts and long necklaces with peace signs, but they seemed friendly and gentle. I felt relaxed among them as bluesy rock music pulsated in the background. A glass counter was filled with pipes and attractive cigarette lighters as colorful as toys. Candy handed me a crudely fashioned joint. "Take a puff of this…it'll make you feel like you're floating," she said.

When I hesitated, she snapped, "Don't be so uptight."

"I don't know," I stammered.

She said mockingly, "Are you worried about what Mommy and Daddy are going to think? Nobody cared when she was pulling your hair out."

I instantly regretted telling her about my mother having snapped. I resented anyone telling me what to do, but I took the joint she pushed toward me; it was easier than saying no, and I was curious about it. Why not, I thought. I took a puff—and inhaled. I immediately felt a warm sensation fill my head and a tingly sense of well-being. For the first time in many months, ever since things started going wrong at home, I felt the anxiety and despair dissipate. The world around me sparkled. It felt as though the music was coming from inside me and everyone was smiling. I started to laugh, and Candy did too. The thought drifted through my head that God had answered my prayers.

We left the store and got a ride home. As the car pulled into my parents' yard I could see my mother's body pressed against the narrow glass windows along the front door. I wished I could grab the wheel and drive somewhere else—anywhere else. My mother was obsessing again. How long had she been standing next to the door waiting for me? It wasn't even dusk yet.

As I walked up to the door, petunias spilled out near my feet. Flowers seemed out of place at a house I thought of as haunted. Thoughts ran through my head that the land was probably the site of an ancient Indian massacre. Why else was everything here named after Indians when I had never seen anyone who was even part Indian?

I opened the front door and like a gargoyle sprinting to life, my mother pounced at me for the second time. Her small fists pummeled my head, but the pot helped numb the pain both physically and in my heart. I was being attacked by someone that I had loved my whole life, someone who had now turned into my enemy. I remember thinking that at least this time; I'd done something to deserve it. It somehow felt better that way. I wished I had smoked more of the marijuana so that I could feel even more numb. I wanted to just drift away and not have to deal with my difficult existence in this troubled house.

There were a lot of secrets around the house, but I would soon learn that my mother was going to various doctors to discover the cause of pain she was feeling in her joints. But even after an exploratory surgery, doctors were unable to find anything wrong. One doctor prescribed diet pills to help give her more energy, but my mom found they made her feel jittery.

In many ways, our family conflicts were part of a common thread throughout the country. Turbulence was raging in the rest of the nation as well. In California, heiress, Patty Hearst, was kidnapped by a group whose professed aim was to rob banks and give the money to the poor. Hearst came to identify with her captors and helped them hold up banks. The Rolling Stones' hit, "Mother's Little Helper" reflected the surge in popularity of prescription drugs like Valium and Dexedrine—downers and uppers—that many middle-class Americans were making part of their lives and in the business world, three-martini lunches for executives were common By now, tailored suits and lacquered hair were giving way to less structured looks in the same way that the tight weave of the American culture finally seemed to have reached beyond its stretching point and begun to unravel.

Chapter 7

Fall 1970

The following fall I started my sophomore year at Arthur Hill High, a large public school. I was 16 now, and a very different person after events of the last year.

I made many new friends at the new school. It seemed like everyone there was smoking pot out on the long school lawn between classes. I knew I needed to get out of my parents house and I worked steadily mostly waitressing along with frequent babysitting jobs.

Tension was still high around the house, and I tended to escape into books and to express my thoughts in notebooks. Among my favorite authors were Sylvia Plath, Emily Brontë, and Gertrude Stein, and I also enjoyed books on Eastern philosophies. A book that I found startling, which happened to be required reading at school, was *Atlas Shrugged*. Ayn Rand sounded shrill and angry, and I was more drawn to the romantic angle than her political stance, but the concept she stressed about an individual striving for his or her own excellence regardless of what the masses thought of them, was a startling notion to me. Fitting in and bowing to the judgment of others had been pounded into me throughout my childhood. I'd been taught that the worst types of people—second to women of dubious virtue—were heretics—or nonbelievers. Now, in school, individualism was being touted as a desirable quality. I didn't know what to think, but I was realizing there was a much bigger world out there, and people with differing opinions.

But the books I was reading would also cause trouble between my parents and me. One afternoon, my dad asked me go with him in his car. He seemed very serious and offered no explanation and I was afraid to question him about where we were going. I remember his steely gaze remained fixated on the road ahead as we drove across town to a run-down neighborhood

We pulled up beside an old house, its paint worn down to bare wood. Cats were slinking around the foundation; a porch railing was tangled in the thistles and choke weed that served as a lawn. Two nuns answered the door and one told me to go upstairs, to an attic room. The house was starkly furnished, with hard chairs and a bare table and the attic room was even more barren. The room had no plaster or drywall, just bare studs and rafters, with a bunk bed in the corner. I looked out through the cobwebbed window high in the peak of the roof and saw my father's car, small below me, pull away from the curb.

I spent the night in the room. I had no idea what I was doing there. I wondered if the nuns were suppose to do some sort of exorcism. Nothing my parents did anymore seemed to make any sense. The nuns didn't seem interested in me; my presence there was obviously an imposition. I no longer felt conflicted about how to react. By now I had discovered tranquillizers, the first ones I got with a prescription from a doctor because of back pain. I pulled a couple of tranquilizers out of the pocket of my jeans, and the night drifted by in a haze.

Only later would I learn that my parents had found a book on Buddhism under my bed during a search of my room. They called my religious uncle who recommended dropping me off with the nuns seemingly so they could reform me.

After an eerie night, early the next morning I sneaked out of the house while the nuns were still asleep and I hitched a ride to a friend's. I stayed at her house and I didn't call home.

A few days later, the police picked me up there and took me home. Because I'd run away, I was assigned a social worker named Mrs. Clark, who to a small degree was able to help things out at home. She instructed my parents to let me go out with whomever I wanted as long as I was back by curfew. My mother didn't appreciate being told what to do, but of course she complied, since Mrs. Clark was an authority figure.

Upset that Mrs. Clark had sided with me, my mother searched my room more diligently than ever, determined to prove to Mrs. Clark that I was using drugs and the source of our problems. She seemed to fixate on me as an adversary and preoccupied herself with trying to catch me doing something wrong. When she found some unmarked pills in my purse, she ran to the phone as if she had a winning lottery ticket. She didn't bother to hide her disappointment when the pills turned out to be the type you could buy over-the-counter. It was then that I realized our problems went beyond the normal teenager–parent conflicts of the day. I wished that someone else could understand what was going on besides a mildly interested, overworked social worker. It hurt that my mom's troubled emotional state was aimed so predominantly at me. During this time, I noticed my father's hair turn white almost overnight.

A TALE OF TWO LIVES

One day I returned home from work to learn that my mother had shattered my John Lennon albums. My sister told me that the record, "Come Together," was the first to go when my mother interpreted the title to have sexual connotations. I ran to the closet to check on my clothes, some of which she considered hippyish, and was relieved to see my sheepskin coat, mini skirts and paisley rayon shirts still hanging.

At school I took a photography class, and my teacher recommended me to a photography business that had a job opening. I already had a work for credit job at Kmart by now but I dreamed that photography might be my destiny so I accepted the offer and now had two part-time jobs after a full course load at school. I went directly to the photography studio after school each day, then to the department store until 10 p.m. After that, I would go out with my friends. I kept this schedule for months with the help of my mother's discarded diet pills, and it took awhile before I realized how they brought about crushing lows when the buzz wore off. Of course, the lows fueled my hunger for more pills, which were easy to find at school.

When my parents weren't arguing with me they ignored me—these were the only ways we interacted. Most of the arguments centered on how my lifestyle threatened to undermine their standing as a "good" family. In my mother's eyes, Jim's kids, my younger cousins, were excelling at everything they did. She felt strongly that if she punished me enough I would straighten out, but of course the more hostile my parents were, the more disillusioned I became and the more I rebelled. My mother lashed back by telling me, "We don't need you—we have other kids who will make us proud."

All I could think about was saving enough money to get out on my own. I managed to save several hundred dollars despite having to buy my own clothes and school lunches, and I was only a couple of paychecks away from being able to buy a car.

It was around this time that I met a guy named Keith at school. Tall and lanky, with a protruding lower lip and thick blond hair that reached the middle of his back, he bore a resemblance to Mick Jagger.

After weeks of stealing moments with Keith after school, I asked my parents' permission to go on a date with him now that I was 16. They said I would have to wait until I turned 18. To circumvent them, I arranged to sleep over at a friend's house and then to meet Keith at Daniel's Den, a highly controversial night spot that was admitting 16-year-olds. Parents all over town were protesting its existence. "The Den" featured hard-rock groups whose band members wore black leather jackets and long hair and their music made the walls vibrate.

My girlfriends and I made it to The Den, but Keith and his friends never showed up. When the club closed at 11 p.m., we went to a party nearby hoping to find them there. At the party, everyone was passing around joints and sipping soft drinks. A guy in his late teens handed me a drink and a little later said that he had put something in it. "You're gonna like it," he said.

Uneasy, I went to search for my friends in the crowded house so that I could go home. When I entered the living room, a lampshade seemed to be circling around to the beat of the music. The music was pulsating as if it was my own heart, and it seemed to move the walls and ceiling. Other people at the party appeared to be in the distance, their faces contorted like live cartoon drawings. My head felt heavy and someone guided me to a bedroom to lie down. I began to have a vivid dream that I was a flower growing in the sun.

When I regained consciousness, I found myself lying next to the guy who'd spiked my drink. Some of my clothes were missing, and when I tried to sit up I found that it was painful. I realized only then that he had taken advantage of me while I was unconscious.

He offered me a ride back to my friend's house, and since my friends were gone by this time, I had no choice but to accept. The trip seemed long and ugly as we drove down lifeless streets just before dawn. An anemic light in the distance indicated that the night was over. I couldn't go back. It was too late to change things. All my life I'd been taught that a woman's worth was her virtue, and now mine had been stolen.

An added blow was that Keith heard about my having sex at the party, but not about my having been drugged. Shame enveloped me, and I couldn't find the courage to call him to explain. Not only was my virtue in question, but I was consumed with worry about being pregnant or having a disease. My family would never forgive me for that. I knew that I was now what my mother called "damaged fruit."

It was not much later that I learned that Keith had gone into the army, and shortly thereafter came the news that he'd been killed in Viet Nam. It was hard to accept that my first love was gone forever—and that he had died never knowing the truth about what really happened that night.

Chapter 8

Despite all the heartache of these years, I also remember it as a magical, wonderful time. The music was transforming. A line in a song by Buffalo Springfield captured it well; "*All across the nation, there's a strange vibration.*" The music was about our generation and our dreams of an ideal world. It energized us, amplifying our hopes and dreams, as well as our frustrations. The music seemed to understand us when the adults around us didn't.

We were standing up to the corrupt "establishment," the older generation that was responsible for sending young people off to a war that we thought had more to do with the profits to be made by selling helicopters and napalm. The glory of World War II couldn't be re-enacted. We were sure what we were doing but we felt that if we stayed the course and didn't let ourselves "sell out," we would triumph and could change the world into a better place. As teenagers raised in a vacuum, we had every reason to think we were capable of a transformation and could escape what we saw as a repressive era.

At the end of a long, gray winter, a friend from work invited me to a place called Ojibwa Island. It was a small hidden park connected to the mainland by a stone bridge, which was partially hidden from the main road by a sprawling ancient willow tree. The island is pretty, but the view across the murky Saginaw River was of defunct foundries attached to large concrete chutes that at one time emptied industrial debris directly into the water. Apparently, the practice stopped after the Cleveland River caught on fire a few years earlier and new laws were enacted.

A friend from school was sitting on the grass with some other kids and called over to us to join them. The small group was sitting in a half circle around a guy playing guitar and singing. He was ruggedly handsome, with intense steel-blue eyes and a square jaw, and I couldn't take my eyes off of him. His eyes caught mine, daring me to look away. After flashing me a brief smile, he sang,

"I've been walking my mind to an easy time...."

He paused to take a hit off a joint being passed around, then glanced at me again.

"I've seen fire and I've seen rain,
I've seen sunny days that I thought would never end,
I've seen lonely times when I could not find a friend,
but I always thought that I'd see you again."

When the joint reached me, I inhaled deeply in order to relax.

Then he paused and looked at me again before singing,

"Susanne the plans they made put an end to you".

I wondered if he knew that was my name. Next, someone yelled out, "Yeah, 'Sweet Baby James,'" and a few people clapped their hands. Others began talking, but I was aware only of the boy pulling strings on a guitar. Everything else was a blur.

Finally, someone introduced us. His name was Robert.

We started hanging out. Robert's friend Joe, a big guy in his mid-20s who worked on an assembly line, had set up amps and a mike in his basement, along with a drum kit. Robert played lead guitar; Joe and another friend, Robert, sang, and a guy named Tom played bass. There were always different drummers. The band, which they never bothered to name, was broke a lot, high a lot, and then high some more. They mostly played other people's music, but Robert believed it was his ticket out, even though months of practicing hadn't gotten them a gig.

We spent a lot of time sitting around on Joe's sagging couch smoking, listening to Hendrix and the Stones, and talking. Robert had a high number in the draft lottery, so that, at least, wasn't hanging over him. But the alternative seems just as lethal: working in a factory for 30 years like his father, only to get a watch and a push out the door when they'd used him up. Robert was angry—angry at the war, angry at how my parents were treating me, angry at the shitty part-time jobs he couldn't hold. "I'm changing tires on these big semis and I find out that they're liable to blow up and kill someone," he said. "That's the kind of job they get you down at unemployment."

"You're just gonna have to deal with it, man," Joe told him between tokes. "If you don't want to live with Daddy, you gotta deal with the j.o.b." But Robert's anger was the purest part of him, and it was comforting to me because despite all the conflict with my parents, I was not quite at the angry stage yet. I was still asking myself what I had done to incur such wrath from my family. My parents quickly added Robert to the list of people I couldn't see, but since they were hostile to me most of the time anyway I had little to lose, so I found ways to sneak out to see him.

When we were together, Robert just wanted us to forget about how fucked up things were, and sometimes we could.

Sometimes we even remembered that we were still kids. A storm one night left everything covered in a thick, shimmering blanket of snow, and I met Robert on the street with a sled from the garage. We pulled it to a park near the turn-of-the-century Water Department building, whose tall fluted columns and ornate cornices gleamed like a wedding cake. When we found a steep slope to ride down, I wrapped my arms around him as he guided us away through the trees.

When the afternoon grew too cold, we walked back to the Water Department steps and knocked a stiff snowdrift off a stone railing so we could sit down. Robert flashed one of his rare smiles and pulled a small box out of his pocket. He flipped it open and held it toward me. The tiny diamond glinted in the sun. The stone was scarcely bigger than the point of a pencil, but it was the most beautiful thing I'd ever seen. I slid the ring onto my finger, imagining what it would be like it to wear it in public, a declaration that I loved someone—and someone actually loved me back.

I slipped out as often as I could to meet Robert at Joe's or at another friend's apartment. I'd finally been able to scrape together the money to buy a used car, and while it was pretty beat-up, it afforded me the freedom I'd been craving for so long.

Robert often brought drugs, and in the beginning I tried them. I'd already discovered the euphoric boost of diet pills and tranquilizers, which helped when things got especially bad at home, but Robert introduced me to the mellow codeine high of cough syrup. I rode along a few times when he went to score in the rough part of town, usually waiting in the car. But he insisted that I go with him into a small, unpainted wood house to meet a couple he said were really nice. The sparsely furnished living room was dingy, and everything in it was filthy, including the five small kids packed onto a threadbare couch in front of a blaring TV. Robert's friend, a black guy named Jimmy, introduced me to his wife, Peaches, who was barefoot and a little spacey. Both of them had to be using. The whole scene ricocheted around my brain and all of a sudden I felt nauseous. I had to use the bathroom down the hall, but when I stepped in front of the toilet, I saw that the entire tank was quivering with cockroaches. All I could think about was those children.

I ran out to the car and waited for Robert. "What was that about?" he said as he climbed in.

"Did you even *see* that house? Did you see those *kids*? This isn't fun anymore," I told him, my skin still crawling at the thought of the roaches. "You need to slow down with this stuff. You need to stop."

"You're right, babe," he said, pulling me closer to him. "That was not cool. I'm sorry, baby. You're right. I'll quit." He was already high.

A guy named Ritchie started coming by Joe's. A friend of Robert's from school, he was sweet and funny, with eyes that had a twinkle. When I went upstairs to get something to drink one afternoon, he was by my side a minute later. Ritchie was on his way out, and he asked me if he could borrow 20 bucks. He needed it for gas, he said, and he'd be able to pay it back in a few hours, when he got his allowance from his mother.

I didn't know Ritchie that well, but I knew *of* him— quite a few girls I knew had crushes on him. I sized him up, then pulled out a 20-dollar bill and handed it to him. It was a major act of faith, since I had to endure three nights of back spasms standing and folding clothes at the department store to make that much money. But he was a friend of Robert's, so I figured he was good for it.

As soon as he was gone, Robert came up the stairs and asked if Ritchie had hit me up for cash. "Shit!" he said when I told him. "Ritchie's a rip-off artist and you'll never see it again. He's going straight to the dope house now. I can't believe you did that. Why didn't you ask me before you gave it to him?"

He fumed. "Ritchie's a chronic. We grew up together, but I wouldn't trust him now with anything. He uses every day, whatever he can hustle. Off gullible people like you."

I began to realize that Robert was not so different from Ritchie. Despite his promises, he didn't stop using. He just stopped *offering* me what he was using and started trying to hide it. We both smoked cigarettes and we often shared them, so I didn't think much of it when he handed me one a few weeks later, saying, "You gotta try this, Sue, it's *so* mellow." I took a deep drag and felt the same euphoric high that I got from pills. But this was different— immediate. Robert watched my face and laughed. "Heroin rush, babe," he said. "I put it in the tip of the cig."

I handed it back. "Just let me have the pack," I said, reaching past him and tapping out an undoctored cigarette. I didn't like the thought of heroin, but now I knew that this was Robert's new thing—and it was a lot easier to hide than alcohol or pills. I could tell by his eyes that he was under the influence—his pupils were pinprick size—but he didn't seem that different. This was a more subtle drug.

Trying to detect whether Robert was high became a game I learned to play. I had also learned to be a good codependent. Sure, he was using drugs more than socially, but he just needed someone like me to help him to see that he'd be better off without them. If he knew how devoted to him I was, he'd quit overdoing it.

One afternoon Robert poured shots of vodka, drinking one after another until a vein on his forehead stood out dark blue against his fair skin. He started cursing at me and yelling, and finally threw a glass figurine against the wall. *He's as crazy as my mom,* I thought, and ran from the apartment.

He called and called, and when I refused to talk to him, he waited outside my house in the sleet and then outside the store where I worked. Finally, he stopped me as I walked out at the end of my shift.

"Leave me alone, Robert. I can't talk to you," I told him.

He leaned over me, crying. "You're driving me crazy, Sue," he said. "The band is going nowhere and I can't think of anything but you. My whole life is crashing. I need you."

I resisted his pleas. "You have to choose between getting loaded and us being together, Robert," I said. "It's like you just can't quit once you start. I think you need to just quit altogether. I mean, I like to get a buzz like anyone else, but you just go nuts. I'm not going out with a druggie."

"If that's what you want, baby, I won't get high at all. I'll get a job and we'll get a place. Being with you is all I want. I'll be the luckiest guy in the world." He tugged me closer to him and kissed me. I loved the smell of him, and his strength, and the illusion that I was safe in his arms. I didn't push him away. We got in his car and drove to a friend's vacant apartment and spent a couple of hours together not thinking about anything outside of our own little world. I couldn't have been happier.

Chapter 9

The next time I saw Robert, his pupils were the size of pins and I knew he was high. He probably didn't waste a day keeping his promise to quit. I didn't say anything about his eyes, but I told him another truth: It was too hard fighting with my parents all the time over him, and I could no longer deal with their hostility toward me.

"You said they were that way before you met me—they're always going to find something else to bitch at you about," he said.

"Well, I just need to try," I told him. "They're constantly screaming at me about you and listening to my calls, searching my things, obsessed with keeping me from seeing you. I can't live like this."

"I can't live without you," he said. But I pushed him off. I had to get back to work.

When I got home I told my mom and my dad, who was hovering in the background, that they'd won—I'd broken up with Robert because they hated him so much. I wouldn't be seeing him anymore and he'd accepted it. I waited for my mother to say something positive, but she just sat there, lips pursed, staring at me as though she thought I was lying. *But she'll see,* I thought. *I won't talk to Robert. I'll get into college and we'll put these hard times behind us.* My father had said he'd help me pay for college if I finished high school and now I was going to make him remember, even though it was more uncomfortable to talk to him than to my mother.

Robert came to see me at work a few days later. He swore he was going to quit getting high for good this time; I meant more to him than the drugs. I left with him in his car to tell him that I'd promised my parents I wouldn't see him and I was going to honor that. But I added that maybe there was hope for us yet. "You need to get your life on track, babe, show me that you can get a job and go straight," I told him. "We can get back together then and no one can stop us once we're paying our own way."

We stopped at a gas station so I could get a soda, and I saw someone who knew my parents, but what did it matter? We were just saying good-bye a second time.

When I graduated from high school the next week, my parents didn't attend the ceremony. Mom wasn't feeling well, they told me. So I went alone. My sister and friends were there, but Robert stayed away. I figured I'd survived one more hurdle.

Two days later I was in stockings and pumps, getting ready to pick up job applications so I could find some kind of work that was less of a strain on my back. My mother stopped me just as I was leaving the house. "I have had enough!" she yelled. "I want you to get the hell out of here and not come back." She had an armload of my clothes and she threw them out onto the lawn. She kept pulling things out of my closet and drawers and throwing them until everything I owned was scattered on the grass.

"I never want to see you again!" she shrieked. "You're no longer part of the family. I know you're still seeing that Robert, and I'm sick of your lying. Get out."

My father stood wringing his hands behind her, but he seemed more afraid of her than I was and he didn't make a move to stop her, or me. I scooped up my things as best I could, retrieving undergarments hanging on a blue spruce and shoes caught in the rose bushes. It was apparent she'd gone out of her way to make it more humiliating for me. As I pulled out of the long driveway I knew I would never again live with my parents under their roof. I had a few hundred dollars in the bank, but no place to go. I didn't even have a bag to put my belongings in.

As I drove away from the house, my suspicions about my mother were confirmed. She was ill. I wondered whether the physical problems she said she was suffering from caused her emotional disturbance or vice versa. I would probably never know the answer—I just had to accept that this was now my reality and deal with it the best I could. It was especially hard because no one else would talk about it. Even the details of her physical pain were often kept secret, so it was unthinkable that she would discuss her emotional problems—even with a doctor. There seemed to be no gray area for our rigid family. People who weren't right mentally were committed to asylums or locked away in an attic. My family lived in a world that was rigidly black or white. If something wasn't 100% right, it was wrong. There was no in between.

As I drove along the open road, I felt a slight sense of relief and although I had no idea where I was headed, I knew I was leaving behind an environment that was toxic.

I located a phone booth and tried calling Robert. At least we could finally be together without interference from my parents. He seemed serious the last time we talked about quitting drugs. When his mother answered the phone she was unusually cool towards me and sounded upset. She said she didn't know where he was and hung up.

I dialed Joe's number and he told me the news. He explained that Robert had packed up and headed for Florida and wasn't coming back.

I leaned against the dirt-smeared glass of the phone booth and looked out at a drab, alien world. I felt completely alone. Where would I sleep that night? I didn't relish the idea of showing up at one of my friends' houses with everything I owned scattered in the back seat of my battered car.

As it began to rain, I retrieved the newspaper from under the clutter of clothing in the back seat. I turned from the page that listed job openings and found the section for roommates. The rain was pelting harder against the glass as I dialed, and when a girl answered I could barely hear her voice. Her name was Jane. She sounded pleasant. She invited me over to the apartment to talk about the available room.

The apartment building was an older-looking two-story fourplex with small wooden balconies and sliding glass doors. It was unattractive and close to a noisy highway, but I hoped desperately that the situation would work out.

As the rain continued to beat down, I rang the doorbell. The smell of stale garlic wafted from the apartment across the hall. The door finally opened partway and I could make out the face of an attractive girl with a dark tan and long sun-streaked hair. She saw me standing there with the newspaper over my head and smiled as she opened the door wider.

I glanced around the room. I could see the entrance to the tiny kitchen alcove, the living room, and adjoining dining room from where I stood. The furniture was simple but clean. A stereo and a stack of albums sat on a few wooden boards held up by bricks, and a tie-dyed cloth attempted to hide a large wooden spool that at one time was used to hold electrical wire and had since been reborn as an end table. Posters of Jimi Hendrix and Jim Morrison hung on the wall. The vines of a hanging plant in the corner trailed down to the floor. The room had a musky sweet smell that reminded me of the incense at mass. I liked the place.

"Go ahead and sit down. It's not fancy, but we try to keep it nice. You don't want to look under the slip covers," Jane said as she disappeared into the kitchen to get us something to drink. Her shiny hair fell to the middle of her back, just inches above her faded blue jeans. She was wearing a halter top, which suited her slim figure.

Jane was a couple of years older than me and obviously very together.

"I brought you a little glass of Chablis, Boone's Farm's finest."

"Thank you." A Bob Seger record was playing. *"Two plus two is on my mind."*

"You seem like you've had a rough day," she said. I realized my eyes were still moist from tears. I had hoped she would think it was from the rain. The last thing I wanted her to know was that I was 18 and still fighting with my parents. It was pathetic.

Jane glanced at my dress shoes and nylon stockings curiously.

"I had a job interview this morning," I explained.

"Have you ever lived away from home before?" she asked.

"No, but I'm fairly neat and easygoing."

"That's good. Sandy, my other roommate, is usually with her boyfriend and I travel a lot. I just got back from Jamaica last week, but when I'm home I like to have a few people over and just kick back, you know? I don't want a bunch of drama or shit out of place everywhere. You know what I mean?"

"What was it like in Jamaica?"

"It was amazing. We went canoeing through back country that tourists rarely get a chance to see. It was the most incredible place…and I thought the West Coast was cool. I lived in California for awhile last year, you know. Some people call me Caligirl."

"Oh, you're Caligirl? I've heard of you. Didn't you used to date Guy Grayson?"

"I used to; we're still friends, but I haven't seen him for awhile. Do you know Guy?"

"I've never talked to him, but I know who he is. My mom always talks about his family."

"Yeah, I think they sort of founded Saginaw or something. He's a total stoner, you know. I like to party, but he's insane. Do you like to smoke pot? You know, turn on?"

"Yeah, sure."

We talked for awhile, and later that day I carried my things in and placed them in the empty bedroom. A mattress lay directly on the floor and a few posters were tacked on the wall. I could start going to the community college nearby in a few weeks and I had my own room in an apartment with two older, rather beautiful roommates. Things were working out after all. With her good looks and easy smile Jane was a popular girl, and two or three of her friends came over to the apartment most evenings.

Chapter 10

Jane's friends were more sophisticated than most kids I'd met. Sitting in the living room, listening to records and smoking pot, they talked about trips to Florida, the Caribbean, and the West Coast; I'd barely left Saginaw's city limits in the four years since we'd moved there.

One guy who'd been coming around was particularly good-looking. I notice Javier's eyes first— just as I had with Robert. They were dark as onyx and sparkled when he smiled, which he often did. He was Hispanic, and never having met anyone from another culture, I was intrigued. Javier wore jeans like everyone else, but unlike theirs, his were always ironed, a crisp crease running down the middle of each leg; instead of the typical T-shirt he wore a well-pressed button-down shirt, and his shoes were always polished. Even his name sounded exotic to me. He traveled with the same friend and although that guy was taller and much larger, it was obvious that Javier was the leader, always sure of himself, somehow relaxed and ambitious at the same time.

Javier was even older than Jane, probably his mid-20s, and I was attracted to his maturity and his knowledge of the larger world. He began to come over quite often and brought food like tacos, chimichangas, and burritos. The most "ethnic" food I'd had before was frozen pizza. When he didn't show up for a few days, I mentioned it to Jane, trying to act casual.

"I wonder where Javier is."

"He's usually working on that restaurant he's starting. Do you want me to take you there?" she asked.

"I don't want to make it obvious or anything. I just think he's nice."

Sandy laughed. "Nice, eh? I think Susie Q likes Don Juan."

"I don't even know him; he just seems nice."

"I know—we could ask him to get us some pot. He knows where to get the best stuff. We'll just say we ran out, and wondered if we could get some from him," suggested Jane.

Javier's restaurant was on the other side of the river in an area called the South End. As I looked out the window of Jane's car, we passed several Mexican restaurants. The houses became smaller and lots of kids were playing in the front yards. We pulled up in front of a small, white concrete building on a corner lot. It looked more like a bunker than a restaurant, but it was freshly painted and had its own parking lot. Inside, I could see sawhorses and a stack of plywood. A long, shiny car was the only one in the lot. Javier saw us as we pulled up and walked out to greet us. I waved from the passenger seat and said hi, and Jane asked about the pot. He grinned and jogged over to the shiny car.

He came to the window of Jane's car, handed her a baggie of pot, and looked at me when he said, "Are you going to be around this evening? I'll come by if it's okay."

It was definitely okay.

When Javier came over later that night he brought his friend. Javier had pot rolled neatly like cigarettes that he brought out in a gold cigarette case. We all sat around our glass dining room table and talked. Robert had mostly carped about the war or problems in the country, so Javier's talk about his future and his plans to start a chain of restaurants was refreshing.

After awhile he reached into his shirt pocket and took out a glass vial.

"You want to try some coke?"

I had never tried coke. Cocaine wasn't readily available in Saginaw, but I'd heard people describe the great high. "Yeah, okay," I said.

He opened the vial, laid out several lines on the dining room table, and handed me a straw. I noticed his friend didn't do anything but sip a beer, and he only rarely cracked a smile when Javier joked around. I went ahead and did a line, and instantly I felt a remarkable sense of well-being. All was well with the world, and I felt good about myself and everyone around me. I felt alive, as if I had just awakened to a better way to live.

Javier did two lines right after me and became more talkative. He told me all about his family and how he was starting the restaurant so that his mother and brother could earn a living since his father had died years ago, after he and Javier's mother came over from Mexico. As he rambled and opened up to me, I sat quietly.

I thought about my family—and the pain associated with them. When I'd finally contacted them a few week's after the move, I thought they'd be relieved to hear that I was okay; instead, my parents' response had been cool. I envied his close-knit family, which sounded united despite so much hardship. Mainstream white families didn't seem to have that camaraderie, and I envied that, too, much in the same way I'd admired the way black people called each other sister or brother. I knew they suffered through many challenges in a white-dominated society, but they seemed to do it with a united front. I felt that my family found reasons to fight with each constantly, as if looking for differences.

As I thought about all this, I began to panic. The cocaine high was wearing off, and I'd never felt a descent like this before. I felt crushed under a great weight, as if the whole past year had fallen on me at once. I was desperate to break that fall, and Javier was quick to lay out two more lines on the table. Even as I snorted them, I was alarmed at the drug's strong effect. I'd never felt a compulsion like that before.

Javier left around 2 a.m., but he left a small pile of coke on the plate. I stayed up, alone, and snorted the white powder until it was gone. I rode the crash all the way down and it was terrible, but I was more terrified that I hadn't stopped myself before then. I told myself I'd never use coke again—its instant control had scared me worse than anything else had before, and I never wanted to feel that powerless again.

At that time in my life, I saw myself as an experimenter, someone who wanted to embrace different aspects of the world. The new path that I'd taken had seemed easy, and there was no one to judge me anymore. It was a kickback lifestyle and I thought we could party every night. But I knew now that I'd been fooling myself when I thought of it only as an adventure. It began to occur to me: Do other people start out being curious and, before they know it, realize their "visitor" status has been revoked and they can't find the exit? I thought the cocaine was just a temporary wrong turn, one that I wouldn't repeat, not another step on a path of quick gratification without consideration of the consequences. True to my vow, I didn't do cocaine again, but I found other ways to walk down that path.

A TALE OF TWO LIVES

Drugs were the centerpiece of our days. We used them and we talked about them. Jane had a friend who showed up with a bag of several pot plants torn out at the roots. He offered her a whole grocery bag of pot for $10. The pot was so mediocre she turned him down. He left it anyway, and Jane cleaned it up and put it into baggies. She was amazed at how quickly people were willing to buy it, even when she told them it wasn't very good stuff. Jane and I pooled the money and bought more pot to sell to friends. We barely make enough to cover our own stash, but her friends were always generous about bringing over the latest types of Thai stick, sinsemean, and other pot that mostly was being brought back from the war in South East Asia.

This new lifestyle was seductive, like a never-ending party. I felt like I belonged again. I was more confident when I was high, and I could make everyone at the table laugh. I didn't see that my life was crumbling around me. There were signs—but I would tell myself I'd take care of the problems later. The highs I experienced seemed more real than reality. They were my new reality.

I didn't attempt to talk about problems with my parents anymore; we barely spoke. I no longer believed in anything I once had. I felt betrayed. As far as I was concerned, my parents had turned their backs on me to impress other family members. I didn't feel trust in the government anymore, either. The war was a mechanism to funnel money to powerful business conglomerates who knew how to kick a generous amount of it back to the officials who helped out. Taxpayers were too busy fighting about being on the left or right side of things to notice they were being looted.

And God, I felt that was another ridiculous hoax, I felt. Where was God when innocent soldiers were being killed in the war, and where was God when I was punished for something a priest did? I knew I was angry... but at the time, in my mixed-up state, the anger felt like a strength. Anger felt better than being confused.

The world had turned out to be a hostile place, a big disappointment for me. The only times I felt good were when I was with my friends and we were getting high.

When Javier and my roommates brought out heroin—or "junk," as we called it—it was just another substance. It made me nauseous, but if there was nothing else around and I felt like getting high I'd use it. I preferred tranquilizers, but they were harder to get and more expensive. I just wanted something to help me get rid of the anxiety I felt when I was straight, something to help me deal with what I perceived as my grim reality.

Javier was attentive and took me to nice places— jazz clubs, card games, dancing. I was spending more time partying and was finding it hard to make it even to afternoon classes on time. My lifestyle had changed incrementally, so it didn't occur to me that I was getting high—on something—almost every day. I was getting pulled in, but at a pace so slow I didn't realize it until one morning, when I felt particularly hung over. As I reached for the door of the medicine cabinet, hoping to find something there to "pick me up," I was startled by the face in the mirror. I hardly recognized the girl I saw—she looked old and had a weary sadness in her eyes. Her skin was sallow. It wasn't a vision into the future—it was what I had become. I felt I'd gone through a metamorphosis, but in reverse. I was a butterfly who'd turned into a caterpillar. I went back to my room and knelt beside my bed like I had when I was a little girl. With little confidence that my pleas would be heard, I prayed to be rescued from myself. Like a drowning person, I was desperate to try anything.

I left the apartment to go to class but decided to stop off to talk to a woman I knew through Javier. She was about 30 and seemed to have her life together. In her living room, I spotted a picture of her younger sister and Javier together. I learned that Javier was seeing her sister long before me and had never quit. I was devastated. Even though we'd been dating for only a few weeks, I'd been living with the illusion that we'd been sharing something special.

I knew I had to make some drastic changes, and the first one would be breaking up with Javier. The second would be finding a new place to live. I need to get away from this lifestyle in the fast lane.

I'd met a girl at school who had talked about wanting to move out of her parents' house, and I approached her about getting an apartment together. She was excited about the idea and, best of all; I knew she didn't get high. This would be the first step in the next phase of my life.

I found a two-bedroom apartment a few blocks away from my parents, far outside of town and away from my usual haunts. If my parents saw that I was managing on my own, going to college and living on the west side, maybe they wouldn't be so critical of me. Maybe they'd realize I was a normal teenager, and even more responsible than most.

I told Jane and Sandy that I was moving out and started packing. I was ready to move into the new place when my new roommate told me she needed another two weeks to save the rest of the money for her share of the deposit and first month's rent. I would have to come up with the money on my own. Now, instead of triumphantly telling my parents that I lived nearby, I had to ask them for a loan.

My mother was home when I got there. I was still hoping that she'd be happy to hear that I was moving closer, but instead she looked horrified, staring at me as if I'd brought some kind of contagious disease into her clean house. She handed me the money in a zombie-like way, as though she had no choice. I was upset by her reaction, but I was still her daughter, and I thought: *I just have to be patient. If I can prove that I'm doing better, she'll accept me again.* I wrote down my new phone number and address, and asked her to call if she felt like it. Neither of my parents liked to communicate through words, but I wanted to give her the chance.

Once I was moved into the apartment, I felt confident that it was a first step toward pulling out of my tailspin. I was distancing myself from the fast crowd I'd fallen into when I was confused and angry at my parents. I'd also realized that smoking pot was holding me back from the ambitions I'd once had.

But as I worked toward making these positive changes, a hand reached out and yanked me back in, one last time.

Grandfather Albert (standing center) with College Basketball team

Susan Marie Ohio 1955

103

Susan Marie Age 4   **Grandfather Albert Lefevre**

Albert & Gerry 1985

**Susan Marie - 12th Grade
6 months before arrest as a drug kingpin**

**Susan (far right) and family (1974)
2 months before the arrest**

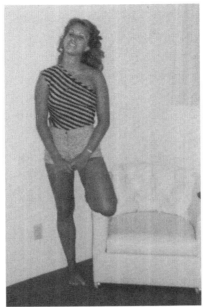

Susan Marie 6 months after escape

Marie & Alan - early years

Our Wedding Day

Maureen's Baptism

Maureen & Katie

Maureen, Alan, Katie & Bailey

A TALE OF TWO LIVES

Walsh Family 2000

Maureen College Graduation June 2008

109

Walsh family 2008

Marie in holding Las Colinas, San Diego

Alan and Katie react in Courtroom The Saginaw News. December 3rd 2008. Copyright 2008. All rights reserved. Reprinted with permission.

Backyard supporter party for Susan Marie a week before Parole Board Decision

Marie in Chicago with supporter Kathy Morse – February 2011

Chapter 11

As I spent the next few days unpacking boxes in my new apartment, I felt alone and in a funk. I missed hanging out with my partying friends, but I knew the only way to get my act together was to stay away from them, particularly Javier.

School was out for the holidays and to keep away from them, I hadn't given my new phone number to anyone other than my mother. I would start the new year headed in a new direction, but getting to that point was proving harder than I'd anticipated. The weather had turned bleak and so had my mood. I was having trouble shaking a miserable cold. But what was worse was that I missed getting high. I began to weaken and to think I might need to taper off more slowly from the drugs. Maybe there was something in one of the boxes I was unpacking that I could smoke or take just one last time, something that would take the edge off. I found myself unpacking boxes with a passion, hoping to find something to tamp down the anxiety. I considered calling someone but resisted. I had moved away from everyone for a reason. I had to stay focused.

Several feet of snow fell and the new apartment was disturbingly quiet. Every noise I could hear was made by me. The old television I had was broken so I played music, but I still felt alone.

One night about a week later, the monotony was shattered by the phone ringing. I answered, thinking it had to be my mother. Instead, I heard a strange man's rough voice. "This is Mark from Jackson, I wanna buy some drugs. Is this Sandy?"

I told him there was no one named Sandy there, that he had the wrong number, and I hung up. I assumed the last person who'd had this phone number had been selling drugs.

About an hour later, I was startled by the doorbell chiming and loud knocks on my front door. It was almost 10 o'clock, so it couldn't be my parents, and no one else knew my address. I opened the door and saw Robert's friend Ritchie standing there.

I had seen Ritchie around a few times after he ripped me off at Joe's apartment a couple of years earlier. The first time I saw him after he took off with the money, he had admitted he took the $20 because he was strung out on drugs and went into a passionate explanation about trying to get help. He said he'd gone so far as to check himself into a hospital that supposedly dealt with substance abuse. "But all they did," he'd said bitterly, "was strap me to a bed for a week till my parents' insurance ran out and then they showed me the door. I felt so rotten, the first thing I did was go get high." He got emotional and his eyes teared up when he said, "I don't know how to quit, Sue. I hate living like this. I didn't want to do that to you; I know you're a cool chick."

I knew I wasn't going to get my money back and I felt sorry for him. Even now, as he stood in my doorway, I found it hard to shoo him away, and besides, I hadn't talked to anyone all week. But I was still baffled as to how Ritchie knew my new address and why he was here. We weren't really friends.

"How did you know where I lived?"

"Billy told me," he said, referring to a mutual friend.

"I didn't give Billy my address."

"I'll tell you all about it in a minute...I got some good smoke. You want to get high? I hear it's some far-out shit." He removed his glove and pulled a tightly rolled joint out of his shirt pocket, displaying it in his palm like a rare gemstone.

"Ritchie, I'm curious—how did you know where I lived? I just moved in last week and I didn't tell anyone my address yet."

"Hey...It's freezing out here. Can I come in and light this up? Then I'll answer all your questions."

I stood away from the door as he pushed past me and took off his coat. He said, "I was wondering if you heard from Robert lately. I haven't seen him around all summer. Is he still down in Florida?"

I pushed some packing material off a chair so he could sit. "Sorry, I wasn't prepared for company. I've had a cold and haven't left the apartment all week; it's been so miserable. It's just weird seeing you here...and no, I haven't heard from Robert. He probably wouldn't know how to contact me now."

He lit up the pot and as he handed it to me, a trail of smoke followed it like a tail. "I needed to talk to someone, Sue. I think Joan's going to leave me for good."

Maybe he had changed. Ritchie didn't have that haggard look most chronics acquire by now. We were all struggling in our own way. His girlfriend Joan was from the west side, like me. He had talked to me about her a few months earlier when I bumped into him. I liked it when someone asked for my advice.

"Her closet at her parents' is bigger than my bedroom at home." He said, "Her parents hate me."

"If you're still using, couldn't that be the reason they're not crazy about their daughter being with you? It might not have anything to do with the size of her closet," I said sarcastically.

"Sue, I'm trying to quit and I'm not doing that much right now, but I can't stop completely. I don't know how. It's just so hard."

"That's what you told me last time I saw you, Ritchie. A lot of us are seeing the downside of getting high. That's why I moved the hell out here to the sticks—away from everything and everyone. This joint's the first buzz I've had in two weeks. I knew I had to quit seeing people who partied all the time, at least till I got my shit together. It's not easy."

He handed me back the joint after he took a puff. It was unlike Ritchie to offer anyone pot—he was more of a taker than a giver. And it felt good to get high again. The Stones were playing "Gimme Shelter," a great song for a buzz. All their songs were. The pot made me feel part of the music. I could lose myself, and the world was at ease again. I thought about Robert, wishing he were here with me instead of his childhood friend. I hated being alone.

Ritchie and I continued talking. The only news I'd had all week was the weird phone call I'd received just before he came over. I told him how my phone had been connected only a few days and some strange guy called asking for someone named Sandy saying he wanted drugs.

"I would have talked to him," he said. The same old Ritchie, I thought—first claiming he wanted to get away from drugs, and a moment later figuring out a way to score. Of course, we were both talking about getting away from drugs—while we smoked a joint. Ritchie continued talking about his problems with Joan and her parents and after

116

spending the week alone in my new apartment, only a block away from my own parents, I could relate to his situation.

But I wanted him to leave, so I told him I had things to do. Instead of getting his coat, though, Ritchie asked if he could use the phone. I pointed him to the kitchen. I could hear him talking, but I didn't want to know who he was talking to. Drug users with a habit didn't socialize, they hustled. I figured that was probably what he was doing.

When he came back into the room, he started putting on his coat. I was surprised when he said, "Hey, you want to go with me down to Luigi's for some pizza? It's on me."

"No way—it's freezing out"

"Aw, c'mon, Sue, come with me. It'll be good to get some fresh air if you've been stuck in here all week. A nice hot pepperoni and cheese."

I'd never gone anywhere with Ritchie before, and it seemed strange that he would ask me now—and even stranger, that he offered to pay. It should have been a clue.

But he kept insisting, and hot food sounded good. The pot had made me hungry and although I had misgivings about going anywhere with Ritchie I began pulling on my coat.

Then Ritchie said, "I got dropped off here, can we take your car"?

This should have tipped me off that something wasn't right. Ritchie wouldn't have known anyone this far out of town. Why would someone have driven him here?

"Who dropped you off all the way out here?" I asked.

"I'm starving. Can we talk about it when we get there?"

"You still haven't told me how you knew where I lived."

He continued to evade my questions *Whatever,* I thought to myself. I would figure it out later. "Whatever" was a word I used frequently.

I grabbed my car keys and we walked out to my cold car. If I didn't let my old Chevy warm up, it would stall when I put it into gear, so we sat there in my driveway, waiting. Ritchie looked out the window without saying much, and he seemed suddenly quite sober.

A TALE OF TWO LIVES

Chapter 12

I remember thinking how dark and deserted the restaurant parking lot was when Ritchie and I pulled in. I didn't see anyone else around. Ritchie left the car and I fumbled with the radio, scanning up and down the dial. I was still buzzed on the pot and it was important to find a good song. I finally found John Lennon's "Imagine." Perfect. I kept the engine running to keep warm. Next, Marvin Gaye's "I Heard it Through The Grapevine" came on, another great song. But after awhile cold air started to come through the vents and the radio filled with commercials. I could see Ritchie inside Luigi's through the plate-glass window, waiting at the counter. I thought, *what the hell am I doing here with Ritchie Anderson?* My teeth were starting to chatter. I got out of the car, slamming the door behind me, and went into the restaurant to see what was taking him so long.

Ritchie was looking at the guy behind the counter as I swung open the glass door. As I took a step into the restaurant, a bunch of armed men leaped out from the shadows and from behind the counter, their guns pointed at Ritchie and me. There were at least a half dozen of them, all dressed in dark clothes, and they looked like a paramilitary commando squad. Various members of the SWAT team shouted conflicting instructions at us. Strobe lights of red and blue flashed rhythmically thru the glass. They screamed, "Hands over your head."

Terrified, I raised my arms and waited. Next, a commando stepped forward and pulled a wad of money

119

from Ritchie's back pocket as he leaned forward with his hands on the wall.

The commando thumbed it quickly and announced, "Three hundred dollars—right rear pocket."

Another agent jotted it in a notepad he had ready. We were handcuffed and led out to two separate police cars in the parking lot. I felt as though I was watching a movie. Nothing seemed real at this point.

At the jail, I was led to a darkened cell where women lay in stacked metal bunks lining the cinder-block walls. The focal point was a stainless-steel toilet–sink combination.

I was surrounded by prisoners, probably hardened criminals, I imagined. I kept asking myself what I was doing there. I didn't know anyone who had been arrested or gone to jail. It was something you saw on TV or that happened to other people. Just then, one of the women got up to use the toilet right in front of me. Now it was really getting weird. The effect of the weed had completely worn off. I thought, one minute I was listening to Miles Davis in my apartment, feeling a little blue, and here I was now— locked in a jail cell, with a stranger sitting on a metal toilet a few feet away from me. When the woman flushed the toilet it sounded like an explosion, echoing off the concrete and metal in the room. The sound seemed to go on and on, and I couldn't help equating it with the sound of my life exploding into a thousand pieces.

I lay down on the thin mattress on my bunk and felt deeply ashamed. I realized I had been going the wrong direction for awhile. I had finally hit bottom. My parents' tawdry opinion of me was now validated. Their fears had become a reality. I had fulfilled their dire prophecy.

This time I knew that my situation wasn't my parents' fault. I was in jail because of drugs, and I had been the one to make the decision to use them.

A million questions flooded my mind. How had I gotten in so deep? Was I as obsessive as my parents? Had I screwed my life up just to get back at them? Was I trying to show them I could make my own decisions, no matter how foolish my choices were? Or was I just a weak person? Either way, it didn't matter. Maybe at one time my parents were to blame for my problems, but now I had sealed my fate on my own. I couldn't blame anyone else.

I felt horrible. My life was now hell, and I just wanted to bail out and end it all. It wasn't worth the pain. But I couldn't. Flashes of my earlier life suddenly flooded my mind and I knew it wouldn't be that easy. I thought of people who had loved and respected me, however long ago.

My thoughts turned to my aunt Mary Alice, who was severely crippled with cerebral palsy. I was the only family member besides my grandfather who could understand her stammering speech. She was always loving and good to everyone. What strength did she draw on? Every moment of her life was difficult, yet she managed to laugh more than anyone I knew. I'd never seen her angry. Here I was in perfect health, and I now I realized how angry I had become behind the image of a happy-go-lucky party girl.

I thought of how my grandfather had taken me aside for walks and talked to me about the old days. He affectionately poked fun at his own grandparents, who he said kept a small tin of soil from Germany, the old country, on the fireplace mantel. When someone nearby uttered words like "gosh" or "darn it" or "Hell's bells," they would run to the tin and touch their fingers to the dirt, sighing about what other family members in the Father country would think of them in America around such vulgarity. My grandfather would mimic a face of woe and gesture as if someone were nearly fainting as a result of such "strong" language. "What is the world coming to?" he would say, imitating their despairing voices.

My grandfather had loved to talk about the past. "When I was a kid," he would say, "my father gave enough money to the church so that we had a plaque engraved with the family's name on it, reserving the first row. When we got to mass, an usher ran over to pull across a little braided cord for us to enter the pew, so we had to be on time. With eight sisters, every Sunday seemed like a near calamity to avoid being late, but my father loved having that front pew."

I'd heard the stories about my great-grandfather, a prominent Detroit businessman, many times, but I had let my grandfather tell them as often as he wanted. Other family members had also achieved prominence as mayors, postmasters general, and county supervisors. I was the first family member to be a prisoner, the first to sully the family name.

It was a long night, but in the morning a bondsman arrived and I was released on a bond of $150. Ritchie's was $300, extremely low amounts even by 1970s standards.

Soon afterward, the *Saginaw News* would print an article about my arrest, and the arrest of some other people, most of whom I didn't even know. The headline would say we were drug kingpins. Since the amount of drugs and money involved were tiny, these facts were conveniently omitted. Nine years were somehow added to my age, which was listed as 28 instead of 19.

Chapter 13

Within a week I was assigned a court-appointed attorney named Joe Amato III. He called and directed me to meet him at the courthouse. When we met I was surprised to see how young he was. I guessed he was still in his 20s. He worked at a personal injury law firm and had never had a criminal case before. As I introduced myself and talked to him he didn't look up from a file he was reading in his hands which I could see by the name on it, pertained to another case.

"Follow me," he said a few minutes after we met. He directed me down a hallway to a small windowless room where a man also in his late 20's sat behind a plain metal table. The room was barren except for the table and two metal chairs. There were no introductions, but I assumed this was the assistant prosecutor, Mr. Ebert. Amato didn't enter the room after delivering me, and he shut the door when he left.

Ebert had a gaunt face with large tinted aviator glasses and hair that touched almost to his ears. "I don't sell drugs," I told him right away, "I was only with Ritchie that night to get pizza."

Ebert spoke in a raised voice. "We know you don't sell drugs, LeFevre…but we know that you know someone who does. We just need you to give us information on your Mexican boyfriend and his connection, and we'll drop the charge against you completely."

"Are you talking about Javier Carreras? He's not a big dealer. He can always get good pot and other stuff but he's not a dealer... and.....I quit going out with him a couple of weeks ago. Even if I wanted to set him up I couldn't.

"Well, if you're no longer involved with him that should make things easier for you. We need you to set him up."

"You don't understand. Javier isn't a dealer. He can get stuff if you ask him but he's not a dealer. If he did have a big connection, he certainly wouldn't tell me their name. Why would he do that? He used to bring drugs over to our apartment for us to party, but it wasn't that much...and I didn't buy drugs from him. I didn't need to. I don't know anyone who's a dealer. They wouldn't talk or sell to someone like me. I just use drugs to party. I'm not an addict."

Ebert shouted, "That's too bad for you, because we're not going to drop the charges against you unless you help us out. If you don't do what I tell you to do, we 'll put you in jail."

I kept thinking how none of this made sense. I heard my uncle say that he knew Ebert personally. Why would a friend of my uncle's, be upset that I didn't know any real dealers?

I was clueless.

I couldn't imagine being responsible for sending anyone to jail and I felt by the way Ebert referred to Javier as my "Mexican" boyfriend that they were targeting him more because he was Hispanic than anything else. I explained to Ebert that I didn't buy drugs from Javier and now that I'd been arrested he and anyone in town would suspect I set him up.

"You'd better give us someone or we'll crucify you,"

It was apparent to me they didn't care who I targeted or whether the person was innocent or guilty. It seemed to me they just wanted more arrests.

We went back and forth. He continued to shout. I'd never been shouted at by a stranger before. None of what he said was making sense to me.

Finally he said, "We're not going to drop the charges if you don't set up Javier but if you agree to plead guilty we'll give you probation.......we'll give you probation for one year."

I was still of the mindset that when I explained that I wasn't a dealer that they would drop the charges. I figured by now Ritchie had explained to them that he had asked me to come along at the last minute and that I wasn't part of the transaction. I thought it would be like I'd seen on a thousand TV shows, that every effort would be made to get at the truth and the charges would be dropped. Of course I was naïve. A couple years of getting high and a childhood filled with delusion made me quite ignorant.

Not happy about getting probation, I continued to argue, "But I'll have a record for the rest of my life for something I didn't do!" The idea of having a record was upsetting. I added, "If I go to trial I'll be able to clear my name."

"That's not an option."

"What do you mean, that's not an option? There's no evidence against me. I had little to do with the transaction that night. There were no drugs at my apartment or on me. I have no money or assets. I drive a car I couldn't sell for $300. I had to borrow money from my mother for last month's rent. Ritchie can explain that I wasn't involved. You said you knew I didn't sell drugs; why would you give me probation for something I didn't do?"

The next thing Ebert said would go through my mind a thousand times over the years. "If you take this to trial we'll crucify you. It doesn't matter if there's no evidence; the agent on your case is a state trooper who is a legend around here for his ability to convince a jury of anything, -no matter what the facts are. You won't stand a chance against him. If you take this to trial, we'll crucify you; you'll go to jail for sure."

"Are you saying the agent who arrested me would lie under oath?"

A sneer came across his face, "Who do you think the jury is going to believe, the word of a druggie over a cop's?" He looked at me as if I was a crumb. "If you take this to trial I can promise you, we'll put you in jail for a long time."

It took me a moment to comprehend what he was saying. I felt that having associated with Javier, a "Mexican", was my real crime.

I couldn't understand why a prosecutor, apparently a friend of my uncles, would tell me it was my bad luck that I didn't know anyone in the drug trade I could set up. That a policeman would lie about evidence against me made my head whirl.

I was 19, but the years of escaping to drugs when things got rough had made me significantly more immature. To me policemen were still the heroes and protectors of innocent citizens. Except for a few obscure news articles about brutality against hippies and war demonstrators, I had no reason to believe that law enforcement, even drug agents, weren't a lot like TV characters such as Sheriff

Andy and his side kick deputy Barnie from *The Andy Griffith Show especially when they were dealing with someone who was obviously not one of the bad guys.* I felt as though someone had switched the channels on my life and suddenly Sheriff Andy, Opie, and Aunt Bea had given way to a scene from The Twilight Zone.

I sat there in a daze. I couldn't comprehend pleading guilty by saying I did something I didn't do. I couldn't figure out why I was talking to him while my attorney waited outside the door. It seemed like an attorney should have been in there with me.

Finally I said. "I need to think about this and talk to the attorney."

"The probation would just be for a year." He reiterated. "I'm sure Mr. Amato will know how to advise you."

Amato was leaning against the door as I opened it. Without discussing the details of my case, he asserted immediately that I should plead guilty. It was obvious he knew beforehand what Ebert was going to tell me and he said without hesitation, "Probation is no big deal."

I remember thinking that as an attorney he wouldn't have wanted a mark on his record for selling drugs. To hear him say probation for a felony drug charge was no big deal made me feel that he also saw me as someone inferior because I used drugs and probably even more so because I "hung around with Mexicans". I felt like I was in the deep south in the days of "To Kill a Mocking Bird". I had so little knowledge of the outside world but I knew many doors would be closed to me if I had a record. I had many ambitions including possibly becoming an attorney who fought for good causes like the character Atticus Finch. I had had so many day dreams about what I wanted to do with my life and now I worried that they had all been in vain.

I continued to resist the idea of pleading guilty and argued my point about not wanting a record for the rest of my life. The next thing Amato said would baffle me more than everything else that had been said that day: "If you don't plead guilty, they're thinking of including you in the other charge they have against Ritchie."

"What do you mean? What other charge?

"Ritchie sold sixty dollars worth of heroin to Greely a few weeks before the arrest with you, some time in early December," Amato said but suddenly his voice trailed off as if he realized he was saying things that I wasn't suppose to know about. He began to backtrack immediately when he saw the baffled look in my eyes.

"What are you talking about? Why would Ritchie have sold drugs to an agent who had arrested him a month earlier? Ritchie hadn't mentioned to me he'd recently been arrested. Why wouldn't he have said something? It would have been big news. He wouldn't have been talking to me about the size of his girlfriend's closet. No one we knew had ever been arrested."

Amato stumbled over his words and his sudden anxiousness spoke volumes. I thought back to the strange things Ritchie had said to me the night of our arrest that hadn't added up. Why had someone dropped him off? Why had he been so insistent that I go with? Amato's slip about Ritchie's earlier arrest, stirred my suspicions up again about Ritchie's role that night. Had Ritchie intentionally lured me to the restaurant because they'd busted him before and they were pressuring him to set someone up just like they were doing to me? Was this all to get to Javier?

So many questions spun in my head. Why would my defense attorney deceive me about what was going on? Why did he know what the prosecution was doing and now he seemed to be covering up what he knew?

"Why didn't Ritchie mention to me that he'd been arrested?" I asked.

I started wringing my hands. I knew that asking Amato was pointless. I could tell he was lying to me but I had no idea why.

Still, I kept asking questions and getting nowhere. "Why would Ritchie sell to Greely a second time if Greely had busted him once?"

Amato was extremely uncomfortable and stammered out," I ah, ah, I don't think anything's going to come of it; I doubt anything will come of this other charge. I don't really know that many details."

"Mr. Amato, I hadn't seen Ritchie for months before the night at Luigi's. How could Greely say I was involved in a charge against Ritchie in December, a month earlier?"

"Like I said, I don't know that much about it but he's not claiming that you were there when Ritchie sold him the dope the first time but Greely says he called you on the phone beforehand and you told him to go to Ritchie's."

"That's a charge their considering bringing against me? I don't remember talking to this guy. And I don't even know Ritchie's address. He lives with his parents—how could I send him "to Ritchie's"? Just ask Ritchie, he can tell you."

"I ah….I… don't know, it's just something I heard." Amato stutters again.

"I have no idea what this agent sounds or looks like yet he's saying all these things about me? A guy called me the night of the arrest and I realize now it was probably Greely, but I hung up on him immediately. Why is he trying to make me involved?

"I only know what they told me."

"Ebert just told me they knew I didn't sell drugs and the only reason they brought me into this was to help them set up my former boyfriend. If you get a statement from Ritchie all of this can be cleared up. He has nothing to lose. He can tell them I wasn't involved."

Amato flinches at my suggestion that he get a statement from Ritchie. He's well aware that Ritchie has been offered leniency for his part in allowing them to bring me into this.

"We don't need a statement from Ritchie. I'm sure nothing will come of it." He repeats again.

I started to piece things together and my head felt like it would implode. I knew what I needed to do. I needed to get high. A joint and maybe a tranquillizer, anything would do. This was too much to deal with. I couldn't imagine such a cynical truth. But I continued to ask Amato to get a statement from Ritchie to 'clear this up'. Since Amato knew from the beginning that Ritchie was working as an informant he naturally couldn't get it and it became an issue between us. I inquired about it every time I saw him but he avoided talking to me in order to steer clear of the subject.

Only later would I realize that during the time Greely was claiming to have called me –I didn't have phone service. I could finally prove Greely was fabricating evidence against me. At the preliminary hearing I would ask Amato to ask Greely for the number he claims to have called me, and I would show phone records that would show it would have been impossible for him to have called me on that date.

I felt relieved but it also felt like a terrible blow to know that a police officer would make up information against me. I knew I was breaking the law by using drugs and a number of times I had bought drugs in small quantities for my friends, but almost all of my friends had more access to drugs and used them as much or more than myself and I was the last person anyone would think of as someone to get drugs from. I was getting high every day and worried about them taking control, so I would have been relieved if the prosecutor had offered to send me to a place like a rehab for a while, but they were instead trying to pressure me to put people in prison who I didn't think belonged there. They were threatening to lie about evidence against me. They were screaming at me and lying to me. It was a terrible, disillusioning experience. Who were the bad guys, I kept asking myself.

I had no reason to doubt Ebert's offer to give me probation. I had never been arrested and the amount involved was small considering that a report later showed that it was 96% non-narcotic.

I was still having a hard time comprehending everything. All I knew for sure was that a rogue cop was fabricating accusations against me and likely Ritchie to pressure us into setting up others, whether they were guilty or not. Our being young drug users made us easy slam-dunks. And they were threatening to include me in another charge against Ritchie just to get me to forfeit taking my case to trial. I felt that I had gone overboard that summer and my partying and drug use had gotten out of control, but I didn't deserve this punishment.

I was now living an hour and a half away in East Lansing and going to a community college there with Ebert's consent. I didn't tell anyone in East Lansing that I'd been arrested, so I had no one to talk to about the day's events.

On a subsequent trip to the Saginaw courthouse, where I showed up for what would be a myriad of hearings, arraignments, and preliminaries, I was approached by Mr. Kelly, the town's bondsman in the hallway outside the courtrooms. He was a small framed, friendly-looking guy who I had met when he'd posted my bail. I stood leaning against the wall outside a courtroom when he approached to ask how my case was going. I told him the court-appointed attorney and the prosecutor were pressuring me to plead guilty. He looked alarmed and said, "Listen, Sue, the first thing you need to do is talk to another attorney. Amato has a major conflict of interest representing you. Trust me—get a second opinion. The judges are on a witch hunt right now. They've made a pact that they're going to give ten-to-twenty-year sentences to anyone with a drug charge regardless of the details of the case. There's a lot of hysteria about drugs and they want to look like heroes."

"What do you mean?"

"The drug agent who arrested you has incited people by saying that Saginaw has five organized crime syndicates run by Mexicans."

"What do you mean, syndicates? Like in the Godfather?"

"What's really happening is, the Italians have been running the dope over to the East Side for years and they see the Mexicans as muscling in on their territory. Heroin used to be white, now there's a lot of Mexican brown from south of the border. The people behind many of the arrests are traffickers themselves and they're aiming at the competition. Amato's family is one of the old guard that's been in the trade for awhile. It's essentially just a turf war.

He leaned closer and in a low voice said, "The way I see it, Greely's nothing more than a front man for the old-guard traffickers who are going after upstart Mexicans trying to weasel into the business. He's probably working right with the Amato family. Trust me, you need to get another attorney to represent you. "

"I've already talked to my dad about hiring someone else, but he said my Uncle Jim said he knew Amato from his church and that he was a good attorney. They already told me they would give me probation if I agree to plead guilty."

He raised his eyebrows when I mentioned my uncle and said, "Just tell him it's important that you talk to another attorney."

I liked Kelly and felt immediately that he was well-meaning, but the things he was saying seemed almost too bizarre to be true.

Isn't the concept of five syndicate families trafficking drugs the plot line straight out of the movie, *"The Godfather"?* Do people really believe this about a town the size of Saginaw?"

"People are anxious. Jobs are dwindling for the first time in decades, and they have to have someone to blame— it doesn't have to make sense. Greely's stirring things up like this merely ignites already existing fears."

"It sounds crazy."

"You seem like a smart kid. What're you doing mixed up in this shit?" he asked just as Amato started toward us. He turned to leave quickly before Amato got there, and said, "Remember what I told you."

When we got in the courtroom, I asked Amato to point Greely out. I wanted to see this individual who was wreaking havoc on my life. Amato gestured toward a gruff, potbellied, unshaven man in a faded plaid hunting jacket. He looked like a homeless person and I judged him to be at least in his late 40s, although I learned later he was only 25 years old. After Greely was sworn in and under oath, I listened to his mind numbing accusations that didn't make any sense and that I knew were false. Amato seemed to offer arguments that had little to do with what Greely was saying. I had to insist that he ask questions as to whether Greely had any proof about what he was saying. In every case Greely admitted he didn't. Nothing was recorded; there were no police notes or witnesses. Amato kept saying we'd have a chance to offer a defense later.

As soon as I left the courthouse I drove straight to my parents' house. My dad was on the screened porch, and I told him that I'd been advised to get another attorney. I attempted to tell him a little of what Mr. Kelly told me, although none of the part about a drug war between suppliers sunk in. He looked at me as if I were talking about Martians from outer space and said, "You're uncle says Amato already got you an offer for probation and we should stick with him. We don't want a public trial. Your mother is already very ill. An embarrassing trial would kill her."

I argued further about what Kelly told me about Amato, but I couldn't get him to budge. My father couldn't bear the thought of my mother having to be exposed to a potentially protracted trial smeared across the headlines.

Meanwhile, I continued smoking pot and taking other drugs occasionally during the time I was in East

Lansing but I was slowly pulling out of my tailspin, and felt I was gradually getting my life on track.

In May, when I attended another hearing, Greely again made contradicting and false statements. Since this was a preliminary hearing and the defendant isn't able to speak to the judge, I wasn't able to respond. Amato assured me again that I would get a chance at a later date to defend against what Greely was saying. He said, "This is how the process works and since all the evidence is on Ritchie, it's necessary for them to focus on ways to tie you in."

It was like a bizarre sport for which only the participants of the justice system knew the rules.

These accusations made by Greely were kept in my file and while I never got a chance to refute them as false, they would be used against me many years later by a *Saginaw News* reporter and a longtime business associate of Greely's, the Saginaw prosecutor.

Chapter 14

In Lansing I met a new group of friends, and I loved living there. My grades were good and I continued to pull my life together. I rarely used drugs or drank alcohol anymore. Looking back, I think pot was the worse drug of choice considering my circumstances. I wasn't thinking things through.

The continuing court hearings grew more tedious. My father contacted me, reiterating my family's opposition to my desire to hold out for a trial. It would be embarrassing. He wanted me to plead guilty. I had endured many months of intense pressure from everyone around me who knew about my arrest. My uncle's name continued to get brought up as a driving force that I should take the plea deal. I was surprised that my father didn't want to clear the family name. He was fully aware that I hadn't been selling drugs, especially since I had asked my parents for money for rent just days before the arrest, but he was adamant that I do as the prosecutor and my uncle recommended. This was the first time in a couple of years that my father had really reached out to me. I felt that at least this terrible incident had a small silver lining if it brought my father and me a little closer. Since my family and uncle felt so strongly about it, I finally decided to go ahead and plead guilty and accept the probation offer. It seemed the easiest thing to do. It had been almost a year since my arrest.

After my decision to accept the plea deal, I was required to drive back to Saginaw to meet with a probation officer. She was an unsettling woman with oily hair and what seemed to be a permanent scowl. She gave me a legal pad and directed me to write a statement about what happened the night of my arrest. After I'd written a few sentences, she read the page and ripped it up. She sniped, "You can't plead guilty if you're not going to say you were there in the car."

"But that's what happened."

"Do you want to cooperate or what?"

"But I didn't go over to the car with Ritchie. Can't I just say I knew what Ritchie was doing? I didn't know, but I can say that. There were a lot of witnesses that saw that I didn't have any contact with the drug agent."

"What witnesses?"

"Mostly the SWAT team members that were in the restaurant."

"You don't have to worry about them as witnesses. Unless you want the plea deal pulled off the table you need to say you went to the car. You don't do it the way we want it—you'll go to jail."

If she had asked me to say that I handled the drugs or the money, I probably would have refused, but to say I accompanied Ritchie to the transaction didn't seem that big of a deal. I had been told I would get probation for only a year, and that didn't seem out of line for a teenager who had never been arrested before.

Looking back, I can see how easy it would have been to pressure me into saying just about anything if they leaned hard enough. I wanted this over as quickly as possible, and avoiding a trial would be the quickest way, so I wrote the statement the way they'd requested and then drove back to Lansing, relieved it would all be ending soon. That night I brought out an album my father liked: Dave

Brubeck's *Take Five*. I was happy my parents and I were getting closer again.

Soon afterward, I received a call from Amato, who gave me a number to call in Lansing for the vice squad there in case I had information I could give them. There was an obnoxious guy who hung around at school and tried pushing kids to use drugs and buy them from him. He was the only person I'd ever met who fit the stereotype of a drug pusher.

I called the number and gave someone there his name. A vice agent told me to come fill out papers at the station. I would later discover that the campus "pusher" was an undercover agent himself who was selling drugs to people apparently to get them to trust him.

Meanwhile, after another hearing I ran into Ritchie, who was also at the courthouse that day. He told me he was getting probation too, adding that the prosecutors kept saying they would crucify him if he didn't cooperate with them. He said Greely was picking him up regularly, giving him drugs or cash and pressuring him to make "buys." Ritchie complained, "Greely always says it will be the last time I have to do it, but then he comes over again and says I have to make more buys or he'll put me in jail. Sue, if I go cold turkey, I hear it's really awful. But if I keep doing this, I'm afraid I'll get a habit I'll never be able to quit."

I felt repulsed. Ritchie seemed oblivious that the people he was setting up, none of them actual drug dealers and they were going to be put through the same hell that he and I were going through now. The people he was targeting were mostly small-time users and Greely was getting convictions based solely on his testimony. Drug users rarely give up their actual connections, for obvious reasons and agents like Greely seemed not to care as long as he could chalk up a conviction.

My father and Amato were already at the courthouse when I arrived to change my plea. I hadn't seen my father in weeks. His face was drawn, and he looked older and forlorn. Amato was looking as smug and callous as usual. He never looked me in the eyes. They were both quiet and started to walk toward the courtroom as I approached. Suddenly, Ebert appeared and asserted himself in front of us. His eyes darted from side to side as he addressed me before my attorney and my father. "The probation's all been set up with the judge like we discussed. But it's important that you don't bring it up in the courtroom. You can't say any deals have been offered...but don't worry...it's just the way we do it." I looked at him, puzzled. This was the first that I'd heard that I would be speaking. I was taken back at the prospect, especially after having taken a tranquilizer. The attorney stood mute and Ebert spoke again: "Like I said, the probation has all been set up. You just can't mention it on record...but don't worry, it has all been arranged."

I wondered why he was repeating himself. I'd already agreed to the probation, even though I thought it was a bad idea. Still, I didn't suspect a thing, and I did exactly as I was instructed.

About a month later, I returned to court for sentencing. The guy I was dating in Lansing, a third-year college student at Michigan State, was planning on our going skiing the following day with a group of friends. I hadn't told him about my arrest.

Amato hadn't explained to me that I would be asked questions by the judge. I'd anticipated the hearing would be a formality, since I'd been told that probation had been set up with the judge.

While I clearly remember the events leading up to this moment, and have played them back repeatedly over the years, the day I was sentenced is as blurry as a fading nightmare.

The transcript says that the first thing the judge did was make sure the public was kept out of the courtroom. He said to me, "Your attorney says that you have requested a closed courtroom." The subject had never been brought up with me, but I agreed. At this point, I would have agreed to being the second shooter in the Kennedy assassination if they'd ask me to. Why would a 19-year-old request a closed courtroom, and how would I have been aware I even had that option?

The next 15 minutes was a kaleidoscope of surprises. The judge asked me if I was using heroin, and I truthfully told him no. I had no idea I was helping the prosecution, the judge, and the drug agent portray me as a ruthless "pusher" who didn't use drugs but sold them to others for profit. The judge was careful not to ask me if I'd been using drugs when I was arrested a year ago to complicate things.

Every copy of the transcripts I was able to see over the years was illegible, but I do recall a few things clearly. I remember the prosecutor asking for the maximum sentence, in direct contrast to his repeated assurances that my probation was "all set up." My defense attorney stood mute, and only then did I realize fully that he was working with the prosecutor, and probably the judge, against me. I was still unaware of what was about to happen to me. It was too much to grasp. I just knew that it didn't make sense, and that my attorney was shunning me while making a lot of eye contact and whispers with the prosecutor and others in the closed courtroom.

The biggest secret in the courtroom that day was that my public defender, Amato, was keeping me from seeing the probation report that went to the judge and listed all the statements made against me. I was unaware that the report quoted Greely as saying I was a high-level syndicate member making thousands of dollars a week with a crew of men selling drugs for me. Another entry in the same three-page report listed my only assets as a 10-year-old car worth less than $300, a broken TV valued at $10, and an antique mantel clock, but apparently this wasn't relevant. Nor was the fact that my parents gave statements about having to subsidize my rent and expenses days before I was arrested.

The report also stated that the prosecutor was asking for the maximum sentence, and there was no mention of the plea deal he'd made with me. Why would I have pled guilty if I wasn't told I would get leniency, when there was no evidence I'd sold the drugs? This report would stay a secret from me for 33 years despite my requests to access my records. As long as Greely remained on the force, I was unable to learn of its existence and use it to defend myself later.

So as I stood before the judge, expecting to finally get the nightmare behind me now that I was getting my life on track, and I heard the judge say, "Although you're young in age, I have a duty to society and I am sentencing you to prison for a period of ten to twenty years."

I didn't scream out or cry. I stood frozen, then turned to see my attorney run to the back of the room and reach for the door. My father was next to him as they opened the door and disappeared. Guards moved in immediately and put chains on my wrists.

Chapter 15

Once I was handcuffed, I was immediately and roughly escorted through a door on the side of the courtroom that leads directly to the jail and put in a jail cell. I was able to make a collect call home, but no one there accepted the charges. In desperation, I called my Uncle Jim. I thought that as an attorney, he should be able to straighten this out since he knew I was supposed to get probation. He agreed to come to see me and when he arrived, I talked to him through a wall of bars. I needed his reassurance so I that I wouldn't go out of my mind. *Ten to twenty years in prison.* I had plans that afternoon. I had plans for a life. But now...

What my uncle said next made me feel much worse: "Since you pled guilty, you won't be able to appeal your sentence." The words played out in slow motion in my mind. He said it as if he'd forgotten that for months he'd advised my father to have me plead guilty. I'd never heard him say it directly; it was my father relaying the information to me...but I did hear him say that he knew everyone at the courthouse involved in my case, especially the prosecutor and Amato, and I should do what they told me to do. That much I knew for sure.

He shocked me even further by adding, "I'd recommend you escape from the prison when you get there and leave the country."

This was a man who was so righteous that he'd cringed when I mowed our front lawn on Sunday, and now he was telling me to break out of prison. I realized that he saw me as little more than fringe that needed to be eliminated. I saw myself and my friends as kids who were drowning and needed help, young people gasping to survive in a complicated world. My own family members saw themselves as patriots and kids like me as the counterculture, who needed to be disposed of to make the country a better place.

Having heard that I couldn't appeal what felt like a life sentence, the idea of death seemed welcoming. I had no idea what to actually do, but I rested my neck on the cloth towel in the dispenser in my cell to see what it would feel like when it tightened around me. The thought of dying helped distract me from thinking about my prison sentence.

A guard walking by the cell opened the door and angrily grabbed me. He ordered me to strip off all of my clothes, and he and another guard roughly directed me to another cell with a large observation window. The cell was freezing cold and I sat on a bare mat, naked, with no undergarments, towel, or bedclothes. The Saginaw jail was notorious for its inhumane treatment of prisoners.

I put small squares of toilet paper on my private areas to cover my nakedness and huddled in vain to get warm. The guards peered in through a large window and seemed only to sneer at me. I had wanted someone to feel sorry for me, to care. Once again I was being naïve.

Chapter 16

Detroit Prison, February 1975

I was 20 years old when I arrived at the Detroit House of Correction. It was Michigan's only women's prison and housed about 300 inmates. The prison was a dilapidated group of buildings referred to as cottages and inhabited an area the size of a football field surrounded by a chain-link barbed-wire fence. Between the tawdry cottages and the stench-filled air, the facility reminded me of a skid row intersection cut out of a ghetto and deposited onto a remote field. The smell of rot and decay would linger with me for the rest of my life. I felt as if I had reached the end of the world.

After being taken off the bus, the other new prisoners and I spent a short time in the processing building being weighed and signed in. On one side of the room was a large cage holding a group of inmates. One woman looked at me and said, "C'mere."

She introduced herself as Lisa and asked my name.

I told her, "I'm Susan," I was glad to meet someone friendly.

She looked at my left hand, at the ring Robert gave me. "That's a pretty ring. Let me see it."

I held my hand up to the bars, showing her the ring with the pinhead-sized diamond. I remembered the day I got it and thought it the most beautiful thing in the world.

"Take it off and let me see it," Lisa said.

I took off the ring and handed it to her to look at. She quickly put it in her pocket and moved to the back of the cage behind the other women. I told a guard standing nearby that the girl had taken my ring. The guard looked at me incredulously and said, "Ain't that a bitch. Sounds like your problem."

Foolishly, I argued, "But she's right there in the cage. Her name is Lisa. I saw her put it in her pocket." I blathered on, but I didn't get the ring back. But this wouldn't be the last I see of Lisa.

Each of us was put into a different cell and an iron door slammed behind us. The concrete block rooms were about five feet wide and eight feet long, and at the far end was a small window covered by a grill that was so thick I couldn't see through it. The door had a small window for guards to look in. The thin mat that would be my bed rested against one wall. It was only a little better than lying directly on the concrete block. A metal combination toilet/sink resided in the corner. I would spend two weeks isolated in this graffiti-strewn concrete closet. This was the quarantine period. At night I could see the faint lights of a house beyond the prison through the window grill, a house in the real world. I wondered if the people inside knew how lucky they were to be on the other side of the barbed wire.

I tried to read books, but the selection was dismal. Most of the books were battered, with missing pages. They were also mostly third-rate mindless romance novels or unsuccessful memoirs. On the spine of the books, the word "discard" was written in thick black letters. Seeing the word *discard* bothered me.

The cell was bitterly cold, which made sleeping difficult. Most inmates had warm clothing that had been sent to them by their families, but my family had yet to contact me and I had only the clothes I wore to the courthouse the day I was sentenced—the day I thought I would be getting probation and go skiing with my new boyfriend. Thankfully, I'd been wearing a suede jacket, which I alternated moving from my head to my chest according to which area needed warming the most. I keep my shoes on throughout the night. I kept asking myself, *how did I get here?*

The other women in quarantine yelled back and forth through the narrow space under the door. Many of them were young also and seemed to be there for drug possession or sales. One of the girls called out that there was alcohol in the tiny bottle of mouthwash we received in a care package. I realized she was talking about drinking it to try to get a high.

I kept thinking someone would be coming to save me soon.

The weeks passed, and I while I wrote long letters to my parents trying to explain what had happened and to say how sorry I was about everything, I didn't hear back from them until I got a brief note from my father. He wrote that a girl knocked on their door shortly after I was sentenced and said she was a former roommate of mine and had left something in my apartment in Lansing. For some reason, he gave the key to the apartment to her, and when he went there later to pick up my belongings he discovered the place had been cleaned out. He wrote that everything I owned was gone.

I thought about my favorite outfits and my jewelry that were now gone. They hadn't been expensive, but they were things I liked and had memories attached to them. I thought of a long suede burgundy coat and matching boots that I had bought and been so excited about, my chandelier earrings with tiny beads of turquoise and matching bracelets, the beaded halter top that Robert used to love me in. Now everything I had in life was gone. I had lost it all: my family, my personal belongings, and any confidence I may have had.

I questioned why my father had written only to tell me this. I didn't have to guess that my parents felt extreme anger toward me. They had been hysterical when I wore faded blue jeans and listened to the Beatles—frightened that I would become "one of them." My getting sentenced to prison for 10 to 20 years had no doubt devastated them. The fact that they knew I'd been promised probation and that I hadn't been a drug dealer didn't seem to matter.

My expectation that many people in prison are criminal masterminds quickly disintegrated, and I realized that the majority of prisoners are from backgrounds of deep poverty. Almost everything I'd seen on TV about the justice system was a Hollywood creation or an exaggeration. Most of the offenses that brought the women to the prison were related to their being frustrated, uneducated, and poor. A huge majority had made relatively trivial bad choices that allowed them to get vacuumed up into the system, and they weren't a threat to anyone but themselves. Most were not so different than I. Of course, a small percentage of women were bona-fide predators who deserved even more time than they were serving, but they were in the minority.

Another amazing irony I saw was that the more corrupt prisoners were treated far better within the prison than the small-time offenders. The prisoners who ran extortion rings, sold drugs, and terrorized weaker inmates were often treated as premiere customers at the prison.

They were the gold card members. Girls like me who were neither street tough nor chronic lawbreakers were considered novices and were vulnerable targets of the guards and the other bullying inmates. By the time the women were released it, was obvious they would likely be joining the ranks of the chronically corrupt types and end up back in prison. The system seemed to ensure its own growth. This realization was like learning that a hospital was making patients ill in order to increase business. Who could imagine something so diabolical?

A large number of the women suffered from mental disorders, most of which could have easily been dealt with through therapy and possibly the right medication. The stress of prison made emotional and physical disorders worse. Many of the women wore helmets for spasms they never or rarely experienced on the outside.

We were unreycled trash—a few real criminal types and sociopaths, but primarily a collection of odd remnants. Year after year, teenage drug users, women with minimal personality disorders, vicious predators, and con artists sat together around cheap metal tables or lay on bunks before getting dumped out on the street. It was a manufacturing plant for corruption. Relevant educational classes and programs were scarce, or hobbling along until the next budget cuts eliminated them entirely in favor of building more prisons and hiring more guards.

The primary pastime was smoking cigarettes and picking on weaker inmates.

I learned the true definition of "ghetto fabulous." It was the belief that ruthlessness ruled and kindness was weakness. Being "ghetto" in many ways guaranteed a higher social standing within the prison environment among both guards and inmates. I viewed the attitude cynically until I realized that in many neighborhoods, this way of thinking guaranteed survival. Trusting or being "nice" could mean losing your life. Who was I to judge a world I knew so little about?

As a woman barely out of my teens, I was a prime target for guards as well as aggressive prisoners. My being white was definitely a liability in a Detroit prison, but I realized soon that it was the white inmates whom I had to fear the most. Some of the black prisoners taunted me as if they felt they were evening the score from past offenses perpetrated against other blacks, but it was the white inmates who made actual threats against me and seemed more motivated to lash out at me—primarily to prove their allegiance to the more dominant black and Hispanic inmates. The inmates who most often came to my rescue and felt empathy for me were also black inmates. I felt that they knew what it was like to be trodden upon. They were quick to tell me to keep on stepping forward and not let anyone see my tears.

I knew it was only a matter of time before I was attacked and likely injured, so when I learned about a live-in rehabilitation program that operated in a separate, cleaner cottage that was run with strict rules, I applied immediately. I didn't see myself as having an actual drug problem, but I figured it would be worth dealing with all the bizarre learning experiences for which the program was famous if it meant residing in a safer building.

I had been using drugs socially for a few years now, sometimes every day, but I didn't see myself as a chronic druggie like Ritchie. I'd resorted to drugs as an answer to frustrations and boredom, but I didn't consider myself to have a problem. As long as there were people around me who seemed more extreme, I saw myself as someone who just liked to "party." It was the 1970s, and I was just getting a buzz. That was the way I saw it even then, in prison on a drug charge. I had no idea about rationalization and denial.

Chapter 17

I moved into the rehab program, and my announcement during my first group therapy session that I didn't have a drug problem sparked off a firestorm of punishments. The "learning experiences" included wearing humiliating signs that said "I am a dope fiend," as well as tasks like scrubbing mountains of dirty pans, polishing floors with a toothbrush, and a day of digging holes for 12 hours in the grueling heat. My hair turned blond and my skin tanned to the point people had to take a second look to recognize me. The extra workload also kept me busy and distracted me from the persistent questions I had about my strange conviction and my family.

I lumbered through the rehab program determined to handle whatever they threw at me. Somewhere among the ridicule, therapy sessions, and monotonous work, I had a revelation. Maybe I did have a drug problem. Maybe I was using drugs as an answer to my problems and they had become a big part of the problem. Maybe I couldn't see what I was doing more clearly because I rationalized and made excuses to myself about everything. What may seem elementary reasoning to most was a revolutionary thought process to me at this point. The program had wonderful counselors, and I learned how I had deluded myself about my own weaknesses and blamed everyone else. I learned that it wasn't my parents or the government that I was mad at and running from, but myself. This information provided tools I would use to help me the rest of my life.

The important part of the therapy was that the people in charge truly cared about helping us. They worked hard to take us to a picnic at a lake outside of the prison one day, where we could swim and feel like normal people. I swam out into the lake and looked back to shore and saw that no one seemed to be looking. I was a strong swimmer and knew it would be easy to swim away and escape, but I knew the program would be closed down and the leaders would lose their jobs, so I didn't do it. I would look back on that day and how wonderful it felt to feel normal again, if only for an afternoon. The counselors had struggled a long time to make this day happen and it was a day that made me feel stronger. I didn't want to deprive others of having a day that they could feel normal also.

At group therapy, five to ten inmates sat in a circle and a counselor led the discussions. On one occasion a counselor asked us to discuss our life goals during a session. When it was my turn, I said, "I want to travel and go to places like Paris and Rome, and then get married and have a family that really cares about each other." The counselor knew I was serving a 10-to-20-year sentence; he knew I had no visitors and no money in my account, and that my only income was my seven-cents-a-day salary working in the kitchen. He looked at me and said, "I think you have illusions of grandeur, Sue." His words hit me like a punch to the throat. Mainly because I knew he was being logical. I had varying degrees of hope, but I knew the odds of turning my life around was not a bet most people would put money on.

The term *illusions of grandeur* resonated with me, and I wondered if I would ever be able to prove him wrong.

During other group sessions, I learned a lot about people's inner selves. Women talked of their personal experiences and struggles. A heavy-set girl with a smooth brown baby face from inner-city Chicago described the frustration she had getting control of her life. She yelled at me, saying she would rather have my problem of a long prison sentence than have to keep dealing with her addictions. The group talks made me realize how much we were all the same underneath the clothes we wore and the lifestyles we adopted. Caring about others helped me care about myself.

After a couple of months I heard from Robert. He'd finally returned from Florida to come and bring me back there with him, only to learn I'd been sent to prison on drug charges. I was struck by the irony: I'd broken up with him because of his drug habit. He wrote that he had quit using drugs and was trying to go back to school. The news he reported from Saginaw wasn't good. Greely, the rogue narcotics agent, was infamous now for his successful convictions and had already received a big promotion. Most of the people he targeted were young, and all were poor. All the same people who were in business selling dope before were still operating. Robert had also heard that Ritchie was escorted from prison to testify against people he was claiming had been drug dealers in an attempt to get out early, or possibly to get drugs while he was in prison. Robert wasn't able to come and see me since he'd been arrested for having pot and was on probation, but he wrote to me several times a week and said he would wait for as long as it took for us to be together again.

I stayed in the rehab program for about eight months, until it was closed because of funding cuts despite its very high success rate. I was transferred to a cottage called MC on the grounds. More than one of the girls in MC had escaped over the barbed-wire fence in the past.

Amazingly, they went directly back to their old neighborhoods and were picked up a few months later, sometimes at a dope house. The penalty for escape was a 30-day lockup.

It was a shock being back on the grounds. It was not uncommon for male and sometimes female guards to enter the prisoner's cells and shower areas and molest or rape inmates. The guards had unlimited power within the prison and were especially exploitive of the youngest inmates.

At night when it got very quiet I could hear noises through the wall of my cell, muffled cries of girls begging a guard to leave them alone. Some nights, the rhythmic pattern of something being pushed against the wall reverberated through the long, hollow hallways and like most of the inmates, I wondered who would be the next victim. After a while I heard details about a guard named Rick. He would enter a girl's cell and instruct her to remove parts of her clothing and pose for him in different positions. The girls had little choice but to do what they were told. As a guard, he had the power to make things extremely difficult for them, including write-ups that could sabotage a release date by years, placement in a cell with inmates that were mentally ill and violent, or weeks of solitary confinement in the hole. One inmate told me that the girls never knew what Rick would do. Some nights he might force intercourse or demand oral sex or molest the girls, but a lot of times he left after forcing them to pose for him in demeaning positions, as he told them they weren't worth fucking. He made a game out of demeaning the girls. I pictured his greasy hair and the calf-high boots that he wore over his pants as though he thought of himself as a rock star. Everyone knew what the noises meant, and it didn't take long for me to learn that Rick had an added agenda. He worked as a guard during the day, but only to supplement a second business in downtown Detroit: a bar where he ran a prostitution business and recruited girls from the prison. The disillusioned young women leaving the prison made for a constant supply for the trade. Now I understood why he spent so much time humiliating the girls—it was part of the plan to break them in for work on the streets. None of the girls had legitimate jobs waiting for them, and they were often on their own in the world. When the prison dumped them out on the street, Rick was there for them. This explained why he had left me alone so far: my long prison sentence meant I wouldn't be available for a while. He focused on girls who were getting released to "turn out," the term used for getting a girl to sell her body in exchange for protection from a pimp. This was one of many terms I learned in prison at a time when most girls my age were worrying about sororities or college homework.

Rick was the most flamboyant of the predator guards but certainly not the only one. Sex with inmates was common, and inmates who got pregnant were forced to have abortions. When an inmate hid her pregnancy and had the baby, it was taken away at birth and she wasn't allowed any contact with the child while she was in prison. Nevertheless, a number of inmates defiantly hid their pregnancies and later faced brutal retaliation within the prison system. One inmate whose case would ignite a major class action suit was routinely denied release 10 years after her first out date while the suit malingered in the court system, stalled at every turn by the state's attorneys despite hundreds of witnesses and difficult-to-explain pregnancies.

I was amazed to learn that the parole board was hand-picked by the prison industry, and at least in Michigan the board was not required to offer justification for keeping an inmate behind bars years longer than a judge ever intended. Many times judges ended up fighting for an inmate's release, but they were usually outmatched by a prosecutor trying to make a name for him- or herself.

I was looking at spending at least my entire 20s in prison, only to be paroled to Saginaw as a disgraced ex-con, and since none of my family had contacted me and I didn't expect that they would, I was looking at a pretty miserable future. Parole was probably the worst joke of all. Parole regulations were designed to keep people *in* the system, reeling in violators for even small amounts of drugs or alcohol in their system, missed curfews, or an inability to pay restitutions. Once you were pulled into the system you rarely got out.

Not all women became more corrupt within the system—just most of them. I felt that if I had to stay there for years, along with getting raped I would probably cave in to the pressures and come out of the experience as corrupt as the worst of them. I saw the small number of women who stayed above the fray. I admired them, but I felt they were stronger than I was.

Now that I was back in the general population, however, the immediate future was a more pressing concern. On a regular basis I was receiving threats and taunts from inmates and guards. My former sheltered childhood was now my biggest liability. My lack of street savvy made me an easy target.

One afternoon I was walking on the sidewalk of the prison grounds and without warning, a girl jumped onto my back and began to hit me about the face and pull my hair. I had never seen her before and had no idea why she was attacking me. Her friends stood on the sidelines. It was apparent that she was trying to impress them. She was pulled off by a guard and we were both put in solitary confinement. While I was in the cell, a guard who sat outside began making insinuations, then threats that he would soon be coming into my cell in the night. I wasn't sure if it was to beat me up or rape me. Since no one believed convicts, he could have done anything—the cell door was bolted from the outside and he had the key.

I spent 24 hours a day looking at the walls, which were covered in profanities and lewd drawings. Waves of anguish and despair washed over me. I could never have imagined life as being so difficult.

Then one night I experienced what may have been my darkest moment. All I could focus on was dying and getting relief from my intense suffering. I found myself praying for the courage to end my life. Then, I was suddenly struck with how foolish I was being. I didn't have much faith in the existence of a higher power, but in case there was one, I realized I might as well ask for something better than imminent death. In the solitude of the stark and ugly cell I begged to be delivered from this place, and this darkness I felt in my heart. I just wanted a second chance. If there really was a spiritual entity somewhere up there, I begged it to give me another chance to lead a normal life. I could hear my pleas as if I were screaming.

It may have had something to do with the depressing jail cell, or a mechanism in my mind helping me to cope, but a change came over me between the concrete walls and I suddenly felt exceptionally awake. All I could think of was that I wanted to live and to have a husband and children to share my life. I could feel the room light up, and it seemed warm and glowing, as if the sun had burst through black clouds on a stormy day. I felt that I could finally breathe and my heart felt light. I knew something was being revealed to me—I wasn't sure what, but I felt a sense of happiness and calm that I knew was going to stay with me.

The concern flashed through my 20-year-old mind that this might have meant I had turned into a religious zealot, the type of person I had a hard time tolerating, but I knew this was not the case. I had no idea how things might change for me, but I knew that somehow I would be all right. Only time would tell whether this feeling would last, but for that moment I felt warm in a cell that had been so cold a few minutes earlier. I felt confident my life would change for the better somehow and that I had much to live for. I felt ecstatic just to be alive.

Chapter 18

A few days later, guards called out that that I had a visitor. This was the first time anyone had visited me in prison. Dressing quickly, I wondered who it could be.

The prison visitors' room was a run-down, windowless chamber with a high ceiling. Its once white walls were yellowed from years of cigarette smoke. The only furnishings were a few worn plastic chairs and some small battered tables.

I entered the room with the other prisoners who had been summoned for visits. As always, we were made to sit before the visitors were allowed to enter. I had no idea who had come to see me, and I was elated to see my grandfather among the group that entered through the double security door. His tall, solid frame, his shock of silver-white hair, and his still rugged handsomeness would make him stand out anywhere, but he looked especially distinguished here in the prison. As he stood there wearing a tender smile, the sight of him gave me a warm feeling. Beside him, as delicate as my grandfather was imposing, was my Aunt Mary Alice. Her mouth was slightly contorted because of the cerebral palsy, but she looked lovely all the same. Affection coursed through me like an elixir as I rose to hug them both, and for just a brief moment, I felt young and happy.

We sat, holding hands. I expected we would make small talk. I supposed that, as always in my family, we would avoid discussing topics that might force us to look beneath the surface of our lives, topics such as why other family members—my own parents, for example—had neither visited me nor answered my letters.

"You look well, sweetheart," my grandfather began, "considering what I know you must be going through." Then he lowered his tone, and his voice took on an edge of seriousness more profound than I'd ever heard from him.

"I need to speak to you. Do you know if our conversations are private in here?"

I nodded, reached for my pack of cigarettes, and pulled one out. "Yes, it's fine," I said. I fumbled with a match and lit up.

Grandpa's face was troubled; his eyes burned intensely into mine. I wanted him to tell me that it had all been a mistake, that the family was going to get me out, that all the misunderstandings had been resolved and I would be home shortly.

"Susan, you need to get out of here," my grandfather said. "They're building a maximum security facility nearby. If they move you there, you may never be able to escape."

I took a deep drag on the cigarette until the menthol burned my throat. I let the smoke out slowly.

What planet was I on? Had I really just heard my grandfather tell me to escape from prison? My grandfather—who in his entire life had never violated a law or bent a rule—was telling me to break out of there? I still hadn't fully absorbed the reality that I was actually in a prison. I kept waiting to wake up from this unbelievable nightmare, and here was the most beloved person in my life telling me to run from the law.

A guard strolled by and glanced our way. I took another long drag on my cigarette.

"What about an appeal?" I said. "This is all crazy. There were witnesses who can testify that they promised me probation and threatened me to get me to plead guilty. My dad and my lawyer were standing right there when the prosecutor said the probation deal was all set. Why aren't they threatening to sue or something? Grandpa, I wasn't a drug dealer. I want you to know that."

"I do know it, sweetheart. You don't have to explain anything to me."

My grandfather shook his head. "Things didn't used to be like this in Saginaw, I guess your defense attorney was likely working right along with the prosecution because he was trying to get a break for his own father who'd been arrested for selling ounces of heroin. This would have been more than a hundred times the amount involved in your case."

"My attorney's father was a drug dealer? What was his name?"

"His name was also Joe Amato except that he was the II. Your attorney was Joe Amato the III."

"Apparently he was well known as a supplier and it was obvious that you had no idea about him. It seems anyone who was actually involved in running drugs would have known about someone like Amato in a town the size of Saginaw. There was never any doubt in my mind about your innocence but it seems obvious they were well aware that you didn't know who was in the business since they went ahead and assigned you his son with the same name to represent you."

"I had people like the bondsman and attorneys at the courthouse who were waiting on other cases approach me who told me Amato shouldn't be defending me. I thought they were mainly meaning because he was a personal injury attorney and didn't have any background in criminal law. Since I was told I would get probation, Dad didn't think it was worth paying for someone else. So his father was at the mercy of the prosecutors while his son was representing me, I was a sitting duck, I guess. What happened to his father?"

He got a 10 to 20 year sentence but no one knows how much time he actually did. It was all kind of hush hush. I knew when I heard about him that something was seriously wrong with what happened to you. With this same group of cronies in power at the courthouse, I don't think you have a chance through legal channels."

I saw that he understood it all only too well, and suddenly, I also knew something else he understood: that no one else in the family was going to lift a finger for me.

I leaned closer to him and Mary Alice. "How can they get away with this? I could get shot trying to escape from prison, and even if I make it, I'll have to live my life hiding out. Where will I go? How will I support myself?"

My grandfather's look was forlorn. Mary Alice didn't speak. These were people who were stunned to find themselves disagreeing with a police action. They had always seen the police as the front line of defense against the bad guys. Police officers risked their lives to keep the rest of us safe. How had it come to this? A world in which the government could do this to an innocent member of their family was a world in which my grandfather and aunt felt like strangers. "You will have to do the best you can," my grandfather said simply.

But if so many old truths were gone, one remained: Someone they love needed their help, and they had the power to act. "Find a way to get over the fence," Grandpa said, "and I'll meet you."

It wasn't hard to come up with a plan. My work assignment was at the medical clinic, which was located on the outermost edge of the prison complex, right beside the 20-foot-high chain-link fence that separated the prison from the outside world. Beyond the fence was a large expanse of thick forest. Even in winter, when there were no leaves on the trees, a person just might be able to get lost in there.

We set a date. Two weeks from now, early in the morning. I was supposed to be at work before dawn. If you were more than 15 minutes late, they started looking for you. I would use those 15 minutes to climb the fence.

"Morning," Grandpa confirmed. "I'll be there."

Chapter 19

The days crept by. I feared I would lose my nerve—the idea of running from the law for the rest of my life was daunting. But in fact, my resolve grew firmer with every passing day. The prospect of up to two decades in prison was almost unbearable. Besides, I had that well of hope to draw on, and I now had something else: two people—my grandfather and my aunt—who were solidly on my side.

Each day, I tracked my walk across the yard to the clinic, looking for just the right spot, scaling the fence mentally a thousand times a day—until the day came.

It was still dark, stars still sprinkling the February sky, as I headed for the clinic. My breath came in rapid puffs of vapor that quickly vanished. This was the darkest part of the yard, the darkness deepened by the forest beyond the fence. I was wearing jeans, tennis shoes, a shirt, and my thick suede jacket—good clothes for climbing a chain-link fence. One glance over my shoulder: no searchlights, no warning gunshots, all quiet.

This was it: do or die. It was a phrase I had never imagined would literally describe my own life. I took a deep breath and began to climb. My anxious panting broke the quiet of the morning. I reached the top in less than a minute. It felt so high up there, scary high, but I felt higher still—on the edge of freedom.

There was a double strand of barbed wire at the top of the fence. Balanced precariously, I took off my jacket, folded it over the barbed wire, then hauled one leg over onto the other side, then the other.

I pulled at the jacket to lift it off the wire, but it was stuck on the old, rusty barbs, and I could not run the risk of it being spotted. *Work it,* I told myself. *Be calm.* I wriggled and pried at the jacket. *Ow!* I choked back a yelp as a metal barb punctured the base of my thumb. I could feel a trickle of wetness down my hand. I jammed my palm to my mouth to suck up some of the blood. The wound would have to wait.

Finally the jacket came loose, and now I was heading down the fence on the forest side, the freedom side. The tight links cut painfully into my feet through my tennis shoes, so I needed to jump soon. But not too soon. The ground was frozen, hard; I couldn't afford to break or sprain something.

Now! I pushed myself back from the fence and dropped through the darkness. I hit the earth and ran, feeling a surge of elation. I was free of the bars, the stench of despair, the windowless cell, the bullying inmates and the crooked guards with their groping hands and brutal threats. I was free, and I was *running!*

Somewhere ahead, my grandfather and Aunt Mary Alice were waiting in his car at the edge of the woods. How far away? How long could I run? The thumping of my feet, the pounding of my heart: it all felt like a dream. I was racing over hard ground and patches of slippery snow, and I was dodging branches I could barely see in the dim light. My lungs were screaming for me to slow down, let me catch my breath. I did not slow down. I kept running.

Nor did I look back. I refused to look back. I commanded myself: *Even if they start shooting, keep running and do not look back.* If they shot at me, I wanted them to kill me. I was not going back.

The sky was changing from gray to shimmering pink, and I was thinking that maybe it really was a new dawn, full of possibilities for me—and then I heard a sound. It was the sound I'd been dreading. *Whup-whup-whup-whup-whup.* A helicopter. It meant they were looking for me. It meant they'd sent out the posse and they were looking for me. *God, help me,* I prayed.

I froze beside a tree. My jacket was decorated with butterfly appliqués, so I had to turn it inside out so the butterflies wouldn't show. I put my face against the tree trunk, right up against the bark, so that it wasn't illumined by the chopper's lights. I held my breath and waited. Amazingly, I thought the sound was diminishing. It seemed to be heading away from me. I exhaled, waited, listened again.

I heard a distant sound, but it was not the sound of a helicopter. This time, it was a car engine. I ran toward it. There was my grandfather in his old silver Cutlass, waving to me. Mary Alice was in the front passenger seat, holding her rosary close to her face. I swung myself into the back seat, using the open door as a springboard. The car smelled of Old Spice, like my grandfather. Still panting hard, I breathed it in.

Morning broke at last, just as I felt the idling car roar into action.

Chapter 20

My grandfather shifted into reverse, pulled away from the woods, and pointed the Cutlass for New Baltimore—home. The drive was not a long one—some 30 miles—but it passed in a blur for me, fear stopping my heart at every traffic light and intersection. Then we were there. As we pulled into the circular driveway, and I saw the familiar circles of rose gardens that Mary Alice, like her mother before her, spent much of the summer tending. In the center of each mound, a four-foot statue of a saint stood with outstretched arms, beckoning, as if to say, *I will protect you.*

On the far side of the driveway was the yard where Aunt Rose Marie practiced archery on her good days, along a long, grassy area where we often played croquet on our many visits when I was growing up. Beyond was the garage that once housed delivery trucks for the dairy business my grandfather and his father had operated, and across the street from the garage were the small cottages my great-grandfather provided for the dairy's surplus workers.

The house was on a hill that rolled down to a breakwater dividing it from Lake St. Clair. On the other side of the lake was Canada. My great-grandfather had built the house over 100 years ago, and his portrait still hung over the fireplace in an ornate frame flanked by braided pendants. Albert II, my grandfather, bore a striking resemblance to his father, except that my grandfather always had a twinkle in his eye while his predecessor looked stern.

I had never been to the house when it wasn't filled with my brothers and sisters and many cousins. We all visited my grandfather and "the girls"—my maiden aunts—several times a year. The Fourth of July was always a special occasion, with hundreds of family members showing up for an outdoor picnic and to watch fireworks out over the lake. One year more than 20 family members piled into my grandfather's small boat, my father at the helm. We went all the way to a tiny uninhabited island my father said belonged to Canada; it was my first time out of the country. On the way back, pastel blue skies suddenly turned dark and the waves rose, tossing the overcrowded boat around like a toy. My father guided the craft directly into the angry waves and diverted it to the home of other relatives farther east on the lake, and eventually we made it to shore safely.

My grandfather's house had been an important anchor in my life since my family had relocated so often as my father took on new positions. It was filled with furniture, chandeliers, a grand piano, and pictures that had been there for generations. The only alteration it ever experienced was the dock on the lake and the small boats that my grandfather left there, mostly for us grandkids to use; they would get crushed against the breakwater in the sudden but inevitable summer storms. My grandfather would spend the rest of the summer repairing the boats or fixing the dock and talking about the violent weather that damaged them. That pattern itself seemed unchanging.

But now, of course, everything had changed, and I wondered whether the enchantment of the house was about to be shattered by an attack from an armed SWAT team trying to recapture me. That image—of a group of uniformed men holding guns pointed at my head—was constantly in the back of my mind. I kept wondering how this would all end. Would my life ever be normal again?

It was risky to be at my grandfather's house, but my parents wanted to see me before I left the area. They were confident that their status as upright and respectable adults would protect them in the event the police did arrive. They saw the law as concerned only with errant young people, drug users, and bad guys—not their kind of people. I had once believed the same thing.

When my parents arrived, I was shocked at my mother's changed appearance. She was unable to walk and sat in a motorized wheelchair. I could see that it was painful for her to use her arms.

But her being crippled came as less of a shock than her next move, which was to hug me. She seemed to feel real tenderness toward me, something I hadn't felt from her since I was child—and even then, only rarely. The rage was gone, replaced by a genuine happiness that I was here. Why did this moment have to come when I was about to leave the country, when I quite possibly might never see her again?

Docile now in the wheelchair, my mother's eyes seemed tortured at what was happening to me. What had caused us to lose control over our lives these last few years? It was as if a powerful cyclone had sucked us up and deposited us, on a whim, somewhere else. Everything we had taken for granted and thought we had figured out about life had dissolved, and we stood watching, helpless to act.

Suddenly we heard the back door open and the sound of footsteps on the stairs. "Go hide in Nuna's room!" my mother said.

I scurried to the room in which my bedridden grandmother had died years before and hid behind the dusty drapes. My mother had actually tried to shield me from harm. Instead of assailing me, she was protecting me—and I was stunned. Although frozen in fear that the police were back in force, a warm feeling washed over me to think that my mother had been ready to defend me.

Suddenly, a sense of serenity about my life and its upheavals washed over me as well, like a soothing silence descending after a maelstrom. Leaping that fence to escape from prison had not been easy. I knew it put me on a road I had never envisioned. I was no longer a party girl struggling through college classes; I was a fugitive from the law. Once I could tell myself that despite using street drugs, I'd never broken any serious law since "everyone else was doing it too," but now I had no illusions: I was an outlaw.

Yet that jump over the prison fence was a leap toward new possibilities. It had given me a chance to reconnect with my mother, if only for a short time. And after making so many wrong turns, it had given me a shot at starting a new life.

When I emerged from my hiding place, my mother hugged me again, pressing my head against her chest almost desperately, as if she were drowning and I were her lifesaver. I couldn't believe that this was the same woman who had lunged at me for smoking weed, who had tossed me out of the house and never visited me in prison. When I was ready to leave, she shoved money into my hand—$200 in neatly folded bills. I realized that this could be the last time I saw her or anyone else in the family, the last time I would set foot in my grandfather's wonderful house. My head was spinning.

"Just a minute," I said to my parents. I quickly stepped around the side of the house and looked out at the lake for one last glance.

Dusk was setting in as the water lapped against the break wall. I looked at the old wooden shanty sitting partially hidden in the trees. I tried to make a mental picture—a fragment of the past to carry in my mind for my long journey ahead. The shanty held fond memories of cold silvery, days out on the ice with my brothers. We dragged the shanty across the frozen lake and cut a hole in a spot of smooth ice. Through our porthole we could see fish swimming blissfully beneath, oblivious that we were preparing spears with nylon cords with plans to impale them. That was how my life would be, living in imminent danger. But the fish had it right. Live without fear. When the end came, it came. At least while you're alive, live it in bliss. I would have to be as unafraid as those fish; worry and bitterness would weaken me and I'd fall prey to the predators again. What was the purpose of all that I'd been through, if I lived out my life in fear.

I don't remember who drove me from my grandfather's house to a small house near Flint, a house that belonged to a friend of a friends, but I wouldn't be able to say their names if I did, because by now everyone helping me in any way was committing a felony.

Robert came to see me every day while I made plans for my departure. We spent our days holding each other close, trying to make up for lost time. As with my mother, I felt that I had found him again only to have to say good-bye. Robert wanted to go with me, but we both knew it was too much of a risk. "If they catch me," I reminded him, "and you're with me, you'll go to prison too." The future seemed as mysterious as an abyss. The only thing we knew for certain was that it would be a while before we could be together again.

171

After about a week, I learned of a couple who were headed out to California in a few days. I had been thinking more in terms of Colorado. From what I'd heard, California was too wild a place for someone to settle and raise a family. There was too much hedonism there, people said, but west was the right direction and I longed to see the coast. The important thing was to get as far as possible from Michigan.

I didn't tell Robert that I had no plans of letting my pursuers bring me back alive. I wasn't sure what I would do if captured, but going back to prison was unthinkable. I worried that Robert would act impulsively, so I told him that I was leaving a day later than actually planned. I hated that I was once again forced to lie. Complete freedom to me would be the day I didn't have keep so many secrets.

Chapter 21

I rose early, while the sky was still cloaked in nightfall. My heart beat rapidly as I stood at the front window, an empty suitcase beside me, and waited for the light, hoping to make it till then. After that I would be on my way west, God willing.

Just before dawn, an old Buick pulled in front of the house and I got into the back seat. As we rolled down the two-lane road toward the highway, I felt better already. I was headed toward my new destiny, to a place where I didn't have to live in fear. The sky changed from gray to a shimmering pink, bathing the road ahead in its glow. Fresh light. A new day.

The car was a big boat, and I had the back seat to myself. Just me and my nearly empty suitcase, containing a few pieces of new clothing and a fresh toothbrush—everything I owned in the world. Empty and new—in a way, it reflected where I was in my life: I was losing everything and everyone I had ever known, and at the same time, this was my opportunity to free myself not only from prison, but also from the hypocrisy and pain of the past.

Just a few more hours and I would finally be out of Michigan.

The young driver of the car had introduced himself as Eddie and said that we had met briefly before. "And this is my girlfriend, Eva." Eva sat in the passenger seat. They were both quiet and, like myself, lost in their own thoughts. We were all going to a place we'd never been and sharing a trip that would change all of our lives. Maybe there was too much to talk about, so for a long time, we said little.

The sky was starting to brighten as the state border loomed. Pre-dawn seemed a good time for escaping: I had left prison before dawn too, watching the sun emerge on the horizon while most people still slept. I remembered the same wet air, the same ink-blue sky.

I would need to call Robert as soon as we crossed the border. Once we were out of Michigan and stopped for gas, I would find a pay phone. I needed to tell him I was gone. I would tell him I would send for him later, though I knew he wouldn't believe me, and I didn't know what to believe myself. I wanted to believe that somehow in the free world I could make my case and overturn the conviction, and that by then Robert would have matured and settled down with a good job and we could live out our lives together.

After we'd crossed the border, Eddie finally broke the silence. He turned his head slightly to say, "We're officially in Indiana now," and I could see his smile. "Michigan is behind us for good." He slowed the car and pulled off the highway at an exit well lit with neon signs advertising fast food and coffee. "We need to fill the gas tank," he said, turning back to face me, "and if you guys would like to get anything to eat..." Eddie never finished the sentence. A police car had pulled into the parking lot behind us, and without missing a beat, Eddie hit the accelerator and headed back onto the highway. It was probably a coincidence, but we felt better staying on the move. The incident sent an ugly shock through me. Was this the way I would have to live my life?

The highway felt safe and except for a few stops, including a painful phone call to say good-bye to Robert, we drove until the light began to fade and a protective darkness wrapped around the car, pushing the outside world a little farther away. The radio was playing "Slippin' into Darkness" by Eric Burdon and the Animals. I tried to focus on the music and relax a little. The small lights on the dashboard defined my world right now, and car headlights along the way seem like guideposts toward a new destiny.

We cruised steadily along the highway in the comfortable Buick. Since we couldn't afford to get pulled over, Eddie kept to the speed limit—65 miles per hour—as cars sped past us. It was a pokey pace, but it was my rocket to freedom.

The next day the road seemed to stretch endlessly in front of us, flanked on both sides by miles of crops that went on forever. There was little to do but stare at the vastness and let our minds wander.

This was perhaps the first chance I'd had to reflect on what had happened and what must happen in the future. As the car lumbered across the Great Plains, past and future sorted themselves out. In the clarity of that air, I knew I would have to forge a new identity. I could no longer be the same person I used to be. The old Susan trusted people indiscriminately and was easily crushed. She wasn't strong. I would go by my middle name, Marie. It was a name used all over the world. Who knew what country I'd end up in? As Marie, I would be someone who accepted that there would be pain in life and I'd face it without numbing myself with drugs.

I realized at that moment that not only the old Susan had to go, but also my parents. Everyone in my past had to be considered as toxic to me now. Letting them live in my head like this would hold me fixed in time, unable to move forward; their influence would drag me down into the same

175

black hole. My family had become for me the rot of gangrened limbs, and I had to cut them off.

As I pondered all this, tears welled up in my eyes. Cornfields gave way to high grassland as my mind's eye envisioned coffins being lowered into graves. Susan's coffin lay next to my parents'. I told myself that my mother and father died to me when I was 14, shortly after we moved to Michigan. The parents that I knew and loved had ceased to exist after that point. Whether it was my mother's illness, my uncle's twisted influence, or airborne mold from the surrounding swamplands that made us all go crazy, it didn't matter now. I couldn't waste time looking backward trying to figure it out. If I wanted to survive, I had to move forward and allow myself to believe that the future would be good.

So, somewhere between the cornfields of the Midwest and the western Rockies, Susan ceased to exist. In the distance, the sky was on fire. That was where I had to look now; my future lay straight ahead, under that fiery sky.

Just before we hit the Rockies, however, I began to feel forlorn. My thoughts drifted to Robert. I could see his eyes filled with empathy and the image stirred a rush of emotions. I thought back to the night—only months before my arrest—when he sat with me outside my senior prom and held me close. I had decided against buying a prom dress and a ticket to the dance, since I was saving my paychecks to move out of my parents' house. We'd gone to the gym where the dance was held to see our friends when it ended, but hearing the music and laughter we were unable to share had filled me with a sudden sadness. Robert could never bear to see me sad, and said, "I'll take you dancing and buy you dresses whenever you want once we get a way from here, babe. Just be patient with me. As long as we have each other, all the rest will come."

But now he was gone, and I had to stop clinging to his memory. I could no longer afford to daydream and delude myself with romantic fantasies. That was Susan's foolishness. I was 21 years old now and with my survival in the balance, I had to focus on reality. I was running for my life, maybe for the rest of my life. Like drugs, fantasizing about what could have been was a dangerous habit.

The reality was that it was Robert who had introduced me to drugs and although he'd said he quit, and perhaps he really had, I knew how easily people relapsed. If I grew lonely and got in touch with him, I might end up telling him where I was, and it could be my undoing. I feared my own weakness.

But I didn't want to continue living in fear. It would not have been worth it to jump barbed wire and risk my life only to end up letting fear and worry engulf me. I remembered one of the nuns in school telling the class that worry was a sin; it meant you didn't have faith. It seemed odd to me at the time, but I saw now how easily my life could be ruined if I let myself live in fear. I had cut the chains I'd been shackled with at my sentencing and could not replace them with the chains of fear and anxiety. This was my second chance. My jail cell the night of my epiphany had been filled with light. I could never let the darkness of fear overcome me again.

Chapter 22

A few hours after crossing into California, we checked into a hotel room in San Diego. It was the wee hours of the morning. At daybreak, I opened the thick drapes to a blast of light and a view of a vibrant pastel sky resting on an ocean of sparkling diamonds. Even the birds seemed ecstatic. I had come to paradise, and I felt immediately at home.

The plan was to head inland to the San Bernardino foothills, where Eddie and Eva had friends. But right now, all three of us just needed to *be*. I needed to stretch my limbs under this lovely sun, to let warmth wash over my skin, and to do what I had not done in months—just be aimless for a while.

We spent the afternoon walking along the beach in Coronado on San Diego Bay. The sand was soft and clean, and the air was light. Everyone seemed friendly. They didn't care who my family was or whom I knew. It felt like an embrace.

Then we headed inland, and very quickly, I got down to the task at hand.

I needed a place to live and could afford very little, but Southern California has always been a magnet for new arrivals, and I soon met Jan—about my age—who had just moved into a small apartment in a complex in West Covina and needed someone to share the rent. The one-bedroom apartment was furnished in a kind of motel décor that seemed appropriate for the perpetually shifting population.

Jan paid the bulk of the rent and rightly took possession of the single bedroom, while my share was $20 a week for the pull-out bed in the living room. The complex was new and clean and in a nice area. There was even a pool, where Jan and I met a lot of the other tenants.

It was comforting to learn that most were refugees, one way or another: young women fleeing parents for the first time, or men in their late 20s or early 30s who had been thrown out of the house by their wives because they took the free love message of the 1970s too much to heart. We are all in transition, and we all seemed to have secrets in our pasts that we wanted to leave behind. There was a vaguely party-like atmosphere many evenings, when we cooked our meals in foil on the outdoor grills and ate on chaise lounges by the pool. The men were very polite; they still seemed stunned to find themselves kicked out of the lives they thought they had.

For me, getting a job was the top priority. But I struggled without a car or license or any type of ID. I managed to snag an interview for a minimum-wage job selling nail polish in a kiosk at a nearby mall, but I was turned down, and the failure deflated me. I had never been refused a job I'd interviewed for, probably because I'd kept my sights low to avoid being rejected, and I took it personally that I'd been thought incapable of selling nail polish. I asked for work at a nearby Reuben's restaurant, but they told me they weren't hiring. I had now been rejected twice, and the thought of their rejection was agonizing. But my stash of cash was down to almost nothing, so what choice did I have?

At another mall, there was an opening to work behind a counter and sell fresh juice. I would have to ride two different buses, and it would take more than an hour to get there, but they offered me the job and I took it. I was happy finally to have a paycheck. I made up a Social Security number and hoped for the best.

My co-worker was named Sherri; she became a good friend. But after a few weeks, the boss said he couldn't afford to have me work during the afternoon hours when the place just wasn't busy enough. I was given a split shift, which meant that I now had to kill several hours in the afternoon just to be able work a few more hours in the evening. Trying to find another job brought the risk of further rejection, so I accepted what was offered.

After a while the business folded, and I was forced back on the job-search trail. Fortunately, one of my neighbors at the apartment complex was able to get me a job as a statistical secretary at a construction firm. With housing developments springing up everywhere in Southern California, this was a good job to have.

My neighbor was able to give me a ride to work until eventually I met someone who helped me finance an inexpensive car. He was a man who was dating my roommate's mother. He owned a dealership and couldn't believe I was living in California without a car. I felt embarrassed, and wanted to explain to him that I was just happy to be free after escaping from a Michigan prison where the guards were raping girls and forcing them into prostitution...but I didn't. I just let him think I was too stupid to save my money for a car.

"I have a trade-in that you can pay me for at the rate of $25 a month," he said. It was an AMC Hornet hatchback. He seemed surprised when I showed up every month to pay him the $25.

The car, of course, changed my life for the better, but I knew that I would eventually have to deal with getting a license. I got pulled over quite often by police, mostly because I was young and blond, but when I explained that I'd grabbed the wrong purse and left my license at home I was sent off with a friendly warning. I managed to remain cool during these incidents, but afterward I would shudder at the close call. I had to get a license somehow. One choice was to go the counterfeit route. I considered trying to seek out someone dodgy-looking and start asking around. I knew I wouldn't be the only one in California with a fake license. But if I did that, and got caught, the fact that I had false identification would be used against me. It would be considered one more piece of proof that I was a criminal, and I would be playing right into the hands of the criminal justice system that had already upended my life.

I decided to take my chances at the DMV. I filled out an application and went through the process, fingers crossed that the license might come through. Amazingly, it did. It is hard to measure—and harder to describe—how much of a relief this was.

I now had a car, a job, and a form of legal ID. It was a new beginning.

I spent four years in the San Bernardino foothills, moving from job to job, from roommate to roommate, but I made many new friends and they asked for no explanation as to why I had left the Midwest.

Southern California felt like a dreamland. The weather was a revelation after Michigan—swimming in the pool, clad in my bikini, in December!—and so were the mountains. My eyes rose to them every morning when I headed out for work, and every time, without fail, the view took my breath away.

So despite the normal setbacks, lonely moments, and self-doubts that I had to chase away constantly, I woke most mornings with a sense of joy. At this time, in this place, it was not difficult to cut myself off from the past. My focus was on the present, on the new me, and on what I needed to do to make my way.

It was ironic to find myself a secretary, typing lists of numbers for construction bids. I'd avoided learning to type in high school, because I never wanted to get stuck working in an office. A career as an anthropologist or a novelist was in my future, or so I had thought. Now I was glad to have this minimum-wage job where no one really bothered me—at least, not until the office manager came to my desk one day and said, "Hey, Marie, you must have given us the wrong Social Security number because they sent us a notice and bounced it back. Get this straightened out, will you?" Instead, I found a reason to leave that job and look for another. I could never stay at any job for very long—certainly not for more than a year—before the Social Security issue caught up with me again.

From time to time, I again thought about getting a forged birth certificate to use in applying for a Social Security card, but instead of taking that risk I would move on to the next low-wage job. I kept thinking that I'd soon be able to hire an attorney who would resolve my legal problems. Somehow, now that I was out in the world again, I felt sure I would manage to figure a way out of my dilemma.

But earning a living was definitely a struggle, and I was never more than a paycheck away from being destitute. I kept track of every expense to see where I could cut back further. Lunches, trips to the local desert, and new clothes were luxuries. I tried to save a small amount from every paycheck in case I ever needed medical care or had problems with my car. Amazingly, the Hornet never gave me a problem. In due course, it would be stolen by someone who smashed it into a tree and abandoned it. When I got it back, it ran fine.

Despite my precarious finances, I was having fun. In Southern California, there was almost no way for people in their 20's not to party. Sherri and I remained close buddies, and Jan and I still got together occasionally. Things were wonderful for me—maybe too wonderful. It lulled me into telling Jan my story one day over a glass of wine when we were both complaining about problems with our parents. She told me her parents were unbelievably critical and controlling, and I told her mine urged me to plead guilty to a drug charge they knew I wasn't guilty of just to get rid of me because I was running around with a Hispanic guy. Then, when I got sent to prison, they didn't talk to me until I escaped...Her mouth dropped open and I realized I had made a terrible mistake. The mistake weighed on me, and in time it drove me away. I moved from West Covina to Azusa—still in the foothills, but to a new start once again.

I was in touch with my parents fairly frequently via phone. My mother was courteous, but I was still the renegade daughter who had let her and my father down. Still, the one time I asked for money—I needed $200 quickly—my mother sent it. I asked my father to talk to my uncle, to see if he would explore some judicial remedy for what happened to me. Nothing came of this—and it didn't add up: Why wasn't an uncle manning the barricades to seek justice for his brother's daughter?

I spoke to someone else in Saginaw and heard the news that Ebert the assistant prosecutor who had helped deceive me had been convicted and sent to prison for selling drugs. The rumors were that Greely had set him up now that he had risen up on the ladder of the force and was cleaning up loose ends. He seemed to be targeting everyone involved in my case.

Questions kept hurtling through my brain about my so called "due process". I wondered if the men involved were truly happy in their lives. Were they ever bothered by their actions? But then maybe it was me who was the fool for not understanding that a kill-or-be-killed jungle prevailed on this earth. I wished I knew someone who could tell me the truth. But I knew that I would rather be victimized a thousand times than to be someone who would victimize others. I had to believe that goodness would win out in the end.

Chapter 23

 F or awhile life ran along smoothly, and I felt almost like a normal girl in her early 20s except for the fact that I had a big secret to hide. Then one night after Sherri and I had been out dancing, I pulled into a convenience store to buy cigarettes shortly after dropping her off. The store wasn't in a rough area, and I left the car running as I quickly made my purchase. As I was pulling out of the parking lot, a blond-haired man jumped into the passenger seat and ordered me to drive.

"I'm not going to hurt you," he said. "I just need a ride." He didn't look like a criminal, but didn't exactly look like a surfer, either. I was terrified. "Turn right," he directed me, turn left, left again—I lost track—and then he ordered me to stop. With that, his hands grabbed my throat and attempted to strangle me.

All I could see was the ceiling of the car and I found myself praying. *God, it is not going to end like this on some back street at that hands of a maniac, is it? Please no.* Somehow, I managed to work my left hand free. I grabbed at the door knob, flung open the door, and rolled out of the car and then under it. "Hey!" said my attacker in an almost reasonable-sounding voice. "Come on out of there. I didn't mean to hurt you. I'm not going to hurt you."

I didn't move. From under the car I could see that we were in a residential area; people were standing in their doorways in their nightclothes as my attacker tried to persuade me to come out from under the car. I tried to scream, but not much sound came out; my throat was still raw from the pressure of his hands. It was a frustrating feeling, to want to scream and have nothing come out. I'd felt that way throughout most of my life.

I saw the headlights of what looked like a patrol car and felt a rush of relief. The car stopped, and the driver walked toward my car. In a split second, my attacker ran the other way and the nightmare was over. I crawled out from under the car.

The driver was a security guard, off-duty and on his way home. "Are you okay?" he asked. I nodded, trying to regain my voice. "Thank you for saving my life," I managed to say. "I'm all right. I'll be all right."

Minutes later, I was back in the car and on the freeway, and in the rearview mirror I could see that my eyes were bloodshot and the blood vessels in my face and neck were broken, my skin mottled and red.

Someone had tried to murder me. Unaccountably. Inexplicably. I began to scream hysterically. I had never screamed like this before. I screamed because this was not the life I'd planned. I screamed because I did not know why any of this was happening to me. When I got home, I called the police to report that a strange man had tried to kill me. The officer told me I had to go to the police station to fill out a form. I responded that I was too distraught to do that; a strange man had just tried to kill me.

"If you don't want to come to the station, there is nothing we can do about it," the officer said.

It was ludicrous, surreal. *Why me?* I asked myself. What had I ever done to anyone? What were the odds of such bad luck…if that's what it was?

I had reconciled myself to the fact that life was going to be more difficult than what my small-town upbringing had prepared me for, but I'd never imagined anything like this.

I stayed home for days. I'd heard from a friend in Michigan that the assistant prosecutor had also had attempts made on his life and that Ritchie was found murdered. I began to question whether the attack on me was random. Even many weeks later when my broken blood vessels and red eyes went away I became panicky; when I was alone in a car with someone who had been introduced to me by good friends. It flashed through my mind that he might physically hurt me. I knew that this wasn't logical but I was not ready to be alone with a man I didn't know well. For the next year I didn't date and spent time with a wonderful group of friends at the apartment complex where I lived.

One of the guys in the group was a Viet Nam vet with whom I felt a special connection. I would have liked to be more than just friends with him, and he seemed to feel the same way, but I never let things get more serious because I could tell he also had secrets. Most of the time he was happy and sweet, but after he'd had a couple of beers, I could see the pain well up in his eyes. He would sit in silence across the room, but I sensed that he was far away—back there, in Asia, in the war. He was the only person I knew whose pain seemed deeper than mine, which may have been why I kept my feelings for him at bay: I knew I couldn't help him, as I was barely surviving myself.

I read a lot, and I found Eastern philosophy to be extremely helpful. It didn't seem to contradict the Christian values I'd learned in grade school. I thought that Jesus would have embraced parts of all religions. East or West, they seem to be saying the same thing about compassion being the key to contentment. One tenet of this ancient philosophy surprised me: that we should thank our enemy, for making us stronger. It was a hard concept to grasp at first. Deciding who's right and wrong and then punishing wrong-doers was the turn religion seemed to have taken when I became a teenager.

I still believed that good people would triumph over the greedy in the long run. For that reason, if for no other, I clung to the hope that eventually I would be able to tell my story to an honest court and find justice. I was continually haunted by images of the women I'd left behind in the prison. Certainly, many were guilty of crimes, but guilty or not, many were victims of the same aggressive and corrupt system that had almost destroyed my life. I felt frustrated at not being able to help them but I didn't know what to do.

I took another secretarial job, but the boss was a lecher who seemed to be able to detect that I was on my own in the world. I made a great effort to dress conservatively at work in the hope that I'd be taken seriously, but he still tried to corner me when others weren't around.

I started looking for a way out, and one day when I was dropping off a contract in Santa Monica, I picked up a throwaway newspaper called the *Argonaut* and saw an ad that one could only find in California. It was for someone to live on a boat and earn extra money by typing the manuscript of the owner's life story; the owner lived in an apartment nearby. I applied for the job and got it. Since the typing was only part-time, within days I got a second job at the Avis car rental at LAX airport.

Overnight, I had become an Angelino—a resident of Los Angeles.

A TALE OF TWO LIVES

The boat was in Marina del Rey, in a slip flanked on one side by a cabin cruiser belonging to Robert Wagner and Natalie Wood, the *Splendor*, and on the other by a huge sailing yacht called *The Sayonara*, one of the largest luxury yachts in the world at the time. I never saw Natalie Wood (who would later drown off the *Splendor*), but Robert Wagner was on board a lot and was always friendly enough to say hello; he even posed for a photo for me. I called my brother and other family members from time to time and was glad to have some news to report when they asked if I'd seen any celebrities.

I had the boat to myself for the three weeks I lived there, and I loved falling asleep to the sound of the lines pinging against the masts of the boats that filled the marina. Under the bright stars over the ocean, I began to feel safe again.

When the typing job ended, I move into another apartment with a new roommate, Annie. Her family lived in the marina and "adopted" me for many of the holidays over the next few years. The holidays were often a difficult time, and this family's kindness was a blessing.

Annie also fixed me up with a friend of her boyfriend—an auto mechanic from Germany who'd been living in the States for about 10 years. Reinhardt was handsome and fun-loving, and I fell for him; he became my first real boyfriend in California.

The first time I went to his apartment in a building on the beach and met his large German shepherd, I told him how unusual it was in this area to find a landlord who didn't object to dogs.

"My landlord loves dogs," said Reinhardt. "That's me; I am the landlord."

189

An auto mechanic from Germany, and he owned an apartment building on the beach! True, his business was well known, employed a dozen people, and was where prominent locals took their cars for repair, but the real key to Reinhardt's wealth was that like so many people in L.A. in the 1980s, he had bought real estate years earlier when it was cheap, and was now enjoying the prosperity that seemed rampant everywhere. The highways were filled with Mercedes and Porsches; massive houses hung from the hills engulfed in tropical trees and flowing flowers; everyone seemed to have a pool and a lifestyle, as the world thinks, to die for.

After we'd been dating awhile, Reinhardt took me to a Japanese restaurant in Beverly Hills where we ended up sitting at a table for four with Jeff Bridges, the actor, and his wife, Susie. We all talked the evening away as if we were old friends. Susie was a photographer, a profession that appealed to me, and they were both exceptionally nice. As I listened to Jeff make a joke and flash his famous smile, I thought back to my time in the Michigan prison praying for a quick end to my life and marveled at how different everything was for me now.

Reinhardt and I went dancing, ate sushi, and walked the semi-private beach under the moonlight. He played soccer every weekend—sometimes against Rod Stewart. Celebration and celebrities: It was all fun, until after about eight months I questioned him about our relationship and his feelings. I didn't hear from him again, and when I drove to his apartment one night I saw that he was with someone else. I felt hurt but foolish. I'd bounced from the drug-using aspiring rock musician to the handsome playboy in Marina del Rey. Why did I see the obvious only in hindsight?

I also suddenly realized that all of "our" friends were actually his friends, so along with the heartbreak came the total disappearance of my social life. Los Angeles, like most cities—and perhaps more than many—can be a lonely place when you're single and the phone doesn't ring. My roommate was in a relationship and gone most of the time. In my loneliness, I thought about Robert, but I knew it was not a good idea to call him when I was in such a vulnerable state, my judgment so in danger of becoming clouded.

Instead, I threw myself into my new job—a sales position at a head-hunting shop called the Powell Employment Agency. My new manager pointed to a group of empty desks and told me to go through the drawers to find old applications. "See if they left references on the back of the applications from friends in the same business," he instructed me. "Then come up with a list of job openings, and start calling them, telling the companies you have some great candidates. If you get the opening, you start calling to get candidates." I compiled my lists and began cold calling. The first time someone hung up on me the pain was searing. I wanted to run out the door and nurse my injured ego. I had never had anyone hang up on me…but through necessity I got used to it, and the knowledge that one client that I sent to a prospective employer was potentially worth thousands of dollars of commission proved to be a huge incentive. Becoming a headhunter became my new dream.

I still watched my pennies, but my financial situation had eased up a bit—that is, relatively speaking. In a place where expensive foreign cars, designer clothes, sailboats, and trips to the Greek islands seemed to be commonplace, buying snack items was a luxury I had to forgo. Since everyone was thinner in L.A., that proved to be a worthwhile deprivation. One day when I was walking out of the dressing room of a store, customers turned their heads to see the outfit I had on and asked for the item in their size. The shop owner invited me to come in on Saturdays and model merchandise in exchange for store credit. I begin to replace the work wardrobe I'd had assembled, some of which I'd made myself on a borrowed sewing machine.

It was a good lifestyle; I had a steady job and friends, and my social life had picked up. The dating scene in L.A. was robust. I suspected I still stuck out as a Midwestern blow-in, but I met lots of fascinating people.

I spent most weekends hanging out at the beach, rollerblading along the sand in Venice, music blasting from the boom boxes people carried on their shoulders. I sailed, played tennis, took hang-gliding lessons, hiked in the desert and mountains, and went horseback riding. The rock music of the '70s has given way to funk and dance music. Michael Jackson dance songs were popular, and on the dance floor I felt on top of the world. My girlfriends and I got complimentary memberships to private night clubs. Several nights, I found myself dancing with well-known athletes or occasionally Lou Ferrigno, the bodybuilder who played the *Incredible Hulk* on television. As we did the hustle or the bump, I considered that the long and winding road of life had some very strange turns in it.

I loved the job at Powell and soon worked my way up from placing secretaries to recruiting engineers, who were much in demand during the 1980s. I was the only female account executive among 40 men, and I made a lot of placements. The old days of cold-calling companies and facing rejection were in the past; now the engineers I placed were glad to refer me to others, and client companies always took my phone calls. I had finally found something I was good at!

I told my parents about my new job, and they were happy for me but still dubious. I'd been forced to lie to them so much as a teenager that they probably didn't know what to believe. Besides, they were overwhelmed dealing with my mother's rheumatoid arthritis and were on a constant search for drugs with less caustic side effects.

My parents spent most of the year in Florida now, where they made lots of new friends at their condominium complex. My mother said that they never did find a circle of friends in Saginaw. They rarely talked to Uncle Jim and his wife—despite their brief alliance when I was arrested and convicted. Conditions in Saginaw had become increasingly harsh. Unemployment was high and as drug usage increased, the town continued to spend liberally to jail people.

Speaking to my parents was oddly comforting, even if the conversation remained stiff. They now had more problems than I did because of my mother's illness, so I found myself in the odd position of trying to comfort them; I never mentioned my own hardships. Certainly, I no longer dwelled on what I expected of them as parents. I tried to consider them now as longtime friends. It was easier that way; I had no expectations. I realized that when I lived with them, I had allowed their disapproval of me to make me disapprove of myself, and I knew it was good that I had gotten away from them. Of course I also asked myself, over and over, why I couldn't have found something other than drugs to ease the frustrations I felt as a teenager under their roof.

At one point I even flew back to Michigan. The family was cordial but not overly enthused about seeing me back home. I was on the fringe—not just because I was a fugitive who could be picked up at any time and sent back to prison, but because I was in my mid-20s and still single. A "normal" girl would have been married by now, as both my older and younger siblings were. I had not, of course, been able to attend their weddings and was told little about the details. Like the holidays spent alone, these events were hard moments for me.

At Powell, the accounting department finally gave me an ultimatum about providing my correct Social Security number. I had been there a year and a half—longer than at any other job—and I loved it, but I knew the end was in sight.

I took my engineer "connections" with me; one of them, a nuclear physicist named André, was interested in a partnership placing engineers in companies that were always searching for new talent. The thought of starting my own business made it a little easier to leave Powell. While I was in transition, working out the details of the partnership with André, I got a job as a personal trainer and aerobics instructor at a Jack LaLanne's Health Club for women. Working part-time at a gym would spare me the expense of a membership for a while and I enjoyed keeping fit. The dress code called for instructors to wear black high heels, black tights, and a leotard. Giving several aerobic classes a day made my muscles a little sore, but I felt emotionally revitalized. The exercise helped to get me through the doldrums.

Then everything changed—drastically.

Chapter 24

By the spring of 1980, I was living in a two-bedroom apartment on loud, busy Pico Boulevard in Santa Monica. For $550 a month, I got a view of the ocean from the living room, proximity to Marina del Rey and the beach, and the area's wonderful energy. Granted, a block or two east the neighborhood got a little rough, as I found out one day when I went for a stroll and the police pulled up to ask if there was a problem. Truly, no one walks in L.A., but in this case, the well-intentioned cops were concerned not just about the fact that I was using my feet for locomotion but also about the area I was walking in. They warned me against walking there after dark.

My roommate, Joyce, was one of the friends I'd kept in touch with from the foothills. She was petite, with exotic dark looks, and she was a magnet for men. Her current flame was a former professional baseball player who appeared to have a great deal of money and time on his hands and lived on the peninsula in Marina del Rey. He went to a lot of parties. L.A. has a dizzying momentum—especially if you are 24 years old, my age at this time.

Joyce talked me into going with her and her boyfriend to a party where just about everybody appeared to be wealthy and, to hear them tell it, important and connected as well. They were either in show business or part of that cadre of newly rich entrepreneurs who were carried along in the current of the California real estate boom. Also present were an assortment of hangers-on who tried to pass as high rollers, although in truth they could barely keep gas in their shiny luxury cars. They passed themselves off as casting agents, producers, or writers, and while there may have been a grain of truth in what they said, it didn't take long to discern that exaggeration was rampant. The casting agents were actually gofers in casting agencies; the producers were assistants; the writers were clerks with fantasies of becoming authors. To me, most of the party guests seemed like elaborately wrapped gift boxes filled with Cracker Jack trinkets. So when I met Philip, he struck me as refreshingly real.

Joyce and I were playing backgammon at the pool when he showed up. Philip was in his early 40s, a big man, average-looking, with ultra-thick glasses that magnified his eyes. He was wearing a three-piece gray suit—unusual in L.A.'s casual atmosphere—that washed out his already pale color, and he had a heavy British working-class accent. "Hallo," he said. "May I play the winner?"

I won—one payoff from the many hours of board and card games played on rainy days during my youth. Joyce went off to circulate at the party, and the guy sat down to play. "I'm Philip," he said pleasantly, and indeed, he seemed a pleasant person—nothing forward about him, very polite. Yet after a few games, I was amused to see how intense he became. He positively glowed, and his magnified eyes lit up when he won; when he lost, it was as if he had lost the farm. He taught me a version of backgammon called Acey Deucey that he said was played a lot in Australia and all over Europe, and he really got excited when I began to win this new version. All I'd done was follow his strategy, which was very good, and I made sure I was efficient. Philip began offering wild odds favoring me if I played him again double down. "You're a hundred and fifty dollars ahead," he said in an excited voice, "and I'll triple that if you win again, and if you lose, you won't owe me a thing." He continued doubling and tripling the stakes until I eventually won $1,700 in a few hours. But since his terms had been madcap, I told him I couldn't accept his money.

"Then how 'bout I take you to lunch this week? Would you join me? I found a fantastic place in Beverly Hills."

"No, that's all right, don't worry about it. I had fun playing. I was just lucky,"

"What about tennis?" Philip asked, not ready to give up. "Do you play? I'm always looking for people to play with. Fancy a match? I haven't been in the States long and haven't been able to find partners." I realized then that he was lonely. I loved tennis, so I was glad to have an opportunity to get out on the court. We agreed to meet the next day—at least for a game or two.

Philip slammed every ball as if it were a bomb he was launching to blow up his opponent, but he kept me laughing and had a sweet personality. "Since you won't let me pay you for winning at backgammon," he said, "the least you can do is let me take you to a nice lunch. You won it fair and square, and I'll feel like a right heel not to pay up somehow. I meet so many flakes; it would be nice to talk to someone like yourself for a change."

We went to lunch at an attractive place in Beverly Hills called the Bistro Gardens. As we entered, Lauren Bacall whisked past us. You don't see many stars in the Midwest and after the experience of the Michigan prison, seeing someone famous was a fleeting sensation I wish I could tell my family about back home. I knew my brother David would love to hear I'd seen a movie star. I wondered when I would be able to tell him. During lunch, I told Philip my story—my recent California story, that is: how I left the employment agency, and how I wanted to go out on my own. "I've been working as a personal trainer at a gym in the meantime," I said, "while I work on plans to start my own search company—specializing in engineers." I told him about all the connections in the industry I had and about André wanting to go into business with me.

"I might be interested in investing some start-up capital," he said. "I wouldn't mind getting involved in something in the States. You need to have your expenses covered for at least six months or you'll have a cash flow problem. Ninety percent of businesses fail the first year because of undercapitalization." He paused. "It's the old adage: it takes money to make money." This was the first of many business lessons I was to learn from Philip.

It was his turn now, and his life sounded far more interesting. Raised in a rough section of northern London, the son of a street sweeper, Philip worked as a carpenter on the docks until he was 20. It was hard work, and the painful chill from the water cut right through him, so when an opportunity to move to Sydney, Australia presented itself, Philip jumped at the chance.

In Australia he lived in a trailer for a time and while working as a carpenter by day he built caravans, as they call them in Australia—trailers that people pull behind their cars—in his spare time. He was paying two men to buy his supplies and sell the caravans, and one day he found they had put him $40,000 in debt. "I had no idea I could have declared bankruptcy, so I took over the marketing aspects of the business as well and within ten years, I began a factory that had more than five hundred workers. But I was spending seventeen hours a day at the factory and it wrecked my marriage." He poured a little more wine in our glasses and his eyes grew excited. "When I found myself single and had a good general manager in place, I felt I needed to get away, so I flew over to L.A. to start enjoying life."

Philip was a serious capitalist who disliked any sort of regulation, yet he wore his own wealth modestly. At the tables all around us were obviously successful people dressed in obviously expensive clothing and sporting obviously costly jewelry and other accessories. Philip seemed different. Apart from his big Rolex watch, nothing about him suggested that he was more than just financially comfortable. He drove an older-model Cadillac Seville in a town where anyone who could afford a luxury car bought a Mercedes or BMW or an exotic foreign sports car.

I liked this about him. In fact, I liked almost everything about him. He had so much to talk about, and the ripe Cockney turns of phrase were a delight. He had been all over the world several times and was full of fascinating and funny stories. Yet charming and sophisticated as he was, there was also something "down home" about him. The first time we went out to dinner—it was also the first time he saw me in a dress: black, simple, and conservative—it was to celebrate a new business deal, and the restaurant was both posh and trendy. Philip seemed nervous in the booth, and when he got up to go to the men's room, he kicked over the wine bucket and sent it flying down the aisle. This broke the ice—literally—and he laughed before I did.

Too bad he's older and a little overweight, I kept telling myself, or I might be interested in him as something more than a friend for tennis and lunch. Still, after a few months of lunches and tennis, I found myself looking forward more and more to seeing him and missing him when I didn't.

Then one day, Philip asked me to accompany him on a special two-for-the-price-of-one Caribbean cruise. I would have my own cabin, he assured me, and he made it clear he just would like to have me along as a friend. But that didn't quite happen, for among those lovely islands, it grew clear that we had become infatuated with one another.

Partly, I think, it was because despite our different backgrounds we had so much in common. We loved the same things: card games, dancing, sailing, and exploring the islands. And partly it was that he was brilliant, larger than life, with a personality like a magnet. When he was up, he soared, but, as I would later learn, when he was down, he was way down. But mostly, I think I fell for Philip because of the way he made me feel. He made me laugh, and heaven knows, I needed to laugh.

Our relationship solidified when we returned to California. Philip got contact lenses, lost weight, and played Air Supply and Billy Joel love songs all the time; he was turning into a romantic swain. I'd also learned his secrets. He was so nearsighted that he was virtually blind without his glasses or contacts and almost completely illiterate. I got my first hint of this one day when he asked how to spell the word "up." I'd already noted that he couldn't spell "Marie," but that seemed almost understandable; not knowing how to spell "up" did not. He eventually told me that he had never learned to read or write and never attended high school. "I've signed million-dollar contracts relying on my trusted accountant and my general manager," he admitted. Only later did I figure out by the way he played games like Rummy Tile that his problem was likely that he was dyslexic.

Despite the poor vision, however, he noted that I didn't have any family pictures at my apartment, and he was curious as to why I seldom spoke of my parents. "I've told my mother you'll take her and Dad sailing if they come out to California," I said, and that seemed to satisfy him.

Philip had found a business venture of interest; he wanted to buy a restaurant, the Bay View Yacht Club, in Newport Beach, down the coast from L.A. in Orange County. If he was going to run a restaurant, he felt, he also had to move there to be on the spot. This was the trigger: Philip asked me to marry him and move with him to Newport Beach.

I said yes, and although I continued paying rent on my Santa Monica apartment so that I was not officially shacking up with a man, I quit my job and accompanied him to Orange County.

My parents were thrilled to hear that I was engaged to someone who had a yacht, a home on the water in Newport Beach, a manufacturing business, and another yacht in Australia. They came out to California and stayed with us. Although my mother was confined to a motorized wheelchair and still battling complications of her disease, she was more content than I had ever seen her. She was able to get onto the sailboat, she drank wine at dinner, and for the first time in years she agreed to play cards despite her arthritic hands. She was so comfortable around Philip and so taken with his charismatic personality that she and my father laughed the entire week they were with us. I had never seen them so happy. My father and Philip played tennis. Philip gave my father a new Prince tennis racket, and my dad's face beamed in the passenger seat of Philip's new Porsche as they drove off.

Finally, I was back on good terms with my parents, just as I had wanted years ago. But the reality was that they were breaking the law to see me and that I still could not go freely to Saginaw.

Philip wanted us to travel. He loved the way I listened intently when he talked about other countries he'd visited. But of course, if we were to go abroad, I would need a passport. And if I was going to marry him, I knew I would have to tell him about my past. But how? How do you mention to someone who wants to marry you— someone who assumes you are a nice Midwestern girl from a good background—that you are in fact someone who broke out of a prison as an accused drug kingpin? How would I even begin?

I finally found the right moment and the right way to tell him. At first, he couldn't believe it and asked one question after another. "They said you were a kingpin? And you were how old? And the local paper added nine years to your age to hide the fact that you were only nineteen? What evidence did they have against you? Nothing—and your uncle told you he personally knew the prosecutor and defense attorney who sold you out?"

Philip had nailed it. He ranted on, his London accent getting thicker with every word: "Bloody Americans and their obsession with vices! Nothing you have done could be worse than the skullduggery I see businessmen up to every day. In America you can invade a country or have a politician in your pocket, but if you get accused of a vice everyone suddenly goes bonkers. Somebody profited from sending you off, that's for sure. It's always money. But now then, I'm sure it's nothing we can't fix. Let's talk to your parents and see what we can do to take care of this."

Eventually we told my parents that Philip wanted to hire someone to review my case and see why I received the sentence I did,.

My parents did not take the news happily. They pleaded with me not to dredge everything up again. "All I have is my dignity now," my mother argued. "I don't have my legs to walk on, but I want to be able to go to church and hold my head up high without people whispering behind my back."

"But Mom," I countered, "why wouldn't you want me to clear our name and show that I was innocent?" She remained unconvinced, and for the moment, I put the argument aside.

The passport issue became urgent when word reached Philip from his general manager in Australia that the business expansion had stretched the company financially. Philip needed to go there—now. Then he would need to go on a buying trip to Asia and Europe for parts and materials to make sure that while he'd been gone, his buying agents hadn't made deals with suppliers. He explained to me, "That's where companies or governments are more vulnerable: the buyers can work a lot of sweetheart deals and rob you blind. I always do the major purchases myself and set things up." He asked me to come with him. I wanted to be involved. I could help him locate the various products, investigate pricing and shipping, provide support—along with his GM—while Philip did the major negotiating.

Obviously, to do any of this, I had to get a passport. I was terrified. I had nightmares about being apprehended at the passport office.

My parents' reluctance to "dredge up" the past only reinforced my resignation; I knew it was going to be a long time, if ever, before my case was resolved and justice done. If I waited until then to get a passport, I might never see more of the world. I finally decided that it was worth the risk, that I would take my chances at the passport office. I sighed with relief when I walked out of the office after submitting my application, and I shouted with joy when I received a passport in the mail. Shortly thereafter, Philip and I flew to France.

Philip loved getting a deal, and one of his favorite deals was to vacation in Cannes the day *after* the film festival, when prices were cut in half. We checked into the legendary Carlton on the famous boulevard known as La Croisette for a fraction of what the rate had been the week before. The first morning, I drank the room-service coffee, not realizing it was espresso—much stronger than a regular American brew. I got wired up. I was reminded of my first cup of coffee ever—when I was 20, at the prison in Michigan. I remembered how I'd sipped the bitter-tasting drink thinking that this was a sign of passage into adulthood. Then it dawned on me where I was, and the absurdity of thinking a cup of coffee meant I was an adult. I'd just been sentenced to prison for 10 to 20 years. It was impossible for me to grasp, even now.

Cannes was beautiful, and I was excited to be in such a luxurious place. The yachts moored out in the marina were picture-perfect silhouetted against the distant hills, and the beach was impeccably groomed, with small tents and chairs from which you could order gourmet food service. We toured the area and visited the outrageously priced shops and exquisite restaurants.

I rented a bike one day so I could get some exercise and see more of the neighborhoods farther away from the water. Most of the homes were hidden behind attractive walls and gates, and many had names. One, behind a particularly formidable-looking gate, was called *Sans Souci*. A person who spoke English strolled by; he told me the name meant "without care." How lovely, I thought, to be without worry!

Philip loved buying gifts for me and loved it even more when I refused them. I didn't want our relationship to get complicated by money, even if we were engaged. He obviously could well afford to buy me these things, but I was troubled by so much extravagance and I didn't want to get dependent on his buying me gifts. While I felt that I had no choice about being a fugitive, I did have a choice about not a being a kept woman. I worked hard as his procurement assistant and would buy what I could afford with my pay. Until we were married, I wanted to keep things proper. This wasn't easy, however. Everything in Cannes was shockingly expensive, and the displays of wealth all around us were staggering.

At the exclusive Palm Beach casino, Middle Eastern sheiks rubbed shoulders with people Philip recognized as European titled royalty, and the money just flowed. Our first night there, we saw the elegantly goateed sheik who had been on our charter flight from Paris and whom Philip recognized at once as Sheik Yamani, at the time the oil minister for Saudi Arabia. Dressed in the traditional white robe, Yamani loaded chips onto the roulette table—each worth $20,000. Every spin of the wheel meant hundreds of thousands of dollars—to either the sheik or the house. I remembered his name because it sounds like "shake your money."

With these kinds of stakes, I was not eager to gamble, even though Philip offered me some chips. I looked around at the well-dressed crowd. Few people were smiling, and no one laughed. There were a lot of older men with younger women. The few middle-aged women were expensively dressed and wore either a Cartier or a Rolex, as if conformity were a requirement—or perhaps as a trademark. It was these older women who looked especially numb, and I wondered what sacrifices they might have made to earn such a look. In such a fast, worldly crowd, what happened to women past a certain age? How would I appear—to Philip and to myself—when I was no longer in my 20s?

Philip was placing a few chips on a gaming table. Our eyes met, and his face broke into a huge smile. He was beaming with happiness, and it was contagious. Suddenly I realized that I was here in the south of France with this charming man I absolutely adored, and who absolutely adored me. I was a long way from cowering in a prison cell, listening to a girl getting raped in the next cell and knowing I would likely be the next in line.

Cannes was a wonderful break from work. Philip and I enjoyed tennis and sailing and playing cards under a beach umbrella. The film festival had recently ended and a few stragglers from "the business" hung around, accompanied by their people. But soon enough, it was time to move on; Philip needed to get to Australia.

I fell in love with Australia. It had the vastness and beauty of California and a friendly down-home feel that I remembered from Ohio; I liked everyone I met.

While in Australia, I discovered that Philip was far wealthier than he'd made apparent in the States. He had several factories and was well known in Sydney. I'd been happier thinking I was engaged to someone financially comfortable, not a mogul. I'd always felt that someone with too much money had as many money problems as someone with too little.

Philip was gruff and at times arrogant on his home turf. I hoped I was wrong in this observation and that everything would be all right.

From Australia we flew to Japan, accompanied by Philip's general manager, Tony. Philip became more irritable as we traveled but I blamed it on our demanding work schedule. Japan struck me as immaculate, crime-free, and filled with wondrous technologies like the bullet train. Every morning, I rose at six; pulled on stockings, heels, and a suit; and began the process of helping Philip and Tony buy needed supplies: tires, bolts, and fabrics for the caravans' upholstered walls and furnishings. Sometimes, the work required days of negotiations over a penny or two per unit, for the penny or two per unit could amount to hundreds of thousands of dollars on the purchase price.

I read a lot of magazines on the long flight that I wouldn't normally read, and many articles were about the unusual way Western businessmen needed to deal with Asian governments if they wanted to do business there. Instead of caring about money, the primary concern in places like China was how many jobs a business would provide. Businessmen in the West needed to put their checkbooks away and focus more on what China viewed as important—getting their population employed.

In Asia, I also learned from Tony that Philip's prowess as a shrewd negotiator was well known throughout the industry. Stories abounded of how he'd made at least one man cry during price negotiations. He used what he called "Australian bargaining," in which he simply raised the price if his terms weren't agreed to instead of lowering it in an attempt to compromise.

I worked long hours and there was a great deal to learn, but I felt a sense of worth in what I was doing.

From Japan, we moved on to Korea and Hong Kong, then flew west across Asia for stops in Berlin, London, and Paris. And suddenly, we were in Elkhart, Indiana, across the border from the Michigan state line, and Philip was pressing me to talk to my uncle about my case.

My parents were still reluctant to rock the boat of the past, but my father's testimony that I was promised probation was vital and their approval was important to me. They finally agreed to cooperate as long as my uncle could handle the case. With him in charge, it could all be handled as quietly and as discreetly as possible. It would save me the chore of trying to find another attorney and torturously explain the details of my unusual conviction.

Philip and I headed into Michigan and connected with my family, and I paid my uncle a retainer. I explained the details of what happened after my arrest, but my uncle seemed only to half-listen especially when my father was in the room. He appeared preoccupied with his brother's presence and when my father left the room, my uncle's eyes glazed over when I spoke.

"They said they would drop the charges against me completely...," I was saying when my father walked back into the room and my uncle suddenly interrupted me. He said, "They say you were clever as a fox, Susan." I realized he was saying this for my father's benefit and I was barely there for him. We were still dancing this dangerous game with each other.

That was when I truly understood how complicated the relationship was between them. Clearly, as other family members had mentioned, there was an intense rivalry that neither brother could admit to, and I instinctively felt that my uncle was not going to help me.

But I managed to override my feelings of doubt. I couldn't bear the thought of asking for help from someone else yet again. I worried that someone might blackmail me, especially now that I was involved with a successful businessman. It was easier to convince myself that I could trust my uncle; surely he couldn't be that heartless and let me suffer through this any longer than I already had. Why would he take my money if he weren't serious about pursuing an end to this nightmare for me? He and my parents were well aware that I had worked hard; they knew I didn't use drugs at all anymore. They knew I wanted to start a family, and family values, religion, and forgiveness were all-important to them. They knew I was innocent. Surely they wouldn't leave me vulnerable to being hauled off by the police again sometime, somewhere.

But I didn't quite believe it, and when Philip and I returned to California, I was in limbo.

We again took up our pleasant California life of tennis, sailing, and Philip's latest hobby of buying restaurants, but anticipation of my case being reopened hung over me like a cloud. If I couldn't get things resolved, I knew that my engagement would end. To distract myself from these thoughts, I tried to keep busy. I had now taken a formal position on the supplies procurement team in Philip's company, and I felt that I was getting a better education than if I had finished college.

More than a year passed in this way and I had heard nothing from my uncle, so I finally pushed myself to get in touch with him. I had never gotten to know my uncle well, but I was still surprised by his response to me, which was full of contempt. He told me he hadn't talked to anyone or filed any motions. Nor did he want or intend to do anything. His wife had asked him not to, he said, and apparently he'd felt no need to let me know he wasn't working on the case all these months while I waited anxiously.

Philip was beginning to sense that the situation was more complicated than he had realized. From other family members, he'd heard about the complex relationship between my father and his brother, and he realized my uncle's friendship with the current prosecutor was an impediment rather than an asset. Phillip understood what I didn't fully grasp yet: that my circumstances were worse because I was innocent, and quite a few people had reason to keep the details of my conviction from coming to light.

Each new revelation seemed a stumbling block, not a path to justice. I was learning that being innocent could be worse than being guilty.

The more the situation stagnated, the more perplexed Philip became—and the more we seemed to draw apart. Jokingly, he began to call me "the crim" and made wisecracks about my being a fugitive. Gradually, his tone grew serious, and he began to use the words against me in arguments.

Around this time I recognized that like Robert, Philip had severe mood swings. In a good mood, he was magnetic and was able to excite everyone around him. Then, overnight, he could revert to a Dr. Jekyll/Mr. Hyde change, becoming scary and miserable and hating the world.

Around this time he began to buy older-model Rolls-Royces. He started off with one he said he'd gotten a good deal on, but when I bought a convertible Cabriolet, he quickly bought a convertible Rolls Corniche. Soon after that, again in one of his moods, he bought another Rolls, and then another. At the time we were living in the Back Bay area of Newport beach in a house with a three-car garage, and we had no place to keep all these cars. He gave one to a tennis pro he'd gotten to know and shipped another back to Sydney. I was in my mid-20s and felt ridiculous in big, opulent car I felt was for old people. But more than this, I was growing weary of Philip's unstable temperament. At a red light one day, I found myself looking out the window of the Roll-Royce at some kids my age in a car very much like my old hatchback and I envied the carefree way they were smiling and laughing. I questioned whether I had escaped one prison only to slide into another?

The arguments between us were becoming more frequent and longer. I could feel the seams of our relationship coming undone. Philip now began to use my past as an angle; it was the hold he had over me—a threat and a weapon. He began to chase other women, knowing I would be helpless to stop him since he knew my secret. What were once passionate, romantic feelings in Philip had turned to possessive, exploitive ones, and although I saw he was no longer infatuated with me, I also saw that he wanted to keep me on the back shelf—and would use his money to do so, retaliating against me if necessary. And this I could not afford.

I now knew I had to escape again and get out of the relationship...but it would be complicated and take time. Philip tried to tell me that many women put up with philandering men in order to have a luxurious lifestyle. It wasn't that I disrespected women who made this choice, but I had to believe that someday I would find someone who wanted only me, someone who didn't want to be with other women even if he had the chance. If I let myself believe that my circumstances forced me to settle, then I would have let the corruption that altered my life in Michigan get even more control.

It wasn't easy for me to stay resolved, though. Philip could be intensely charming, and a few months later he apologized for everything he'd done and vowed there would never be anyone else for him. When he asked me to go with him to Australia to get married, I decided to give us another chance. He said he loved me and there could never be anyone else in his life to take my place. These were the words I'd wanted to hear all my life. In a moment of weakness, I decided that he had changed and that I would go with him.

It was 10 hours into the flight to Sydney when Philip again said affectionately that I would always be number one to him. He took another sip of his scotch and added, "There may be other women, but you'll always be the one I come back to." I realized that I had made a terrible mistake.

I was 37,000 feet above the world's vastest ocean. What were my options? Should I take my chances in Australia? I loved it there, and I knew I didn't have much going for me in the States, but it seemed inconceivable that I could leave America, possible for good, no matter what had happened to me there. As technology progressed and more database networks were connected, it was likely I would never be able to come back to the States, and living in Australia might mean I wouldn't see my mother again. In her condition, she would never be able to make the long flight. We had a painful past, my mother and I, but she had been thoughtful and kind for several years now. Her life was difficult, and she needed me much the way I once needed her.

The plane touched down in Auckland, New Zealand for fuel, and I told Philip that I was going back to the States—this time for good. He watched in shock as I walked off the plane, and I caught a flight back to California a few hours later. This would mean 30 hours of flying within a couple of days and I knew I'd get a little stir crazy on the flight back, but I also knew that I had narrowly escaped a dangerous relationship even though I knew that an uncertain future awaited me. I once again told myself I had to have faith that everything would be all right.

Chapter 25

Back in the States, I rented a house in Tustin, in the middle of Orange County, and considered my situation. I was broke, for one thing. The savings that I had built up had been spent on a car to replace the Audi 5000 Philip had bought me as an engagement present. I had thrown the car title for the Audi at him during one of our quarrels. I'd also left a lot of my clothing in the house in Australia, thinking I would be returning with him eventually.

It occurred to me that I would have been in a better financial position if I had never been involved with a guy who was rich. I had been naïve to allow him to get so much control over my life.

When I had gotten engaged to Philip, I was on schedule for my plan of being married in my late 20s. Instead, at 29, I was effectively starting over. This time, I had a car and a house, but I needed roommates to help pay the rent, and had no boyfriend and no job. Still, it was more than I had at many times in the past.

I soon found work as an accounts payable clerk at an architectural landscaping firm. I found a couple of roommates, too. One of them, a commodities broker referred to me by a friend, turned out to be a drug user who blew through $400,000 in annual commissions, wrote me bad checks for the rent, and refused for months to move out. During this difficult time, I found myself questioning my decision to break up with Philip. Eventually I got rid of the deadbeat roommate and managed to replace him with a couple of great roommates.

It wasn't long before Philip began to call me. I knew it wasn't love as much as his tendency to be obsessive that drove him. *There's no reason we can't be friends,* he argued. My guess was that he was seeing someone else but trying to keep his options open. I accepted his calls, reminded of something I learned in a course in Judo that I had taken after the strangler attack in the Foothills—that resistance can incite a higher degree of aggression. Refusing to talk to Philip would be tantamount to waving a red scarf in front of a bull. The fact that he knew my secret put me in a vulnerable position.

Indeed, Philip's phone calls became more frequent, and one day I returned home to find a message on my answering machine that if I didn't return his calls, he would turn me in to the authorities. I felt frightened again and wondered if I would ever be able to lead a stable life that wasn't one survival experience after another.

I let my mind flash back to the moment in the jail cell in Michigan when I experienced an infusion of spiritual grace and maybe even a jolt of cosmic energy. Who knew for sure? The memory of it had never faded and I drew on that moment now as my freedom was being threatened again. Whenever things got tough, thinking about it helped me put everything in perspective. I felt that my own heart was being revealed to me because I had faith, and I believed the center of my universe was the power of that moment. Not career, not money, not a person. That was my strength.

I had learned at least one more important lesson: Unless and until I could take charge of my own legal case, I would tell no one—no one—the secret of my past. Clearly, to do so was not only to risk discovery; it was also to cede control over my life and jeopardize my future. I vowed never to do so again. Whatever happened, no matter how tempting it might be, I could not share my story with anyone.

I was on my own.

Chapter 26

The landscape architecture firm where I worked gave me a fair amount of responsibility, along with an assistant and a nice office, but I found the job tedious and unrewarding. There was no way out, however; I simply had to make a living. The brief taste of extravagance and luxury I experienced for five years as Philip's fiancée was over. Traveling first class was fun, I reflected, but it wasn't particularly important, and it was certainly not the only way to travel. So, I was back to working hard and hoping to advance.

Though I had a rough couple of months readjusting to the single life, I soon established a new group of friends and began enjoying life again in Southern California. I started dating a little as well, but no one clicked—and that turned out to be all right at the time.

My two roommates in the house in Tustin were both around my age—Laura, a good friend, and John, a sweet guy from Ireland who was teaching me how to operate business software, a big plus for me on the job. In exchange, I agreed to give John tennis lessons, and we arranged to meet at the courts at the apartment building where he used to live with his two younger brothers, also émigrés from Ireland.

We were working on John's forehand when someone called out from courtside, "Hey John, I didn't expect to see you out here. How's the tennis?"

It was John's brother Alan and he quickly introduced us.

Alan was young-looking, had boyish good looks, and, as he proved when he stepped on the court and picked up a spare racket, was a natural athlete. I discovered during our brief conversation that he was an accountant—perhaps not as glamorous a career as globe-trotting business mogul, but my foray into the world of glamour had been disillusioning. I would have liked to get to know him better, but after a few volleys, he was off. "A pleasure meeting you, Marie," he said. A charming accent and good manners, too.

After that evening, Alan began to come around the house quite often, but while he was friendly, I couldn't tell whether he was there to visit his brother or me. Soon enough, however, Alan became part of my social crowd, and we spent a fair amount of time together, as a group, going to beach parties or heading to the mountains on weekends for ski trips. I taught Alan to wind-surf, and he tried to teach me to surf—with limited success. I found him more mature and solid than many guys his age, and I was impressed by the different dimensions of his personality. He loved to dance and laugh—and he found me funny—but was serious about values like integrity and had a strong work ethic.

In fact, our first real date was when we attended his company's Christmas dinner. On our second date, on the way to the beach he stopped at the company yard to see what he referred to as "The Fleet," a vast yard full of purple trash trucks. I thought he was kidding around until I saw how seriously he looked at the trucks as if they were his own proud collection. When we finally arrived at the ocean, Alan gasped at what I thought at first must have been the spectacular view of the sun setting over the horizon. But it was something else that had caught his eye: "There's another one of our bins," he said, and I realized how truly serious he was about all things trash.

Alan was in many ways a conventional guy, yet for an accountant obsessed by his work, he was also full of surprises. I was stunned to learn that he had been a disc jockey at an after-hours joint in Dublin one summer, and that he specialized in playing Motown groups like the Stylistics and the Chi-Lites. He did a great B.B. King imitation: "Don't nobody love me but my momma............and she could be jiving too, " he would say jokingly.

Alan thought I was conventional too, and it was something he valued in me. He got this notion in part from John, who had told him I sometimes attended church. Since the subject never came up, I didn't have the opportunity to tell Alan my misgivings about certain aspects of our shared religion. I still found it hard to square the valuable lessons I learned from the church as a kid with the hypocrisy of what happened to me later at St. Stephen's as a teenager... not to mention the example of family member's who I suspected had a role in getting me convicted, knowing I wasn't guilty, while flaunting their connections to church bishops and their high-profile trips to the Vatican. The lessons of unconditional love and forgiveness had seemed to shift to a focus on sinners and retribution. Alan, of course, knew nothing about my past.

I also liked that Alan was careful with money. Still, I was hard pressed to understand why he had so few assets, given how hard he worked. His car was practically an antique, and his apartment was sparsely furnished.

Then one day I found a check he had written to the African Relief Fund for $800—earmarked to fight AIDS. The amount seemed staggering to me, knowing how simply Alan lived. It did not seem the most logical way for someone his age to spend money, but I couldn't help admiring him for it.

Not long after I began seeing Alan, I received a letter from Robert. He had returned to Michigan from Florida, and had waited outside my parents' house for weeks until he was able to catch my sister at the mailbox out front. "Please send this to Susan," he asked. My sister knew my parents would never pass his letter along, so she gave it to my aunt Mary Alice and it finally reached me.

The letter said that he was doing well but had thought of me a lot over the years and still wanted us to get back together. He gave me his phone number and asked me to call. Although I knew it would be painful for us both, I picked up the phone.

It was wonderful to hear Robert's voice, but it was difficult to talk to him about everything that had happened to us. I still couldn't tell what he was actually up to, and I knew it was too dangerous to tell him where I lived.

It was odd to recall that at one time, he seemed to me to be everything I needed. So much had changed since then; now, I was at a point in life where I wanted a mate with whom to raise a family. That was my focus. I was glad that Robert and I had finally reconnected, and I hoped we could always be friends, but he still belonged to that parallel universe and I still held the fear that the two might collide.

Alan and I dated for some eight months and then flew together to Michigan, where he asked my father's permission to marry me. Of course, my father was impressed by this oh-so-traditional gesture. He was also pleased by the fact that Alan was Catholic—Irish Catholic, even better—and was happy to say yes. So was I. It was a joyous time. All of my family and friends liked Alan immediately, and I felt that my prayers had been answered.

Before we got married, however, I thought it was only fair to tell Alan something about my past. I told him about my having used drugs, and about Robert, the forbidden boyfriend, and the battles with my parents. Alan just shook his head. "What's past is past," he said. He didn't want to know more. He understood that there was a tumultuous period in my life, but he didn't want the details. He loved that my parents thought highly of him, he related to their being so traditional, and perhaps he did not want to see them or me in another light.

For my part, though I trusted him not to turn on me the way Philip did, I was relieved not to have to say more.

In November 1985, Alan and I were married in a local church with my parents, some family members, and friends in attendance. We honeymooned on the north shore of Hawaii, where the waves were said to be best for surfing. Present on the honeymoon were me, Alan, and his ever-present surfboard. At the airport, we had to wait for a special bus since we couldn't fit the board in a taxi. Of course it would have made more sense to rent one in Hawaii, but he insisted it wouldn't be the same.

From our hotel room the view of the ocean was stunning, but the waves were so big it was impossible to swim. There was a storm at sea, and only two people dared to venture into the surf. One of them was Alan. The undercurrent was so strong it took him more than an hour to get back onto the shore. While I worried about his safety, I hoped his determination was a sign that he was someone who wouldn't shy away when the going got tough.

In the beginning, like so many just-married young couples, we struggled with money. When our landlord offered to sell us the house we were renting for $150,000. The down payment alone was out of reach. My parents refused to help—comparable houses in Michigan cost about $40,000, and they thought the house was overpriced. No doubt it was, but California real estate was much higher—we paid a premium for our sunny 70-degree winters.

We put in an offer but were outbid by the owner's secretary. Then one morning, while we were catching the early waves at the beach, the owner brought his secretary to the house unannounced for a second look. We had left the place a shambles, and she didn't like what she saw. This was our lucky break. We were able to negotiate a more reasonable price, and we managed to scrape together half the deposit and the owner agreed to carry a second that we had to pay off monthly at the same time as the mortgage payments. The house needed a new roof, driveway repairs, and interior remodeling, so money was extremely tight for the next few years.

We both worked hard, and spent weekends doing most of the house remodeling and repair ourselves. I learned how to re-tile floors and counters, Alan had the unenviable task of pulling off a shake-shingle roof, and we re-tarmacked the driveway.

Our shared goal was to raise a family, and our first child, Maureen, was born in 1986. Lively and precocious, little Mo began saying full sentences at eight months and, as I tease her to this day, she hasn't stopped talking since. From the very beginning, she exhibited a charismatic personality and a curious nature.

Katie arrived a year and a half after Maureen. The prospect of juggling two babies was daunting, but I got something of a reprieve, as Katie proved as angelic and peaceable as her adored older sister was dynamic. She seemed to have been born happy-go-lucky and content, something anyone could envy.

I was in my late 30s when our son, Alan Junior, was born. Bathed in the affection of his older sisters, he was a happy, easy child—the only baby I ever knew who hugged back when held—as well as being witty and smart as a whip.

Once I became a mother, I left my job to be with the children; my salary wouldn't come close to covering the expense of child care, and I was happy staying at home. When they entered preschool, I was able to work there.

Alan Sr.was up at first light six days a week and put in 12-hour workdays, and on weekends we attended business events, where I'd be dressed to the nines as we mingled with business executives and politicians. We were often exhausted by the end of our long days, but in time, it all began to pay off; Alan was consistently promoted to more responsible positions.

Once the kids were in school I become involved in volunteer activities, including an effort to help a remote monastery stave off a development that would have destroyed 80 years of privacy in the rural canyon area of Orange County. I was also active in Common Cause, the "people's lobby," and in its advocacy of campaign finance reform. I felt strongly that our two-party system was really one party controlled by big money interests; weapons manufacturers, banks, and unions who controlled Democrats as much as Republicans. I learned about entrenched bureaucrats who have more power than elected officials; their primary focus was to ensure that someone more competent didn't get hired who would make the other incompetents look bad. This explained a lot to me about the prison industry, the ills of which I knew only too well.

Family life proved a challenge as the kids grew older, and I gained a new respect for my mother raising five kids at a time when women had few outlets for their frustration. I was determined to negotiate rather than just discipline, and to discuss family problems rather than sweep them under the rug. We had some turbulent times, and some days the problems felt insurmountable, but we hung in there and got through. The tender moments made it all worthwhile. While Alan was good-hearted and full of boyish charm, I gained a new understanding of why a football team would be called the "Fighting Irish" and why t-shirts in Irish gift shops joked, *"You can always tell an Irishman, you just can't tell him much."* Just about the time I learned to deal with my husband's stubborn ways, I saw that our children had inherited his DNA. Raising a family would prove to be my biggest challenge yet.

When finances, in-laws, and other issues strained our marriage at times, I credited having been raised in a religion that stressed the importance of marriage for our ability to stay together. I hope I've been able to pass these values on to the children despite the influence of mass culture and the scandals that have plagued the Catholic Church.

When the girls hit their teen years—especially headstrong Maureen—there were arguments about unchaperoned trips to Cabo San Lucas and how late a teenage girl should stay out on weekends, and of course discussions about drinking and drugs. I made certain these were different from the battles I'd had with my parents: My children always knew that our love for them was unconditional, whatever they might do or say or think.

Because of my past, I made the conscious decision early on to err on the side of being too permissive rather than too controlling. Of course, I often worried that my flexibility might have unintended consequences.

While raising teenagers was incredibly hard overall, I guess you could say our family got along. We seemed to have the quintessentially conventional California family, with our healthy, polite children, our growing material success, our rising prominence in the community—Alan as a business leader, me as a ubiquitous mom and volunteer—and our move to a bigger house as we rode the wave of rising real estate values, we might have been a magazine-cover ad for the delights of life in Southern California in the 1990s.

With a few exceptions.

Alan's family in Ireland couldn't understand why I didn't come with him when he traveled "back home" for a visit. I told Alan I didn't like taking long trips. The fact was that I was terrified that thanks to advances in government communications, I would be apprehended trying to get back into the U.S. The thought of being torn from my children was unbearable. I was even beginning to wonder if I would have trouble getting a driver's license renewed.

In the meantime, Alan's parents in Ireland came to visit us. And we received routine visits from my parents as well. I talked to my mother every week, and while it was a strength knowing I could live without my parents' approval, I was overjoyed to have her and my father back in my life. I was inspired by my mother's success in turning her life around in the face of a crippling illness, and we'd both been able to let go of the anger that tore our family apart in the past. The memories that at one time we almost destroyed each other were far behind us.

But my life had its private ironies. When Maureen and a friend were about eight years old, a man they recognized—the father of a classmate—accosted them near their school after school hours, offering them quarters if they would touch his penis. As he suddenly grabbed Maureen's little hand and pulled it toward his open pants, she pulled away, and she and her friend fled. Alarmed, I reported the incident to the Orange County police, and I was pleased when a female detective showed up at the house to follow up. We provided all the details she requested, including the address where the man, a migrant worker, was staying. The detective was polite and professional, and said she would look into the matter and get back to us.

And she did, calling just a few days later, reporting that when the police went to the address, a woman answered the door and said, "The pervert is already in jail for molesting my niece."

"Great," I said, "so he's already in custody. So now we just have to press charges on this incident and he won't be molesting any other children for a while. How long is he serving on the current charge?"

"He'll be out in a couple of months."

I was stunned. "He'll be out in a couple of months for molesting a little girl?"

"The prosecutor must have given him a deal to make sure they could get a conviction," the detective said.

"Well, with this second charge—and really, who knows how many other children have been victimized who didn't come forward—we'll be able to show he's a serial predator, won't we? What do we do now?"

226

I sensed some hesitation on the other end of the line. "Well," said the detective, "it's not that easy. This isn't the type of case prosecutors like to file. They stay away from cases with child witnesses because kids aren't reliable about showing up in court; their parents often don't want to put them through the experience of testifying. Prosecutors don't want to take on a case they might lose. They don't want a loss on their record."

Her words turned on a light bulb in my brain. No wonder drug-law offenders were so intently pursued while child molesters and even murderers went free or received negligible sentences. Witnesses in a drug case were drug agents—typically, the police officer who set up the drug sale—and they could offer polished, professional-sounding testimony that could persuade a jury. So even when molesters and murderers presented a bigger threat to society, they were tougher to convict. And because law enforcement careers advance based on the number and length of convictions rather than on the seriousness of the crime, ambitious prosecutors had far more incentive to go after drug-law offenses; it was simply a more fertile field for getting promoted up the ladder.

"This man is a degenerate predator hanging out at grade schools attacking children," I argued vehemently. "There is no way Maureen won't show up in court—we'll make sure she does. And she wants to. She's mature enough to understand that this guy shouldn't be allowed to victimize other children. Plus, we have a second witness, the friend who was with her. What more do you need?"

"I'm sorry," said the detective. "I understand completely. I've tried to get them to file charges but they aren't interested. It's too big a risk."

"What about the risk to other children?" I asked. "This guy has a history of molesting children and we can't get charges against him because someone doesn't want to risk a blemish on his record? Doesn't public safety weigh in here at all?"

Over the next months, I appealed to one agency after another—law enforcement, child welfare, and the prosecutor's office. But I hit a brick wall every time. Without a prosecutor willing to prosecute, no one could do a thing.

Sure enough, the molester was released after a few months of detention—free to strike again. I wrote a letter to the *Orange County Register* pointing out that the man would doubtless be in jail if he had been caught smoking a joint; was molesting children less important—a less dangerous crime? In enlarged print, the letter was prominently displayed in the paper's editorial section.

Meantime, while a guy who tried to molest my daughter went free, I lived with the knowledge that I faced 10 to 20 years in prison for being present when somebody sold a teaspoon of a 'controlled substance'.

In addition to the ironies, there is a certain loneliness in being the sole possessor of a past you cannot share. It's lonely having to remember what to say and what to leave out in talking to strangers. And I was lonely keeping a profound secret from the people I loved most.

One rainy Saturday, as I was killing time before the kids' piano recital later that day, I found myself in front of the television, caught up in a movie called *The Virgin Suicides*. It was the story of a Catholic family in Michigan so deeply religious that the family's five daughters were prohibited from listening to music, dating boys, and even having school friends. The mother ends up crushing the rock albums the girls have managed to bring into the house.

The conservative brick house and familiar-looking trees in the front yard were eerily reminiscent of my parents' house in Michigan, complete with the same Catholic pictures hanging on the walls in the background. Because of the repressive atmosphere, within the space of a year, in the story, all five girls commit suicide.

I felt that, short of the suicides, this was a story about me, about my family and my upbringing, and although I knew it was illogical, the story reminded me so much of my high school years that I felt unnerved. It was as if someone had looked into my life. My private island has been invaded. I hurried to get ready for the recital but felt edgy and confused. I wished I could just be alone for a while and work through the emotions that had suddenly surfaced regarding that terrible period in my past. The scenes in the movie seemed all too familiar. I tried to shove my feelings down inside me as I prepared to attend my daughter's piano recital.

It was a fairly formal event. All the little recitalists were dressed in velvet dresses and suits, while the adults were served dainty appetizers and soft drinks. The girls were all adorable as they played their pieces—some ploddingly, some gracefully. But when Maureen began to play a tender number by Chopin, I felt a torrent of emotion well up inside me. Tears rushed to my eyes as I was suddenly and unaccountably pulled back to the bitter memories of my childhood years.

I couldn't help myself; the tears poured down my cheeks. I tried hard to smile, to leave the impression that it was the music and the young pianists that had moved me to tears. My son looked up at me and saw that I was crying.

"What's wrong, Mommy?" His little angel face was solemn with concern. I leaned over and gave him a kiss on the cheek. "Nothing's wrong," I said, and I smiled again.

The music ended, and we were all invited into the backyard for refreshments. The rain had stopped, and the sun was out. I was relieved to have a reason to put on my sunglasses, which obscured my red, swollen eyes.

As I looked around at the other mothers—neighbors and friends, most of them—I think, not for the first time: *If you only knew...*

Chapter 27

One of the most gratifying developments of my life blossoming was that my parents had again become a permanent fixture in my life. I talked to them often, and they often came to visit us in California. Despite my mother's illness, she and my father's lives had settled into something of a comfortable routine, and they spent most of their time in Florida.

My mother's disease was in remission. However, she would never fully regain her health, and she virtually lived in her wheelchair. Her most formidable health issue now was the side effects of the drugs she had to take. One produced painful acid reflex that strained her esophagus, while other medications made her skin puffy and caused sores that wouldn't heal. Yet she showed no anger, and despite her pain, she was able to find happiness in the simplest, most everyday things. The sudden appearance of a strand of orchid blossoms on a dormant plant brought her joy, and my father bungling a joke or mangling a proper noun could send her into gales of affectionate laughter. She was a different person from the mother I knew as a teenager in Michigan, a stronger yet more yielding version of the caring but rigid mom of my very earliest years. Her hardships made my present problems seem small.

My father did not leave her side. A man who in general disdained details—unlike my mother, an ace at crossword puzzles and *Jeopardy*—he nevertheless knew everything there was to know about her disease and its treatment. He seemed to suffer every injection with her, to be there for every pill and blood test and exam. He lifted my mother into and out of her motorized wheelchair and loaded the heavy chair in and out of the trunk of the car. It was strenuous, and growing more so as he grew older. Alan and I offered to buy them a carrier that would transport the chair on a trailer attached to the back of the car, but my mother didn't want it to be so obvious that she was handicapped, and my father saw no point in spending money on something he was "perfectly capable of doing."

Like many of their closest friends in Florida, they lived frugally. They drove older cars and ate out only at restaurants that offered a discount coupon. My father reaped all the benefits of Reaganomics and the exploding stock market and could well afford things like hiring a weekly cleaning woman, but he wouldn't do it. Again, he said he was perfectly capable of doing it himself.

Among the few luxuries my parents did allow themselves were frequent cruises in the Caribbean and other places with their many friends from the condo complex. My mother was also generous about sending us money to visit them in Florida and offered to pay for staying at our house when they visited us. Tearing up her checks became a game, and I urged my parents to use the money to splurge on slightly more extravagant restaurants or hire a housekeeper a couple of times a month. But the checks kept coming. Money was still tight for us, but I didn't feel comfortable taking money that I suspected was my mother's attempt to make up for the past. I wished I could convince her she had nothing to feel bad about. We'd all made mistakes.

We never talked about the past. I tried to focus on looking forward, to enjoying our good fortune. I was happy my children had grandparents that they loved, and it was as if my parents and I had found each other again. The past sat like a train wreck between us; the debris and the stench of tragedy was still there, but we tiptoed around it.

My father was still quiet around me, but occasionally we got into discussions about social issues that quickly became heated. He didn't understand why I couldn't see that life was better in the old days, and that through the use of force the country could get things back the way they used to be. I argued against his views vehemently, but in time we both realized that the other would never change, and eventually we learned to accept that we would never agree. I tried to respect that his positions reflected the way he was raised to think, and I tried not to let it bother me, but during one summer visit when my father thought that I was out of earshot, I was astonished to hear him give relatives his views on prisons.

"Prisons are like a revolving door," he said. "Michigan is finally starting to change laws to take away credit for good behavior that lets prisoners get out early. If we lock up these crooks and throw away the key, they'll get the message."

Knowing that a majority of people in prison were there for breaking drug laws and other nonviolent crimes, I felt that most recidivism was the result of people having a hard time making a living without an education. I thought the biggest difference between myself and others who were in prison was that I had the benefit of a structured and secure upbringing and a decent education.

Overhearing my father's extreme views made for challenging visits at times. I was happy knowing he wasn't in a position to do anything more than cast one vote.

Chapter 28

It was the end of the 1990s, and Alan had been at Waste Management now for more than 15 years. He was one of the rare executives to weather several regime changes. I think this was because he managed to stay out of the politics, was honest, and worked enough hours for two people. Of course, I'm probably biased.

Our new home in San Diego was in a brand-new neighborhood, so everyone on the street was also new and we got to know each other while sharing the challenges of landscaping our dirt lots, installing floors, and decorating. The upcoming New Year would be the turn of the century, and a panic ensued that computers would malfunction throughout the world as they failed to recognize "00" as the year 2000. Rumors circulated that life as we knew it would cease. Our cul-de-sac planned a big party to celebrate Y2K. We organized a tent and food, hired a deejay, and prepared to dance our way into the new millennium.

Once the kids were all in school, I took up several sports. I began playing in a morning tennis league, took bridge lessons and entered tournaments after awhile, and rode horses. The horse I leased was named Goldenwing, and he was like a dear friend. I questioned whether certain friends would still be there for me if my secret was discovered, but I knew Goldenwing would always be glad to see me. When I rode at a nearby polo field, I cut loose and felt a sense of exhilaration that I was free and moving forward, moving against the wind, and nothing could stop me.

San Diego was another new start for us, and I chose to do less controversial volunteer work than campaign finance reform or taking on land developers. I decided that being a hospice worker would involve helping people without alienating anyone. When I began training, I was surprised to find the lessons I learned to be spiritually nourishing and enjoyable.

The kids liked our new neighborhood and were able to walk to a grade school nearby. Alan and I were amused watching them go through their typical preteen phases. Maureen went through a *Gone with the Wind* period; she came down to breakfast one day and asked that we refer to her as Scarlet from now on. Katie had her own heroine, Maria from *The Sound of Music*, and regularly sang songs from the movie, of which she had every line memorized. Alan had graduated from a Barney-the-purple-dragon obsession to Power Rangers and carrying plastic swords in his waist band. Not long after our move. we brought home Bailey, a black and tan dachshund puppy. He was the new family baby. "He's so small you could put him in your pocket!" Katie squealed. We'd lost an identical-looking dog named Oscar to coyotes when we lived in Orange County, and Alan Jr. was only interested in another wiener dog. I knew this was the life I had dreamed of having. My *"illusions of grandeur,"* as they were called by the counselor at the prison rehab, had come true.

Although questions still churned in my mind about my conviction, I didn't find satisfactory answers, and the only way of attaining peace was through acceptance. This was another part of the rehab program that had stayed with me, and I reminded myself of the word over and over.

My real enemies, I realized in an epiphany when I was 21, were anger and bitterness. I had to be vigilant about my thoughts and not let myself dwell on things that could pull me down. Thoughts in the past had drawn me into a depression, and my subsequent escape into drugs had almost ended my life. I couldn't let that happen again. I believed strongly in a higher power of goodness and that justice would ultimately come to people who were unfair to others. It wasn't my responsibility to try to even the score.

Chapter 29

One morning in September 2001, Katie rushed into our bedroom and urged us to turn on the TV. We watched in horror as the Twin Towers in New York collapsed surreally into a ball of dust. A small group of Saudi nationals and Pakistanis were responsible, so the nation quickly declared war on Iraq, a competitor to Saudi Arabia.

Soon afterward we received a flyer from neighbors, (who have since moved out of state), inviting us to their home for a meeting regarding the war. Wanting to be good neighbors, we showed up, as did a dozen others. After a glass of wine, one of our hosts said they wanted us to see something they had in their garage. As we rose and walked towards the garage door she commented, "I would rather die than be forced to wear a burka." In the garage we were shown a corner filled with hundreds of rolls of a thick plastic leaning against the wall and a wheelbarrow full of duct tape. The plan was to seal up the windows and French doors in the event of a chemical attack by Saddam Hussein.

It all reminded me of the fear-mongering in Saginaw that got my parents so disturbed when I was in high school. I found it hard to feel threatened by an impoverished country where most people had trouble owning a car. I was more leery of a government that would mislead its own people and be able to get away with it.

After the September 11th attack, the neighborhood began to change greatly. Neighbors who were experts in bio-tech were forced to move away and downsize, because venture capitalists were no longer funding medical advances as readily as they were lucrative contracts with the government in the war effort. Neighbors involved with companies that could get a defense contract moved away to much larger homes. One family who the year before had been having financial problems was now able to move to a home with a heliport for the new helicopter they were ordering was a result of successfully wooing an arms contract. The war was a bonanza for them.

Chapter 30

Tensions seemed to hang over everyone after the war started, and on my birthday Alan and I had a bad argument. A moment after he ran out, slamming the door behind him, my father called to wish me a happy birthday. He asked, "How are you?" and I blurted out that I was tired of being a fugitive. I told him I was angry with Alan and needed to clear things up in case I had to get a job, since our marriage was questionable right now. "I'm going to pursue this through to the end this time. Since you were there when the prosecutor told me I would get probation and it was all set up with the judge I'd like you to put what you saw in writing in case I need you as a witness."

I was standing in the butler's pantry off our kitchen. My husband or the kids could have come home at any moment, so I had to be careful to listen for them. I knew my parents were reluctant about "dredging it all up," but I didn't anticipate my father's response. His eerily calm reply would haunt me for years afterward. He said, "I heard him say that but I knew it wasn't going to happen." He paused for a moment, and then went on, "Everyone knew." He paused again. I was stunned and said nothing. He then added, "You were running around with 'those' people. The lady who wrote the probation report said sending you to prison would be a good way to get you away from the people you were hanging around with. We had to do something."

His words were like knives slicing into my chest. I couldn't speak. I stared at dried eucalyptus branches in a vase on the desk. The walls of the pantry seemed to squeeze in on me.

"What are you talking about?" I finally responded.

"You were embarrassing the entire family."

I spoke again. "You mean you prompted me to plead knowing they were going to send me to prison for something you knew I didn't do, your own daughter? Did you think I was really a drug dealer?"

"We knew you didn't sell drugs, you didn't have any money, but we heard about the kind of people you were hanging around with. Jim said he'd thought of running for office for district attorney but because of the rumors about Mexicans coming to your apartment he couldn't do it. People thought the stories were about one of his daughters. It was killing your mother to hear about you like this. We didn't have a choice. We had to do something."

"Dad, Mom's illness started long before I tried drugs or started hanging around with people you thought were the wrong crowd. How could you blame her problems on me? And my seeing a Hispanic guy, is that what this was all about? You weren't prejudiced when we lived in Ohio. You knew Angie Borge's parents were from Mexico. But she and Jack were wealthy. Is that the difference? I was hanging around someone from a poor family? A poor Mexican and embarrassing the family, is that what this was all about?"

I wanted desperately for him to argue with me and say he thought I was dependent on drugs, or was somehow thinking of my well-being, no matter how illogical it might have been. If he'd said he believed I was a drug dealer, it would have been easier for me to take. To hear him say that he knew I wasn't guilty of the charges against me yet still didn't support me was devastating. I needed to grasp something other than what he was making clear to me now, that my crime was that I had tarnished the family name.

I'd had my suspicions about my father's role in my conviction, but I had hoped someday to be proven wrong. Now he was leaving me no doubt.

"Do you realize what I've had to live through all these years? Do you realize what this could do to my family, my children, to Alan?"

"If I had it to do over, i would do things differently," he responded. "Things were different then. I didn't feel like I had a choice."

How did this happen to someone like my father—a man who was a devoted caregiver to my mother, a man who never said no to a friend in need? I am a parent myself and can't imagine such a thing. How great a fear could have caused him to side against his own daughter? Seeing this side of my father was one of the most painful moments in my life.

Knowing my parents had sided against me was a deep blow, though my chances in the courtroom might have only been slightly better had they been behind me. My co-defendant's family had done everything possible to help him, and he had helped set a lot of people up yet he got the same maximum sentence I did. He was a little older and had a few previous drug offenses against him, but he wasn't a drug dealer anymore than I was. It hadn't mattered. It was all about racking up convictions and making headlines. The ambitious agent and his cohorts were driving the momentum, and determined to martyr anyone in their path. My own family was pulled along in the hysteria.

I had one last question for my father. "Did the public defender, Amato, also know that the probation promise was a ruse?"

"Of course he knew. I told you: *everyone* knew."

It was quite a birthday. My brain was numb. I felt as I had when I'd fallen out of a tree as a kid and had the wind knocked out of me. The feeling went deeper than anger or bitterness. I told myself that the important thing was that I not take my hurt out on my family.

Alan and I reconciled the next day, but he had never seen me withdraw like this. I think he supposed it was because of our argument that night and his moodiness in the weeks before.

The final question that burned inside of me was where my mother fit into all this. I knew the answer, but I had to hear it from her personally. Maybe she could explain things better. The next day when the house was empty, I closed the bedroom door and called her before I lost my nerve. When she answered, I said in a solemn tone, "I need to know what you knew about my conviction, Mom. I have to know the truth."

She began to cry. I had never heard her cry before.

"It was a terrible time for all of us; I made a lot of mistakes and I know they hurt you. I know you weren't yourself during those years. I just want to know what happened."

She cried harder but didn't answer.

I pushed on. I had to hear her answers to questions that had circled painfully in my mind for more than two decades. How did Ritchie or the police know my new address?

She started to cry harder. "We didn't know what to do." She said. "Your uncle kept showing up that summer insisting we had to do something about you. You were ruining the family name, he was furious."

She paused but I couldn't speak. She continued, " I felt so foolish afterwards. I realized as soon as they took you away that we had overreacted. You weren't doing anything a lot of people weren't doing, I realized that only later."

Overreacted. The word hardly seemed to describe it, but I knew her intentions were genuine.

My mother continued, "I used to see people come on Johnny Carson, and they would say, 'If you remember the 70's, you weren't there, man." And everyone would clap and laugh, and make jokes about using drugs. I would feel sick to my stomach thinking how your father and I had gotten so upset; I think about how hard we were on you dating that boy we didn't like. I saw later that you were trying to help him. I've seen how that's the kind of person you are. You weren't just seeing him to defy us.....I don't know how we got so carried away."

"I know, Mom. I can only imagine how hard it must be to have a teenager using drugs. A lot of people are frightened about drugs. They're a scary thing to have your kids get into. I made mistakes, too. I can never forget how foolish I was to get so heavy into drugs, I don't even understand it myself, but I know it's more important to learn from the past and move forward." I wanted her to know that I loved her and did not blame her, but we were reaching back into a dark crevice and I'd probably never again have the chance to hear the details so I asked her a few more questions about why they didn't contact me at the prison.

She said that as soon as I was sentenced, she tried to block everything out of her mind. She had been so angry during those years, it was a stressful time, but only once the reality of what had happened to me hit her and I was sent to prison she felt paralyzed about what she should do.

She struggled to move on, she said, but when she heard that my grandfather was going to help me escape, she felt a weight lifted from her shoulders.

At this moment, I felt more anguish about what they did to my mother than about what they did to me. She was used as a pawn. She was clueless about what was really going on in Saginaw that year and relying, as she had always been taught to do, on what the authorities told her. I assured her that I understood the pressure she was under and reiterated that I knew I'd made bad choices also.

She began to cry again.

"Somehow, Mom, this was just meant to be. At least I am free and have a good life, probably better than if none of this would've happened." I hoped these words would give her some peace. I knew I'd never tell her about the terrible despair that I felt during those years.

This too shall pass, I thought to myself, but how long would it take?

Like counting sheep to push away sleeplessness, I tried to count the many blessings that I had in order to push away the dread of this latest news. I again reflected back on that moment of light in the dark cell to give me strength. I thought of the people who helped me along the way, the family members who stood by me. Maybe the fire really is purifying; maybe suffering really does bring understanding. It didn't lessen the pain to know this, but at least it helped me believe there was a meaning for it.

For now, I saw that my pain had made me strong, and that poisonous thoughts would serve no purpose. But healing takes time, and I had to be patient. I had learned a terrible secret. What was my next move?

Chapter 31

With the new knowledge gained from the phone call with my father, I embarked on a search for more evidence, tracking down everyone I could reach who might have had any involvement in my case.

I reached out first to Amato, the public defender. He was still a Saginaw attorney, still specializing in personal injury. The first call to his office elicited the news that he was spending the winter at his villa in Puerto Rico and wouldn't be back for some weeks. The wait for his return was gut-wrenching, but not as bad an ordeal as the phone call itself.

I had identified myself as a potential defendant so Amato would take the call. He was not happy when I revealed who I really was, and he grew immediately defensive when I told him what I had learned—that he knew I was innocent, knew I would be harshly sentenced, and went along with it. Why, I asked him, did he insist that I plead guilty knowing the court was planning to give me the maximum sentence?

His answer was the same one heard from my father: He had no choice. He had to do what the prosecutor told him. "They were going to give you ten to twenty years no matter what I did; the judge had made a pact with the other judges to give everyone the max, so what choice did I have?"

"Why didn't you tell me that Ritchie set me up?" I asked next. "You knew he'd been arrested by the same agent a few days before he lured me to Luigi's."

"There was nothing I could do. They said I didn't have a choice—they were sending you to prison no matter what I did."

"Why did you push me to plead guilty knowing what they had planned for me? You must have known that pleading guilty hurt my ability to get an appeal"

"I had never had a criminal case before...and I never took one again after yours. They pressured me to take it. I don't have to talk to you," Amato snapped. "I have to go." He hung up.

His abrupt hang-up left me with one more question I didn't get a chance to ask. Had his father's conviction prior to my arrest had anything to do with his conspiring with the prosecutor? I felt sick after the conversation. It brought back memories of the degrading way he'd he treated me three decades ago—as if I were less than human because I was a defendant.

I now pushed myself to contact the former prosecutor, John Ebert. I had heard by now that Ebert's life had taken strange turns since his days as prosecutor. He was long gone from Saginaw, but I was able to find a location and then a phone number and I made the call—and uncovered still more startling information about the bizarre members of the kangaroo court.

Ebert was much more willing to talk than Amato was, and while witnesses stood by my side, just as they had with the call to Amato, he explained what happened to him in the years following my conviction. He left Saginaw soon afterwards after feeling bullets whiz past his head. He admitted that he and Greely were aggressive in their pursuit of convictions, no matter how flimsy the evidence. He knew most of the convictions were based on Greely's word alone, and they managed to get long sentences because Greely had everyone at the courthouse excited by his claims that there were five organized-crime syndicates operating in Saginaw, despite its population of only 50,000 at the time. I mentioned to him that that is the plot straight out of the movie recently released called "The Godfather". He'd never thought of it like that. Ebert, inexperienced and young, believed Greely was legitimately bringing in major syndicate members. That most of the defendants could not afford a decent attorney seems not to have raised any flags—not for Ebert nor for anyone else.

But the real irony was that Ebert himself was later sent to prison. The charge? Selling drugs. The plea? Not guilty. Then I heard a stunning revelation. Ebert believed that it was Greely, by now the state police chief, who managed to get him convicted and sentenced unjustly.

"I started using coke when people I was defending paid me in drugs," he said. "But I wasn't selling it." In a roundabout way, he said that Greely had framed a lot of people, and he unwittingly was part of it. But the confession came obliquely; Ebert said that many people "changed their minds about Greely" once cases were successfully appealed on the basis that statements from Greely were fabricated.

I didn't tell him that around the same time he was dodging bullets and being framed, as he claims, for a drug conviction, my co-defendant was mysteriously murdered in Saginaw and there was an attempt on my life in California. Ebert went on to tell how he was beaten up pretty badly in prison and now doesn't want anything to do with anything or anyone from Saginaw. To him, the whole experience reeked of the Salem witch hunts of 1692—the same extremism and intolerance, false accusations, and utter collapse of due process.

He told me he did not actually remember my case, but he recognized the trademarks of corruption in Saginaw and asked me to send him the transcripts to jog his memory. Did he not remember telling me that I would get probation if I pled guilty? No, but he said this: "I do remember that we were misleading people at the time by promising lenient sentences and then instead of giving them the maximum sentence, thirteen to twenty, we gave them a more lenient sentence of ten to twenty years." A strange interpretation of leniency

The phone call with Ebert dredged up the past so vividly that it left me feeling dirty. I picked up Bailey, our miniature dachshund, and cradled him in my arms. He was so soft and loving—proof positive that I was home, that I had a family, a stable life, virtually everything I have ever wanted. Life is a series of obstacles, I reminded myself, and I had jumped over most of them so far. I would have to keep trying to overcome this obstacle.

But while the corrupt world of Saginaw—Amato, Ebert, Greely—was behind me, the hideous details of my past could not be put aside for good. I could not let the past drag me down, but somehow, I still had to put the pieces together and figure out how to untangle this vicious trap.

I always believed there was a reason for it all. My volunteer work and my training as a hospice worker were important but in my heart did not seem enough. I wrote articles about rights issues and contributed to advocacy groups—in time as well as money—but it still seemed I should be doing more.

I knew how tough it was to bring about change; my involvement in community issues had taught me something about that challenge. But it was one thing to give dinner parties and participate in comfortable charities that aren't too "gritty" and quite another to do what I felt I should be doing—namely, helping those coming out of prison and struggling with the transition, or working steadily with teenage drug users. At the same time, I knew I would run the risk of becoming too passionate—and possibly blowing my cover. I would be getting too close to the flame. Once I was able to resolve my situation, I would be free to do more.

I continued to call attorneys and continued to hear that I should have nothing to worry about. Michigan was too broke to keep schools going; it was absurd that the state would waste money coming after someone like me…after all these years.

Suddenly, I snap back to the present as the slave bus lurches forward. I become conscious that I am no longer in Carmel Valley, I am chained up in a cage and on my way to a Michigan prison. The nightmare has caught up with me. I feel a surge of dread when the reality hits and I have full consciousness as to where I am. The metal handcuffs cut deeper into my wrists when I lay my head back, trying desperately to fall asleep. I wonder how much longer it will be before we reach Michigan and God knows what will await me there.

Chapter 32

It's early on a Friday morning when at last the bus stops. We are ordered to get off. We're at the Christian County jail in Kentucky, a TransCor hub. The company pays to use the drunk tank to house its passengers until it's convenient to take them to Michigan or another destination state. The black boxes come off, but time moves excruciatingly slowly in this windowless lock-up. It's a dim cement room with a slightly raised four-foot-wide ledge around the perimeter where we're supposed to sit, and throw our thin mats and blankets to sleep.

A delusional man named Brian, who has been in the adjacent cell for four months, screams almost constantly and uses a half dozen different voices. One seems to be his father's: "Brian you idiot, why did you do this, you fucking idiot? I hate you!" the deep voice screams loudly and condescendingly. Then another voice screams defensively, "I don't know why I'm an idiot!"

Apparently, Brian hit a guard at a mental institution, and locking him here in solitary for months is the consequence. He's medicated at night and talks to a girl he can't see in another cell through the narrow slit in the door where food is slid into the cell. She says she is leaving in a few days and will come back to visit him. Brian talks of nothing else. Then Dottie, the guard who delivers food, tells him that the girl won't be visiting him because the condition of her release won't allow her to see people in jail. Brian voices his rage. His screams echo through the walls and in the unit every day for most of the day. He is a tortured soul, and hearing him scream is a torture in itself.

I sit for days in the dimly lit cell. I realize that for more than a week, no one has any idea where I am....

Chapter 33

As the sole female on the bus, I spend a weekend alone in the windowless cell at the Kentucky facility.

One day, a guard escorts me to a 10-minute shower, then returns me to the cell, where there now appears to be a person curled up under a blanket on the floor. The guard says, "That's Diane."

For the next two days, Diane sleeps, covered from head to toe by her blanket. She wakes only when it's time to get back on the bus for the last leg of the trip to Michigan. She is a honey-colored woman, I guess, is in her forties. Seen in profile from her right side, she is rather pretty, but face to face, she's lopsided: Her left eye is lower than her right, and parts of her left side look crushed. Crushed, it turns out, is the right word; she was hit by a car while she says she was crossing the street some years ago, and her left leg and arm have never fully recovered. Like seemingly everyone else on the bus, she is here on a technical violation: She didn't show up for a parole appointment. Her initial offense was for drugs.

We're both chained around the waist and linked together with more chains, then fitted once again with the restrictive black boxes on our wrists. As the TransCor guards lead us up the steps of the bus, a large man dressed in a military-looking uniform again holds an automatic rifle pointed slightly above our heads. Since neither of us has been convicted of, much less charged with a crime of violence, it strikes me as overkill to aim guns at two middle-aged women already wrapped in chains—it's like pruning a rosebush with a chainsaw.

If any of us on the bus had been violent criminals or child rapists, this paramilitary production would make sense, but we're a busload of druggies, deadbeats, and an ex–drug user.

It's a daylong drive to get to the women's prison, with many stops along the way picking up and dropping off prisoners. The noise still seems like it could shatter my eardrums, but I'm happy to be out of the dungeon-like cell in Kentucky and able to look out a window. The bright and colorful world on the other side of the glass looks remote from my seat here on the bus.

We stop first at a large men's facility called Jackson, where the men get out. Then we double back toward Plymouth, where there's a women's facility named Scott.

That's when Diane starts talking. The clanging metal inside the bus seems to echo even more loudly now that the men are gone. Diane is seated behind me, and she has to shout to be heard over the noise. So shout she does.

For a crack user with a crushed body and a history of long stretches of time behind bars, she's remarkably articulate.

"You heard about the prison they're taking us to, right?" she yells. I peer through the space between the two seats to try to see her as she speaks.

I yell back, "No, I haven't. What's it like? Do they smoke at the prison? I won't have to be around smokers, will I?"

"I don't think cigarette smoke will be at the top of your list of worries at Scott. It's supposed to be one of the worst prisons in the country."

I feel a little knot in my stomach when she says this, but I fight against feelings of fear. I assure myself Diane is probably being dramatic and I shouldn't have a problem since I've never had issues getting along with other people, and I don't have a problem following rules.

But Diane is full of details that make it hard to stay calm. "The state just settled a lawsuit against the prison because guards were raping female prisoners. They'd been raping 'em for years, and the lawsuit got stalled by the state for decades. Prisoners were getting pregnant and being forced into abortions, till one inmate who'd been locked up for five years got pregnant and hid her pregnancy so long they had to let her have the baby. Even with this kind of evidence, the state's lawyers said they needed 'further analysis.'

"So one day there's this one woman who runs out of her unit over to the admin building, spits out a mouthful of semen on a desk, and says 'Analyze this!'" Diane screams out with a boisterous laugh.

I guess I can see how it's a funny story, but I flash back to what I saw when I was locked up as a teenager and remember what the guards did to girls then. "They were raping girls in the 'seventies," I yell to Diane. "The guards were coming into the women's cells, into the showers, forcing them to do whatever they wanted."

Diane looks at me, startled. "You were in prison in the 'seventies?" She had me pegged as a novice.

"It's a long story, but yeah. So what happened to the lawsuit?"

"It finally came to an end this year and the MDOC was fined $200 million so far, and the number is climbing. There are still a lot of cases yet to be heard."

"What's the MDOC?" I ask.

Diane looks surprised that I don't know this. "The Michigan Department of Corrections. You know, they 'correct' people," she says sarcastically.

She feels like talking, and she's got a whole collection of salacious tidbits about our upcoming accommodations.

"And you heard about the gun battle between the two guards, in the parking lot at Scott?"

"No, I haven't."

"Just a couple of months ago, two guards got into a gunfight and one of 'em got shot fifteen times right outside the prison and died. The prison is right next to a high-end residential area, so now they're losing their lease."

"No kidding, a gunfight at the prison—by the officers of the Corrections Department?" I say.

"And over at Jackson, the guards baked this guy to death in a cell. They had him chained up for days, at four points, his arms and his legs, and he died from the heat and no water. I saw it on *60 Minutes*. The show said Amnesty International said Michigan prisons are some of the worst in the world. And that's just from the murders that get found out about."

I wonder how much of what Diane was saying could be true, and what she's conveniently leaving out. Surely the inmate who died must have been violent and out-of-control.

I'm 54 years old, I tell myself. Who would pick on a middle-aged woman? I've never had a problem getting along with people or respecting people in authority and I'm unusually frail with all the weight I've lost worrying the last few weeks. Surely I'm not worth bothering.

Still, it's a terrible feeling to think I'm going to a prison like that—or any prison. I ask myself again and again what sense it makes for Michigan to search for me for almost two years, fabricate information that they were responding to an anonymous tip, and then transport me across country to a place where the employees rape and murder the inmates and even each other—it seems absurd. I know the state is hard up for jobs, but this strikes me as a type of social cannibalism.

Diane isn't finished yet. "There's a new warden who's never worked in a prison before. She apparently got the job as a gift from some bigwig at the MDOC. I think that's the only way you get a job anymore in Michigan— you gotta know someone."

"How do you know all this?" I ask, amazed that she would be this informed.

"You learn all this shit in jail."

One of the guards on the bus, a skeleton-thin woman with different-sized eyebrows, comes to sit in a seat across the aisle from us. Her bulky handgun and holster hang on her waist and hit against the armrest as she lowers herself into the seat.

She starts in abruptly, as if she's been in on the discussion all along.

"If they close down prisons and I lose my job, we'll probably lose our house. My husband's business folded a couple a' years ago and he ain't found nothin' else since."

It feels like some cynical game—the poor forced to feed on the poor.

A TALE OF TWO LIVES

It's evening now—about 6 o'clock. In the distance, I can make out fences and razor wire that surround a group of grubby-looking buildings. I remember being on vacation with my family a few years ago and seeing a prison along the highway. We were traveling through the Sierras to go skiing. I remember feeling goose bumps on my arms and I could only look at the prison for a moment; then I turned to look at my children sleeping peacefully in the back seat to reassure myself I was safely on the right side of the barbed wire. As I watched my husband behind the steering wheel, I wondered when I would finally tell him what I'd kept hidden for so long. It was an eerie feeling to look at the prison from the outside and know what it was like inside. I was thankful for my good fortune that I was on *this* side and I never wanted to forget that. Of all the millions of people sucked into the incarceration machine, some guilty and some not, I was that rare thing—someone who had been swallowed up and left as a statistic, but managed to get away and build a better life. I've wondered at times what would have happened if I'd finished out my original sentence. I shudder to think.

Now, as the bus begins to slow and we pull through a gate manned by guards carrying rifles, I cringe, knowing that this time I am on the wrong side of the barbed wire and I have no idea for how long.

The bus pulls into an alleyway where we are unloaded, still in chains and at gunpoint. We enter a nondescript building for processing. Guards take the street clothes we were wearing when we were picked up and the items in our possession, then put them in a box to be sent to whatever address we write on a label. I want mine sent home to California, and I sign a voucher to pay the postage. Diane has nowhere to send her clothing and no money to pay the postage, something she awkwardly tries to hide. I can tell she feels humiliated when her clothing is thrown into a large trash can.

We are each issued a canvas bag containing two sets of the prison uniform—blue pants and a blue shirt with a wide vertical orange stripe, a few sets of undergarments, and a toothbrush. Thus equipped, we are marched off across the compound, and I get a chance to see the rest of the prison layout. It's comprised of a number of low-lying buildings—I can't quite count how many—of maize-colored brick crowned with coiled razor wire. Around the perimeter are several rows of chain-link fences, also edged with coils of razor wire. A sidewalk connects about a dozen one-story buildings, and the buildings too are crowned like everything else—with razor wire. In the center of the sidewalk is broken concrete; in one spot, it looks as if someone years ago had begun to build a small amphitheater but never finished it. Weeds crawl up the sides and through the cracks in the broken cement.

We arrive at the building housing the prison clinic, and there we wait. Other new recruits file in a few at a time, or sometimes in groups of a dozen or more. Eventually, the 40 or so chairs in the waiting room are all occupied, and prisoners begin to sit on the floor and find places to stand along the wall. Again as on the bus, I feel like I'm part of a herd of animals being roughly led to slaughter.

Current inmates coming into the clinic for their medications are told to wait in a line outside. To prevent disease epidemics, new and old prisoners are not supposed to interact, but the crowded conditions make separation impossible, and we continue to be crammed in more and more closely as prisoners keep showing up. Eventually, women are sitting on windowsills, hanging on water coolers, and crouching on the ground. When prisoners in wheelchairs arrive for their meds, the line has to give way, and more prisoners are pushed together. I see more wheelchairs than I've ever seen in a hospital. Some of them are double wide because the women in them weigh 300 to 400 pounds. Such obesity is widespread, and I wonder about the food being served here.

Diane soon sees inmates she knows from previous stays, and there's a lot of "Hey girl!" and "Wuz happening?"

"Have you been here since I left or are you back in?" Diane asks one acquaintance.

"I been home, baby, I was doing all right but it's an election year, you know that."

Diane nods knowingly. Then a few other women chime in; they're here, they also say, because it's 2008 and it's election time again.

Over and over, the women talk about being here because of greedy politicians who compete to look tough on crime. They say it's because of the money prisons get. "Mo' money for mo' prisoners," one of them says. One inmate with a face like petrified wood and the same dead-looking eyes of so many of the prisoners says, "If the prison gets as much money for a minnow as a shark, why go after a shark?" There are a lot of minnows here, and not a lot of sharks from what I can see.

In many ways the prison, the glossy concrete-walled room we are in, and the sad- faced women here look remarkably similar to what I remember from 30 years ago; I see the same stark old furniture and junky conditions. Eerily, it's as if I've been pulled back in time to that terrible period. The only difference in the furnishings is the presence of a boxy computer screen sitting on the desk

261

showing pictures of dilapidated barns as a screen saver. Everything else seems frozen in time except for the many neck tattoos—that and the fact that I don't remember prisoners talking about politics 30 years ago, certainly not so cynically.

Diane catches sight of another old acquaintance—a tall, slim dark-skinned woman with broad shoulders and a square jaw, who introduces herself as Uncle Buck. After a while she begins to sing quietly in a rich baritone voice. Diane joins in with a similarly rich voice that sounds a lot like Gladys Knight.

Singing is against the rules, and a guard orders the women to stop.

We're still sitting and waiting, and the constant hum of conversation becomes almost lulling. I ask Diane, "Why do you use crack if you have such a beautiful voice?" She widens her eyes but says nothing, and I realize it was a thoughtless question.

She tells me that the first time she got caught with drugs, she got probation. A few months later she violated her probation when marijuana showed up in a urine test. She was sent to prison for 12 months. During that time, by her account, she was attacked by another inmate, and the parole board sentenced her to another year.

According to Diane, marijuana is a drug that sends a lot of people back because it stays in your system for weeks and weeks, a much longer time than other drugs.

"Why didn't you just stay away from everything?" I ask.

"It didn't matter," she says. "They were going to put me back in jail no matter what, so I figured I would enjoy what little time I had on the outside."

"Knowing what you were facing, couldn't you have just quit using drugs, they couldn't put you back in unless you broke the law."

Diane shakes her head. "You seem like a nice lady and you've no doubt been through some shit yourself, but you have no idea how it really goes down once you're in the system. Once they get you in, it's a spider web you don't get out of."

"But if you didn't use drugs—"

"I was working for six months sweeping floors and could hardly pay bus fare to get to work and eat, but every time I went to see my P. O. she threatened to put me in jail the next time she saw me if I didn't bring in money to pay off what I owed them."

"Why would you have restitution for a small drug offense?"

"It wasn't restitution, it was to pay off my court costs and for the public defender I talked with for like two minutes. They charged me $1,400 to prosecute me."

"I thought they were required to give you a defense attorney."

"They got all kinds of new laws.

"Where do they think I'm gonna legally get $1,400 to pay for court costs? Not a lot of people are lining up to hire ex-cons."

"I never heard of them being able to charge someone like that."

"When I lost my job and knew I couldn't make any more payments, I ask my PO if I could go to Georgia—I had my people down there—but she said I couldn't go. I think she just wanted to keep a big caseload to keep her job."

"Doesn't a parole officer help you get a job? How do they expect an ex-prisoner to get a job when no one else can?"

"Some parole officers are cool and really try to help, but mine was nasty. A lot of 'em are. The power goes to their head. Who was I going to complain to, the governor?"

I can't believe Diane was sent to prison for having a small amount of marijuana in her system. I tell her this and ask her if I can see her court papers.

I ask this of many prisoners when they also claim they were here for what seem to be unbelievably trivial offenses. And buried under codes and numbers I repeatedly find that just as they had claimed, they are here based on a minuscule amount of drugs or alcohol, or missed parole appointments that violated their parole or probation.

Were the women locked up on technicalities because they were dangerous in other ways, in the same way Al Capone got 20 years for tax evasion? In the weeks and months to come, I find that that isn't the case. I find that many of these women are not much different than me and many should not have been in prison at all.

I feel a small sense of relief sitting in the clinic. It's at least an improvement over what I've been through the last few weeks. However, I can't stop thinking about what my children and husband are going through at home. Newspapers keep repeating the Saginaw prosecutor's allegations that I'm a former high-level syndicate member. I still have no idea where he is getting this information from. At home, I'm not even the cool mom. It took years for my husband and me to give in and sign up for HBO because it was too risqué. When I finally signed up to see Bill Maher's show, my daughter said to me jokingly, "Oh, we're finally getting 'Hell's Box Office.'"

Before I'm able to exhale, Diane and Uncle Buck begin to fill me in on what's ahead. As part of the new herd, they tell me, we will be kept for the next month or two—maybe longer—in a cell, two to a room, for 23 hours a day—maybe 24. There will be little to read and no pens to write with.

The prospect of lying on a bunk in a small concrete room behind a thick iron door for weeks, even months, on end seems overwhelming. How long can I deal with this? I wonder. Another week? A few weeks? Surely when the truth about my conviction surfaces, I will be released from here; it can only be a matter of weeks.

I remember how much I suffered the first time I was in "the system." If I'd had more faith that things would have turned out all right, I would have saved myself a lot of unnecessary grief. Now, in crisis mode again, I have to grab onto thoughts that give me strength if I want to survive. All of life seems like a crisis in a way, with intermittent moments of lightness that make it all worthwhile.

I haven't been away from my family in 24 years. Not having them near feels like part of my body has been ripped away. I haven't been able to talk to my husband or children in weeks. All that time on the slave-ship bus, they of course kept us incommunicado. And now, I can't help but think, I am in Michigan, where the unimaginable has happened before.

My family and the life I led for three decades seem almost as remote as if they were just a dream. But they weren't a dream. In just a few weeks Maureen will be graduating, and the family trip we'd been planning for many months to San Luis Obispo for her commencement ceremony was nearing. Maureen was graduating near the top of her class and had taken on extracurricular projects like recruiting her entire sorority to help run a booth at a job fair and raise money for the American Cancer Society. She had worked hard and looked forward to this day for so long, it seems unbearable that I might be here instead, and that people would be thinking about me instead of celebrating her triumphant day.

By 10 o'clock that night, the clinic is brimming with some 30 new arrivals, and we are shepherded along the narrow sidewalk to the quarantine unit, called Cord. I am assigned to a 9- by-12-foot cell with Diane. We each get a blanket, sheets, and a hard plastic pillow. I have the top bunk. Thankfully, the cell has a window. It is narrow and doesn't open, but to me, with my serious claustrophobic tendencies, it makes the room seem less like a closed coffin. Diane shows me how to make the pillow more comfortable with the nylon jacket we were given. She also demonstrates how to lay out the prison uniform meticulously under the three-inch mattress so it will look almost ironed in the morning. I admire her style, but the last thing on my mind is getting rid of wrinkles in my prison uniform.

My fears of what lie ahead are making my heart pound. I climb up onto the bunk and—somehow—I sleep.

I wake up in the middle of the night. It takes a moment for me to realize where I am. I think again of my family and the terrible things said about me in the paper and the fact that I am facing more than five maybe ten years in prison.

The thin mat I'm sleeping on is old and the stuffing has been pushed to the edges over time so that the middle section has no padding. During the night I have to turn from side to side when my hip bone gets sore from hitting the steel of the metal bunk underneath. With the door closed, the walls of the room seem to sway inward and push out the oxygen. I am aware the anxiety is all in my head. I use my imagination that I'm a journalist on an assignment in a war zone. I think of soldiers who are sleeping in bunks in imminent danger. But the hardest part though is not the physical discomforts. It is whole idea of why this is happening to me and so many others in similar circumstances.

Chapter 34

In the morning, Diane is called out from the cell and ordered to mop the floor of the common area in front of the guards' desk. Getting to leave the cell for any reason is a perk, and Diane excitedly dresses and goes. She returns half an hour later, bursting to tell me that she has overheard the guards at the desk discussing me.

"The guards were talking about you all morning, LeFevre. They're sayin' some shit about you, girl. They said they were gonna write you up with violations so they could send you to the hole and shit. It was crazy."

I notice instantly Diane's sudden shift to slang. "Why would they be talking about me? I haven't even been out of the cell yet."

"Well, they said 'that bitch from California with her Lexus,' and there ain't a whole lotta people here from California with a Lexus."

"Why would they bother with me?"

"I don't want to bum you out, but they were talking some serious shit, like they was gonna make sure you didn't get your out date."

"There must be some mistake."

"I don't know, girl, but there was a bunch of us out there cleanin' and we all heard it. We were all just looking at each other. It was almost like they wanted us to hear what they were saying. One of the guards was Dingle. Remember I told you about the guard who got the inmate pregnant?"

"Yeah."

"Well, that was her husband. He got fired and stuck with paying child support for the inmate's baby. She's hated inmates ever since. She picks on white *and* black inmates.... I heard her tell the other guards," she lowers her voice an octave, "'That bitch ain't never going back to her fancy house in California.'"

She continues standing in the center of the room, her eyes large. I'm not sure if she is upset about the guard's threats against me or just eager to have something to get excited about.

"You got a fancy house, LeFevre? They said you married some rich guy."

"That's mainly something the papers played up."

Diane continues to ruminate, "I've never heard anything like it, the guards just putting it out there like that."

I'm stunned to think that things actually seem to be getting worse. "I'll just have to be careful." Sarcastically I add. "I might have to hold back on my plans to pick fights and kick some ass."

She shoots me a startled look. It takes her a moment before she realizes I'm being facetious.

"Diane, I'm just kidding. I've never been in a physical fight in my life. I've never even seen one except on TV. I'm just trying to find something to laugh about. This is all so crazy. If I don't laugh I'll probably cry—or

I'll go insane. It all seems absurd. I can't believe this is happening to me."

"Yeah, I guess that is a trip, and apparently the guards don't like the noise your case is making. What are you gonna do about Dingle?"

"All I can do is make sure I follow the rules and do my best. I'm sure when they see that I'm not a bad person, it'll be all right."

Diane looks at me straight on, which she rarely does because of the scars on the one side of her face, and says, "Susan, I would advise you don't leave the cell for any reason if you don't have to. They can mess you up, girl. I seen 'em drive women to kill themselves and I hear it happens all the time. Some of these guards enjoy seeing another person destroyed, and they don't need a reason. A few a' these guards are a lot more sadistic than any of the inmates. I mean, like some of the guards are cool people, like really cool, but the ones that are evil are the ones in control."

Just then a loudspeaker blasts out an announcements for our unit to go to "med lines." Anyone who takes medication, which is the majority of inmates, has about 15 minutes to go to the clinic to pick it up. Inmates stream to the front desk to get a pass. I didn't want my body adjusting to the Zoloft I was taking for the last few weeks so I planned to quit it soon, but I was thankful to be able to walk outside for a few minutes to get to the clinic twice a day. After being locked up in the tiny cell all day it was exhilarating to breathe fresh air and feel the sun on my skin. Those few minutes a day that I could focus my eyes on something farther than a wall a few feet away felt like a luxury.

A TALE OF TWO LIVES

As I walk back from the clinic, I close my eyes and feel the sun and the moist Michigan air. I try to imagine being somewhere else, but it's hard to concentrate on the crowded narrow walk. Inmates often talk to me as I pass. At least a dozen times, inmates passing the other way pause to say something, mostly about Jesus being there for me. I'm usually cynical of overtly religious people, but these women express such heartfelt warmth that I'm genuinely touched. An African-American woman with the kindest eyes looks me right in the eyes and says with sincerity, "God's gonna send you home to your family, baby—don't you worry." Just about everyone here uses slang, black or white. In my sensitive mood, it means a lot to hear concern from complete strangers. It's like another tiny hand helping me stay the course.

Seeing me exchange words with the inmates walking by, a large, heavy-set guard yells out, "Hurry up, LeFevre. Get back to your unit." The other inmates stand on the walk talking, smoking cigarettes, but he singles me out by name. It feels eerie enough that a stranger would know my name, much less voice it in a hostile way. When I approach my unit, Dingle is outside the building with a small horde of younger guards smoking cigarettes by the door.

A tall, large-boned girl with an even taller afro approaches me and identifies herself as Angela. In quick succession she says, "Are you Susan? My roommate's Jane Smith; she says you'll know her from Saginaw. She wants me to tell you she's here. I have a note from her," she slips it into my hand discreetly.

The sidewalk is full of prisoners coming back from the clinic. On one side of me near another unit, a young woman standing with a thicket of other young inmates yells out, "You my hero, girl!"

Angela quickly interjects, "I know that girl; she probably read about you being rich and she's trying to play you. Watch out for her."

Then from the other side of the walk, while Angela is still standing next to me, we both hear Dingle shout out, "That bitch is gonna know she ain't in Beverly Hills no mo', driving around in her Lexus. I'm gonna write that bitch up. She ain't never getting outta here." The other guards let out loud howls. "We'll show her our best behavior." More howls.

Angela says, "Damn, girl, did she really just say what I thought she did? I've been down eighteen years and never heard anything like that —and right in front of all these people. Why they hatin' on you like that?"

It's still sinking in that the guards are talking about me. I can't believe I'm in a prison and a group of angry guards are yelling out threats at me. Angela turns to go to her unit in the other direction and says, "I have something else I want to tell you about, but I'll have to tell you later. It might explain why they're screwing with you. Are you going to the evening clinic?"

"Yes," I answer; my head is still spinning.

She walks the other way as I turn into Cord unit and toward the group of guards in front of the door. They glare in my direction and I avoid making eye contact, using the same instincts I learned as a kid when dealing with animals in the wild. One of the guards throws a cigarette butt at my feet.

A TALE OF TWO LIVES

As I pass, the guard who works with Dingle sneers, "You missed your chance to get a shower, LeFevre; I called your cell while you were at the clinic. Better luck tomorrow." I hear a couple of low snorts from the other guards.

In my cell I read the note Angela passed me from Jane. Getting a note slipped in my hand like that felt like junior high—a version of it in hell. Jane's note is supportive, and she tells me how she was busted for drugs two years ago and has been here ever since. She has another two years to go. She has a lot to say about Saginaw. It went downhill drastically since I left, she says. Much of it looks like a third world country with burned-out buildings and the city doesn't have the money to get them torn down. Streets are crumbling and weeds grow several feet high, taking over old neighborhoods. All the same people have remained in charge there for decades –on both sides of the law.

Her note makes me realize that my fate could have been worse had I stayed in Saginaw.

I spend the rest of the day lying on the top bunk in the sickly hot cell. Diane is anemic and doesn't feel the heat; sometimes she wears a jacket on hot days. As a result of years of doing drugs, she says she is almost always cold. She is also hyper, a normal reaction to coming off a long period of drug use. She paces the floor and readily tells me about her life when I ask and sometimes when I don't. She came from a two-parent home, and a mother who was overly strict. I had expected the opposite, of course. Then she got pregnant in her senior year and was kicked out of school when she got into a fight with someone over a comment about her Geri-curl hairdo. Things went downhill after that. Her stories about the streets of Detroit still haunt me.

At 6 p.m. I go again to med lines and I see Angela on the walk. Her expression is anxious and she begins quickly, "My friend does maintenance up at the admin building and she was there last week when the new warden called this meeting with a bunch of the guards. She heard the new warden say that when you got here, the media would be watching your case closely and they needed to be on their best behavior toward you. Apparently when she said that, the guards started screaming and getting hostile. The new warden had only started working here a few days by then and I think the guards thought she was sticking up for you possibly because you're both white or because you got money. Whatever reason it was, they got so loud the warden rushed out of the room. I guess the guards started yelling even louder."

I would hear about the meeting from others also. Prisons don't have a lot of news, and stories circulate rapidly. The rowdy meeting among the guards was only the beginning. I would soon learn of a more compelling force that was inciting the guards' rancor. I would learn about it directly from the guards themselves.

At about three o'clock in the morning, the bright ceiling light is switched on in my cell, waking me from a sound sleep, and I open my eyes to see several guards standing next to my bunk. One of them barks an order for me to get dressed and report to the base, a term for the guard's desk outside in the hallway. I have no idea what is going to happen to me.

At the base, several guards hover around and no one says anything for a few minutes. Then a particularly mean-looking guard wearing pitch-black sunglasses (in the middle of the night) hands me a paper that I am told is a ticket for a major violation. "Just a few more of these and you'll be in the dungeon for a good while. The parole board loves to see tickets so they can keep your ass in here indefinitely. You won't be getting no special treatment from us, Lefur," she says, mangling my maiden name.

"Could I ask what this is for?" I say.

"Read it and sign it."

I read it, and see that it is a ticket for the escape 33 years ago.

Back in my cell, I climb up onto the bunk and wonder what is ahead if this is the first day for me in a Michigan prison.

Chapter 35

Later in the week telephone accounts are set up so new inmates can make collect calls, but I find my application has been "lost" and I have to submit another and wait. I feel as though I've been counting the hours, waiting to get a chance to call home and talk to my family and an attorney. I haven't spoken to my family in several weeks now. Among other things, this means that I have been unable to help my husband choose a Michigan attorney to submit a motion for review of my sentence. Alan sends me the phone number of an attorney he is considering, but I have no way to call her. I appeal to the warden with a note called a kite, a memo that we mail from boxes in the unit. I explain to her that I need to talk to my husband about my legal defense. I include information about the guards' threats to write bogus violations against me to get me sent to the dungeon cells, and add that I'm being denied showers and meals other prisoners are getting. I explain to her that guards are intentionally preventing me from getting phone privileges like the other inmates.

I have little doubt that my latest phone application will also end up getting "lost."

I don't get a response from the letters, but a couple of days later I am told to report to the admin building to deal with the escape ticket. I get handcuffed behind my back and led into a barren little room with cracks in the wall and a sinister-looking woman dressed completely in black, with eyes as small as ants glaring through massive black-rimmed glasses and thick lenses. She glowers behind a laptop computer. After a farcical process, she gives me a sentence of 30 days of 24-hour-a-day lockup that will continue after the quarantine lockup period. Her manner is so odious that even the armed guard who has escorted me there widens her eyes. As I rise to leave, the hearing officer flashes a mean smile and says, "And this will mean you won't be able to use the phone for the thirty days either." She doesn't try to hide that she is singling me out cruelly.

I go back to the cell and lie on the bunk for the rest of the day. The only bright moments are when Diane sings. I ask if she knows a song by Minnie Ripperton -called "Lovin' You." It's a song I remember hearing in 1975 when I was in prison the first time. I interpreted the words then as coming from above, and it gave me reassurance that I could go on after all. This might sound strange. Maybe only people who have been on the knife edge of despair can understand how a song or a small gesture of kindness from others can make a difference that you remember the rest of your life.

Meanwhile, I continue to write letters to everyone I can about my needing to use the phone to contact an attorney, and one afternoon the warden suddenly appears at the door and asks me to come out to talk to her at a small table in the common area.

She says right off, "We're not giving you any special treatment, LeFevre."

The words *special treatment* hits a nerve—I've heard it many times by now. "All I want is to be treated like the other prisoners," I say. "I haven't been able to call an attorney or talk to my family in weeks." Suddenly I find myself breaking down, and in a pleading voice I tell her, "I have to take care of my legal issues. I wasn't guilty of what they convicted me of, and I can easily prove it, but I need to get a motion filed and the guards are intentionally preventing me from using the phone. I have no idea why. I have done everything I can to be polite to them. They just get more vindictive. There must be some rights a prisoner has to contact an attorney. How can they do this to me? All the other prisoners are using the phones and getting regular showers and meals. I haven't done anything and I am locked up in this tiny room, with the guards openly threatening me."

"Okay, calm down," she says.

"I'm sorry to be so upset, but have you read my letters about what they've been doing to me?"

She seems genuinely affected and says that she will tell the guards to allow me to use the phone.

This is all I really care about. I worry about my lungs being exposed to so much smoke, I badly want to be able to shower in this sticky weather, and it feels terrible to miss a meal when my skin is already hanging on me because I've lost almost 20 pounds in the first two weeks, but if I can call home and an attorney, I will be overjoyed.

The warden walks over to the desk where two guards are sitting and tells them that I am to be allowed the same phone use as other prisoners.

I feel a wave of relief.

Finally someone with authority is stepping in and doing the right thing, I think. But again I'm being naïve.

When the "telephone period" comes a little later on, I go to the phone and dial one of the numbers my husband has sent me for attorneys. A lawyer answers, and I talk as quickly as I can because the phone company automatically terminates calls after 15 minutes. Before I get a chance to discuss my case, a large hand comes down on the receiver, and I look up to see Dingle. Her arm comes toward me as if to strike me and she physically grabs the phone and pounds it into the receiver. "You ain't callin' nobody, LeFevre. You don't need to call no lawyer, 'cause I told you before, you ain't never leavin' here." She sticks her face close to mine and juts out her lower jaw. "Now, get back to your cell," she says as she glances over to the other guards hovering or sitting at the desk, cheering her on. "Yeah, LeFevre, go back to your cell!" a skeleton thin white guard with a green tag yells out. Green tags are new hires who wear a green ID tag to distinguish them as novices. They are often the worst for targeting prisoners because they are trying to impress veteran guards.

I immediately write again to the warden, and the next morning I smuggle the letter out with me to the clinic and put it in the drop box there so guards in my unit aren't able to arrange for it to get "lost." I ask myself if I am being paranoid, but inmates would later tell me that guards often go through and steal mail from the boxes.

The warden shows up again at my unit and again speaks directly to the same guards and instructs them to let me use the phone. I feel a surge of confidence once again until I watch with amazement as the guards make gestures ridiculing the warden as soon as she turns to walk toward the door. The room is filled with inmates, who also witness the blatant disrespect aimed at the warden.

I'm stunned by how brazen the guards are, but I assume that they will finally comply with orders since the warden addressed them in person a second time and she is suppose to be their boss. I don't want the guards to be any angrier than they already are so when phone period arrives, I make a point to go to the desk and politely ask the green tag if it is okay to use the phone now. Since prisoners aren't required to ask, she seems caught off guard by my civil demeanor and nods, but a few minutes later, when I am dialing the phone and Dingle again charges at me and grabs it out of my hand, the green tag joins in with the others, yelling threats and jeers at me.

This time I know there hasn't been a misunderstanding and I challenge them: "But the warden came here and told you to let me use the phone."

"I didn't hear nothin'. You got proof a' that, Lefur?" a hard-faced guard blurts out, staring at me defiantly. She isn't even from our unit and came over to join the excitement. Other guards stream in from an adjoining unit and circle around Dingle and the green-tag guard. Dingle echoes, "I don't see nothin' in writing on my desk, do you? Does anybody see anything in writing about letting LeFevre use the phone?" she says louder, craning her neck back and forth like a strutting ostrich.

"I don't see nothing," another guard pipes in. Guards who have apparently left their own units continue to join in, grunting their support for their colleagues. I can tell ganging up in this fashion is nothing new to them.

"But she was just here. Everyone here heard the warden tell you to let me put in a call to an attorney." I realize how futile I sound and try then to appeal to them in another way. "I haven't talked to my family in weeks. Why would you do this to me? I am just a woman who has suddenly been taken away from her children and I want to talk to them. Don't any of you have a family? Do you know what it's like not to talk to your children?"

"Lefevre, go to your cell. This is only the beginning of what's gonna happen to your ass, bitch."

The next day I write to the warden telling her that the guards have ignored her order to allow me to use the phone and I ask her if she can put her instructions in writing. As the harassment continues, I also write to others in the prison administration and even the Michigan Department of Corrections in Lansing. I ask my family to contact the warden and the governor's office and MDOC to tell them what guards are doing to me but our efforts are ignored. We write or leave detailed messages, but it is obvious that legislators or administrators won't take on the powerful prison union. I have always been a strong proponent of unions and I still am. I've always seen them as the only way to fight off certain tyranny in the workplace. But this union is a runaway train. No one seems to have any control over the prison.

I am awakened again in the middle of the night and learn that two more tickets have been written against me by the same guards. The violations say that I used the phone although I was ordered not to do so. The first ticket is written by Dingle and witnessed by the guard who was a green tag. The other ticket is written by the green tag and witnessed by Dingle.

Nothing on the tickets is accurate, and the information makes it clear that the guards disobeyed a direct order from the warden. A guard who is sympathetic, whispers to me that the tickets will never get upheld and the two guards will possibly and finally be exposed. But I forgot I was in the parallel world. The one where nothing makes sense and debauchery rules. The next day, when I see the gangster-like hearing officer again, she almost immediately reads a note from the warden saying she no longer wants any involvement in the issue and that I am not to contact her again. The hearing officer peers over her thick glasses smugly as if to say, "You didn't really think the warden would go up against us for long, did you?" It was obvious the warden figured out that if she wanted to keep her job, she would have to refrain from interfering with the guards if they choose to target me. It is apparent that the guards have full reign within the prison, the tail wagging the dog. I realize no one will be able to stop them.

Not all the guards are cruel, of course. Many of them are normal people trying to earn a living in a difficult place, and I know some of them feel badly about what is happening to me. A few of the guards are even exceptional. What may seem like small acts of kindness to most people are momentous acts of courage in the corrupt environment of the prison, where the mere appearance that a guard is breaking from the pack is taken very seriously. Guards often speak of being a team, as in being team players who don't tell on each other. That's the way the system works; even the warden and elected officials in Lansing don't challenge it, no matter how many people suffer as a consequence.

A few times, a guard catches me alone and quietly says something like, "Just so you know, a lot of us don't like seeing what's happening to you. We don't think you deserve this, and we hope you go back to your family soon."

I appreciate their efforts to tell me this, but it's a little chilling to see that it's a risk for them even to whisper support for me. It's daunting to see how much they fear the belligerent guards who are in control.

One of the good guards whom I will never forget is Officer Johnson. She can see that I'm feeling a great deal of anxiety one day and she pulls me aside and sits down with me at a little table on the edge of the common area. We're out of the way but still in plain view of the other guards at the desk, one of whom is a major player in the aggression against me. She starts a conversation of small talk as if we were in the free world having lunch, discussing our husbands and kids. I know why she is doing it and I begin to cry, but this time the tears roll because I feel touched by her thoughtfulness—I can see the concern in her eyes and that she is trying to make me feel better. She wants to remind me there is another world outside out and that I need to hang on. I know that she is risking criticism from some of the other guards who are targeting me.

She puts her hand on mine and says compassionately, "Just hang in there, dear. They'll move on before long and find someone new to pick on. You'll make it through."

Mrs. Johnson is African American and has the most enormous brown eyes I've ever seen. I look up to see tears spill down her cheek and I think how she is truly a humane and brave individual. I can tell she's been there for other inmates at the end of their rope, too. I know that to her I'm a person who is hurting, and my skin color is as irrelevant as my eye color. Anyone who believes in a higher power cannot believe that people were created to be inferior or superior to others—and that God would bother to color-code them. Both of us, I think, know that behind any type of prejudice are merely angry, fearful people trying to repress others.

Mrs. Johnson has managed to bridge the two colliding worlds I grappled with for so long. Her kindness reaches into the dark pit to help keep me from falling. I knew in this porthole to hell that God had provided angels to help me stay afloat. I just had to keep the faith that they would be there for me.

I already sense the war within Michigan that was sparked off by the collapse of the auto industry when companies first started quietly moving themselves out of the country, politicians helping to pave the way in exchange for contributions. Infighting between various factions in the state is evident in headlines, political debates, and policy almost daily. It is a bitter "us versus them" battle that gives me another déjà vu moment from the 1970s. With the same vigor of the tall weeds that infiltrate once proud cities, a corrupt good-old-boy network has risen up and found a simple solution to replacing jobs on the auto assembly lines: building, staffing, and filling prisons. My case seems to have hit a chord with its influential and usually shadowy members.

Negative comments continue to appear in the news, instigated by Barney Duncan and a spokesman for the prison industry named Strickland. They continue to insist I was a high-level syndicate member, although the evidence would suggest otherwise and neither of the men was in office at the time I lived in Michigan. It is still not clear to me why they are so vehemently against me.

I am soon transferred out of the unit Officer Johnson is in. The last time I see her, she warns me to get transferred out of Scott, saying, "I learned why they're harassing you. I can't give you details, but you need to do everything you can to get transferred to another prison. Have your family write to the governor or anyone else higher. People higher than the DOC [Department of Corrections]. Tell them you're not safe here."

Eventually I would come to understand why she had said this.

A few days after the warning from Johnson, another guard pulls me aside as I was returning from the clinic. She says, "I felt you should know. A man named Strickland came here from Lansing......he's been with the DOC for decades. He came to address the guards, at least on my shift, and told them that you made them all look bad when you escaped all those years ago. He openly taunted the guards to harass you, essentially putting a target on your forehead." She traces a bull's-eye in the air. "Imagine him telling the guards that your escape made *them* look bad. Why, none of them were even working at the prison when you left. How could you make them look bad? Ain't none of 'em working here thirty years ago." She shakes her head in either anger or bewilderment. "You better try to leave Scotts. Even Huron Valley will be better than here after he's done put a target on you like that."

Strickland was the same industry spokesman speaking out against me in the press, repeating the same bizarre allegations that the Saginaw prosecutor was making. When I heard the same story about him from several guards, I knew it was more than a rumor. But why would he travel more than an hour to the prison and incite guards to attack me? I was again being assailed by a man I'd never met over something that happened many years before he was employed in the system. Why were there so many people opposed to me receiving a fair hearing?

It isn't long before I learn that Strickland, Duncan, and Greely are well acquainted with each other and worked together over the years, pushing for new laws that would expand the prison industry. Many of the laws targeted women as a vulnerable demographic. Many women are in prison because they were with a man who committed a crime that they had little to do with. The women are often more compliant than men and give up information that makes them easy to convict and they end up serving sentences longer than the actual perpetrator of the crime. Within 30 miles of Duncan's home is a prison, a prison funds processing center for the state prisons and allegedly another prison decorated in pink tiles through out, that was never opened. The crony network by most accounts relatively small but extremely influential Michigan politics.

The guards continue to prevent me from calling an attorney, but my husband arranges for one, a woman named Cheryl Freeze, to drive two hours to talk to me at the prison about appealing my sentence. There are so many irregularities in my case that I feel confident I should be able to get my conviction overturned. Freeze specializes in post-conviction cases for prisoners who have lost appeals or, in rare cases like mine, never did appeal. I get the impression that she usually works with women who are destitute and have been in prison for decades. Apparently she has helped to get some of them out.

When she arrives, I wait more than an hour and in the next room, the attorney also waits for an hour. The guards play computer games and intentionally stall my being able to talk to her.

I finally get to meet Cheryl. Her first comment is that she is well acquainted with my uncle and his family in Saginaw. "They go to the same church that I do and your uncle is quite infamous for his opposition to having female members of the church staff involved in giving part of the mass. He and some of his family members sit in the front row of church and if a woman steps behind the lectern, they rise abruptly and walk out to send a message of their disapproval. Someone from the church has to call them ahead of time to warn them which masses a female is going to be part of the service."

At least the attorney can understand some of the background of my family dynamics. I am anxious to discuss my case and I immediately begin to explain to her how a drug agent set me up. Her response is sharp and immediate, and not the relief I wanted it to be: "You can't say that a cop lied. In Michigan they'll never let you out of here if you try to minimize guilt."

"But I am not guilty, and the evidence shows that," I insist.

"Evidence, shmevidence; it doesn't matter. You might be able to have this cosmic view of what is justice and truth, but I have to deal with the real world and technicalities that will force them to release you. If you say that a cop framed you and lied about evidence against you, you'll be here twenty years. And in your case, that cop became a state police chief. There's no way you can say a cop lied about you who later became a state police chief. We'll fight this on the grounds that the judges had an agreement to give everyone with a drug charge a long prison sentence. That you were deprived your right to due process. That and the fact that your own lawyer kept you from seeing the probation report and the allegations against you—those are strong grounds to get your sentence reviewed."

My mind boggles. I can't understand why I need to look for technicalities, as if I'd actually been a kingpin trafficker. I want to say that I was innocent—I want it screamed from the rafters that I was not a drug dealer. But once again I find myself being told by an attorney that I can't tell the truth, that I have to play some twisted game. "I've read some of my file," I tell her. "It says right in there that my only assets were an old car and a broken TV. I didn't even own furniture. My parents verified that they had to supplement my rent. I worked at a minimum wage job almost continuously during those years. Why would I live like that if I was making thousands of dollars a week as a high-level syndicate member like the drug agent claimed? Why can't you tell reporters that the drug agent lied about the evidence and we can prove it and now the prosecutor in Saginaw is trying to cover up for him because they've been buddies for many years? Miss Freeze, I wasn't a drug dealer, I only used them. I have a family that has to live every day with these accusations being put out by the press so some politician can look good to the prison industry."

"It's not a matter of right or wrong, it's not a matter of what's said in the media—I have to find technical reasons to win this."

"What's wrong with just using the evidence that is there? It's obvious I was framed. None of the accusations made by Greely in the report they kept secret make any sense, yet you're letting Duncan put it out there like they're proven facts. Why don't you tell reporters the allegations he's making aren't included in any transcripts or testimony under oath? Why is this guy so intimidating to everyone?"

"I'll make the decisions. I've been doing this for twenty years."

"But you're talking about defending me on technicalities as if I was guilty. This is the same defense you'd give someone arrested on a Colombian jet loaded with pounds of drugs. The fact that I was in a parking lot during a small drug transaction makes it evident to most people it was unlikely I was a big drug dealer. I wasn't what anyone would consider even a small time drug dealer. I only got drugs mainly at parties through friends."

"This is the way it works."

"But it's crazy I have to worry that it appears that I'm minimalizing guilt. Is that the objective, to get everyone to grovel whether their guilty or not. I have strong evidence for everything I am saying. I have witnesses. I'm no longer a hapless teenage they can trample over. I want to show what is happening to kids all over the country even today."

We glare at each other for a moment, and then I go on. "None of these comments Duncan is feeding to the media are in the transcripts and that's because they don't make any sense. I have overturned cases and testimony from the prosecutor at the time that Greely was famous for lying about evidence to get convictions. My co-defendant was older than I was, with a history of arrests. Why would he have been working for me? It's ludicrous."

She's unmoved. "You hired me, I'll make the decisions."

"Ms. Freeze, they knew I wasn't a drug dealer. They told me directly that they knew I wasn't a dealer. I scored for my friends a few times, but that's what almost everyone does when they're involved with drugs. No one would have considered me a drug dealer."

"They, they, they!" she snaps. "Who are you talking about as 'they'? Don't you know how to talk?"

For years, I had thought about the lawyer who would finally save me from the monsters of Michigan. I envisioned suave, silver-tongued Jerry Spence or Johnnie Cochran types. But this is a scene right out of Kafka.

"I am talking about the prosecutor and the drug agent," I say slowly, trying to stay calm. "The prosecutor talked to me right after I was arrested, and told me they only arrested me so that I would help set up my boyfriend. They refused to drop the charges when I couldn't do what they wanted, and they told me I would get probation as long as I pled guilty. I resisted for a while but everyone, even my family kept pestering me to take the plea deal and then after I agreed people involved with the prosecutor said in order to get the plea deal I had to say that I knew Ritchie was meeting someone at Luigi's, when we were arrested."

Again the attorney stares at me not happy that I am arguing with her.

I continue, "Cheryl, I talked to Ebert, the assistant prosecutor involved, less than a year ago. He said Greely later set him up too. He said he felt Greely set up a bunch of people by falsifying evidence against them. I have witnesses to our conversation, and I want to subpoena him to testify. He can support what I am saying."

"I said I'll make the decisions here," repeats Cheryl sharply. "I'm the attorney." She's furious that I'm telling her how I want to defend myself. Again and again she repeats that I cannot claim that a drug agent was lying when he said I was a drug dealer. She is going to fight the case based largely on the fact that it was well known that the judges made a pact to give a blanket sentence to all drug defendants and that my defense attorney was incompetent.

When I mention going to the press to dispute the false allegations made by Barney Duncan, she goes ballistic.

"I am not talking to anyone," she says through clenched teeth. "The press is not your friend."

I mention to her also that I saw articles in the *Saginaw News* that twisted many of the facts to reinforce Duncan's statements such as doubling the amount of money involved from $300 to $600 and referring to me as convicted heroin dealer LeFevre while leaving out the small amount of drugs involved or my actual role. Almost all other papers referred to me as a "fugitive mom," and pointed out that the amount of drugs involved was paltry. I felt frustrated that my version of what actually happened was not being heard. Once again the paper was misquoting the facts like they had 33 years ago. I had always considered Saginaw as my hometown, making the misreporting especially disheartening.

I continue to try to get the attorney to understand my position. It seems ridiculous not to stand up for myself. "We're paying for assistance and this is something that is important to me," I finally tell her. "I asked my husband to write or call the paper, but he said you ordered him not to talk to anyone."

"It doesn't matter what they say about you in the media," she retorts. "No one pays attention to what's in the media."

It is a replay of the past, the same paralyzed system that I'd dealt with three decades ago. My stomach sinks. I know Cheryl is speaking from years of experience and has no doubt learned the hard way that a subservient defense is what works in a city where the prosecutor has held office for more than 20 years and brags that his office sends more people to prison than many much larger cities with the same crime problems. It seems more about repression than justice.

After an awkward pause, Cheryl half stands and throws a stack of manila files in front of me. "That's your file and your co-defendant, Ritchie's."

As I begin to look through my file, she comments, "It's incredible that in '75 the police could claim anything and there was no requirement for evidence. The only time in Saginaw they arrested anyone who might have been fairly high on the trafficking ladder was a Colombian national they pulled over as a fluke and found pounds of heroin, cocaine, and $50,000 in cash. He had a history of drug offenses and was sentenced to prison, but supposedly someone at the Corrections Department 'accidentally' let him walk away within a year after he was transferred to a facility with no fences. Everyone knows it was a payoff." She shakes her head. "Almost no one who is actually a high level person gets kept behind bars long."

"But they pursue people like me instead."

"They don't even want the real traffickers. They're harder to catch and convict, since they rarely go near the drugs themselves. They pay other people to actually handle the drugs. If they do arrest someone at a high level, he hires a high-priced attorney who gets him off anyway, which makes prosecutors look bad. Prosecutors who are ambitious prefer the slam-dunk cases. The poor people—or like in your case, someone already convicted. They are far easier cases to prosecute. And the fact that you were white was a real bonus. The industry is trying to get out from under the rap that it's biased against minorities, so there's a premium on whites they can lock up."

"I keep hearing that."

"No one really cares about the drug problem; that's why there's very little rehab in prisons. They just need convictions to keep getting promotions and more funding."

It's some small comfort to know that at least the lawyer and I agree on the big picture. I figure that even if she can't help me like the crusading attorneys I'd imagined spearheading my defense, she might at least be able to help me with my most pressing problem regarding the abuse from the guards.

"The guards are getting worse towards me," I tell her. "They're manipulating it so that I'm in an overheated cell. I feel like I'm going to have a stroke or a heart attack. I'm getting really sick."

When she doesn't respond, I tell her about Strickland encouraging the guards to harass me. "There has to be someone we can call who can intervene," I say. "What if we told reporters?

"No one goes to the press," she says again. "Do you understand?"

"Okay, okay, forget the press, I forgot how you feel about them—it just seems crazy they can do this stuff."

"Keep writing to the warden," she says.

"The warden is afraid of the guards and Strickland too." Cheryl just stares at me without saying anything. I might as well be complaining about the mafia.

Chapter 36

Summertime, and the livin' is anything but easy in the Scott prison of the Michigan gulag.

The intense heat wave takes hold early in the season and maintains an iron grip for weeks on end. Even on mild days the temperature inside the unit is stifling, and I learn that the ventilation system in the ceiling has been broken since last year and the staff member responsible for reporting the breakdown forgot to submit a work order.

The guards at the unit desk sit in front of a three-foot fan on a pedestal and inmates use desk fans in the cells, trying to circulate the air.

As the weather continues to heat up, I am transferred to another cell where for the hottest part of the day the sun shines directly into the room through a window that doesn't open. And the new room doesn't have a fan. The concrete walls and thick iron door hold the heat so it feels like a pizza oven. Because of the trumped-up tickets, I am restricted to the cell 24 hours a day for many weeks and months. It is oppressive.

When I ask for a fan the guard says I need to put in a request for one, even though I can see a storage closet full of fans. Like other inmates, I put a cover over the window to block the sun, but a guard quickly comes into the cell. "If I catch you putting anything over the window, you're going to the dungeon cells," she says in a hostile tone, "and they'll make it even hotter for you there. You have no idea what they'll do to you in there.... I'm sure you've heard the stories about all the prisoners who have died in seg." Her face lights up and I realize that keeping me overheated is intentional and she knows exactly what she is doing; she enjoys that I am being tortured. "You think we're fucking with you here? Wait till we get you sent to the hole. You're gonna wish you never came back, LeFevre. You and your fancy house …ain't nothing gonna help you now." The temperature is far above 100 degrees in the tiny room and although I have to stay there all day because of the violations written against me, the guards keep careful watch to make sure I keep the door tightly shut.

As the hours pass and the mercury rises, I feel increasingly nauseated and begin to feel faint. I can sense the blood draining from my extremities. I know these symptoms as the precursor to heat exhaustion and heat stroke, and I again appeal to the guards. This time, the response is wordless; the guard simply laughs. As my heart begins to beat rapidly an added feeling of panic rushes over me, I begin to fear that I will bake to death in the cell. I begin to fear that I will bake to death in the cell. My head is pounding. I've splashed water on my clothing so many times that my skin is raw and swollen with rash. The heat makes the rash burn more, and the feel of the thick material of the prison uniform makes it sting.

The bottom bunk is empty and a little cooler, but the guards smirk and tell me they will issue another violation and threaten me with seg if I don't stay on the higher level. After a few days my symptoms worsen, and as I try to climb down to get help I collapse to the floor, hitting my head on a metal table. On the dirty concrete floor, my head pounding, I feel a minor relief. I have barely any feeling left in my hands but I flatten my palm against the gritty concrete, thinking how comforting it feels. I realize I must have lost consciousness and notice inmates congregating outside the cell door. A couple of the guards push through and stand over me. One guard has her hands crossed over her chest. Her head sways away from me and with a half-smile she says, "Now you know what it's like, bitch." I know it is a racial slur, but it takes only a moment before a white guard is quick to join in the assault. "What's wrong, LeFevre, can't take the heat?" She bellows out a hollow laugh at her own remark. It's no a secret that racial issues are rampant at the prison but just like years ago, as a white inmate, it is the white guards I learn to fear most. A number of them try desperately to appease the more predominant black guards. When my face begins to turn as white as a pillowcase, a guard who is new to the unit, a large woman who had initially been staying back, breaks from the clique and orders everyone to clear the area around me. "Give her some space to breathe. Someone get some water!" she yells out.

Another guard, this time a black guard I recognize as a friend of Officer Johnson, rushes in from the adjacent unit and brings over some ice. The small horde of hostile guards step away now, but still let out mean sneers in the background as if they were hyenas robbed of their prey.

I start to come around more, but my hands and arms begin to shake uncontrollably, and the helpful guard orders one of the inmates to bring a wheelchair to take me to the clinic. I am wheeled past the angry guards, many of whom I've never seen before, and they toss cruel remarks at me as I sit crumpled in the wheelchair. "You're nothing but a crack ho', bitch!" Another one says, "You ain't no better than us, LeFevre."

When I get to the clinic, a white male nurse refuses to allow me to lie down on the gurney. He says he doesn't want to have to change the paper. "Please," I beg, "let me at least lie down on the floor."

"Sit in the chair, it's illegal to let you lie on the floor," he barks at me. Sitting is painful; my limbs are bloodless, and I am quite certain I need to lie down to stimulate some circulation. In this vulnerable condition, I am unprepared for his extraordinary rudeness, yet I don't take his bitterness personally. I don't think he even knows my name. I think that he sees me as an anonymous low-life prisoner and this is his standard treatment. He seems angry that he is stuck working at a prison. The stress and weight loss has made my face look drawn, my cheekbones hollow, and my hair is unkempt and frazzled. I look like hell and like all prisoners to him, I am worthy only of contempt.

A female nurse tries to convince him that I should lie on the empty table to allow the blood to circulate, but the male nurse refuses. In time, I feel the blood surging back into my head, which begins to pound even harder as I am reviving. The female nurse's kindness is a balm.

A few hours later I return to the unit to find that the guard who helped me earlier is still on duty. Not only that, but she brings me a fan. But as soon as she goes off shift, the other guards announce that I am being moved into another cell. I gather up my stuff, including the fan, but a guard pulls it away from me. "No fans!" she shouts. "Fans have to stay in the cells!"

The guards don't bother to hide the fact that this is sheer harassment. I still feel weak and nauseous, yet I am forced to pack up bedding, clothing, books, and toiletries and move everything into another cell. This one, too, receives direct sunlight, and again I am without a fan. I continue to feel sick from the intense heat, and I collapse again the following week and end up back at the clinic. Inmates tell me stories of prisoners dying after complaining repeatedly to staff that they were suffering from complications of the heat; the families of these prisoners were told the deaths were from "natural causes."

I collapse a third time over the next few weeks. I beg my husband to do whatever he can to stop the guards from torturing me. He desperately reaches out to anyone and everyone—the governor's office, the MDOC in Lansing, the warden—but there is no response. A friend who is a doctor writes letters to prison officials warning of the danger to my health. No one responds.

I feel so ill that I wish I could die and get it over with, but at the same time I am terrified by the thought of dying here in a prison cell. I think of all that I have been through in my life and again I ask, "Is this the way my story ends, God, in a prison cell at the hands of these cruel people?"

The outside world seems obscure and far away. I think of the few people at the prison who have been kind to me, and it helps give me strength. I know they are probably aware of what is going on but helpless to intervene as they too, could get pulled down by the angry sector of guards who rule. When the misery seems endless, I try to focus on Officer Johnson's advice that I hang in there, that this too shall pass.

I have to keep the internal dialogue active to block out the fear and doubt. *Thank your enemies, because they make you stronger. Suffering is an opportunity to grow.* This advice sounds hollow when I am feeling such despair, but I know I have to keep strong. I have many wonderful people supporting me; I have to believe I can make it through.

Meanwhile, I am regularly denied showers and meals and am put in closed cells with cellmates who chain smoke. Every day prisoners have to report to their cells for several intervals that last over an hour. Inmates have to lie on the bunks with the door locked, to be counted. During "count" they light up, and I have no choice but to inhale their smoke. My throat is sore and I'm congested from all the toxic smoke, and I submit repeated requests to be placed in a unit that has nonsmokers. My requests are ignored.

Violations continue to mount against me, one more inane than the next. In the ultimate irony, I get a ticket because a guard claims she saw me smoking. When I ask to see the rules, a supervisor hands me a paper stating I have read the rules and orders me to sign it. When I tell her I want to read the paper before I sign it, she writes me another ticket for disobeying a direct order. Each ticket is accompanied by harassment: 3 a.m. wakings; five-hour waits in a chair to see the ghoulish hearing officer, my hands chained behind my back; 24-hour lockups, denying me the ability to call my family or attorney. This was the most difficult part—being isolated, with no means of communication.

I have never cried in front of others, but I simply cannot help it now. I don't expect the guards to be affected; tears are commonplace here, but I am unprepared for the sheer glee in their eyes when I break down. It strikes me as fiendish that the sight of despair in another human being excites them. Just as the other prisoners have warned me, tears seem to encourage them. They respond like beasts to the smell of fresh blood, circling their prey, preparing for the kill.

Its little wonder that this unit is known as the "Rat's Nest" by both inmates and staff. It is the place where the long-term prisoners are kept and where the worst guards are assigned.

When I spot the warden on the walk one day, I seize what could be my only opportunity to tell her about the guards ramping up their harassment effort even more after her attempted intervention a few weeks earlier.

She says, "There's nothing I can do to control them. We'll be able to get rid of a lot of them when we close down next year, but I can't do anything about them till then. You can appeal the tickets to Lansing, where they'll be able to get the charges dropped."

"I'm worried mostly about them getting me sent to seg. I hear terrible stories about prisoners sent to the segregation cells. They keep threatening that they're gonna write up enough tickets on me to get me in seg where they'll seriously be able to hem me up. They're still keeping me in an overheated cell without a fan or letting me keep the door open, it's getting much worse instead of..." I begin to ramble desperately.

She interrupts, "I won't let them put you in seg. They don't legally have to give you a fan. They are obviously going to keep torturing you...I'm going to get you transferred to Huron Valley, another prison forty-five minutes away from here."

"Things could be just as bad over there. I heard from a number of guards that an official with the headquarters of the DOC is coming here from Lansing intentionally encouraging the guards to harass me. The guards who told me this were upset about what he was doing."

She looks alarmed. I expect her to ask me who the person from Lansing is, but instead she asks, "Who are the guards who told you that?"

"I don't want to get them in trouble. I know they took a risk to warn me. But I know it's true—several different guards have told me this. Could you just let the guards know that you'll scrutinize the tickets written against me, and that they'll have to answer if they're baseless? The hearing officer that reviews them is worse than the others. They're like a gang that feed off each other knowing no one will stand up to them. "

"Did they tell you the name of the person who was here from Lansing?"

I feel she already knows, but I tell her, "His name is Strickland; he's a long time acquaintance of the drug agent who lied about evidence against me thirty years ago."

"I can't get involved in that." She snaps quickly, "Why don't you tell the guards who told you about Strickland to contact me? I'm going to keep working on arrangements for your transfer. I have to go."

She takes a turn on the sidewalk leading to her office and is gone.

The next day, I get a chance to call my attorney. I plead with her again to contact someone about the abuse and I tell her about Strickland's involvement. Like everyone else, she tells me that if the guards know I'm complaining, things could get much worse. And again, she warns me against talking to the press or saying anything about my case. It seems ironic that I am inundated with mail requesting an interview from every media source I can think of—*60 Minutes, Oprah, Larry King,* CNN, Dr. Phil, two British magazines, and newspapers—yet even as I fear for my life, I'm kept from telling my story.

During the hours outside the administration office waiting for hearings on the tickets written against me, I hear a male guard say, "Birds of a feather stick together." He says it over and over as if it's a tune stuck in his head. He comments to other guards, "Michigan is a union state—they'll never go private." It's apparent quite a few of the guards are aware of the many problems in the system. But while comments about "sticking together" are common, high recidivism rates, costly prisoner lawsuits, and runaway expenses are topics I never hear discussed.

Finally, I decide to defy the attorney. Hoping it will help curb the harassment, I agree to do an interview with a *Detroit Free Press* reporter, Jeff Gerritt, who has been a proponent of prison reform for years. I want to counter the false statements issued by the prosecutor and Strickland about my being a former drug kingpin, but since the attorney was so adamant that I not discuss my case, Jeff agrees to discuss only prison conditions, which are my most pressing concern. I tell him that the prison is far worse than it was 30 years ago and the rehabilitation efforts are a sham.

By this time, I am aware that the rehab program, GED prep, and all other classes have a year's waiting list and inmates are often unable to get in at all. The rehab program is available only six months prior to a prisoner's release date, and therapy sessions, which once involved six to ten people sharing intimate insights about their personal lives and history of abuse, now herd 40 to 50 prisoners together in what is clearly a meaningless endeavor.

The GED preparation class is even more of a joke. Students receive a workbook and sit in a room where another inmate is responsible for helping them. The teacher is sympathetic to the women but since there are so many ages and different levels of uneducation, he or she is overwhelmed. Since statistics show that 80% of inmates have less than a high school education, few inmates are qualified to teach and the women struggle by themselves. Although throngs of guards congregate in thickets there are only two teachers to service a facility of more than 2,000 women. Classrooms exist primarily for the purpose of making prison brochures look good to visiting bureaucrats eager to justify the obscene amounts of money they shovel out to an industry known for its generous contributions.

On numerous occasions, women quietly approached me to ask for explanations about basic grade school math problems or help in spelling simple words. A young mother of four I realized had waited patiently on the outskirts of the dayroom in order to catch me when I was out of earshot of the other inmates so that I could help her reduce simple fractions. She had undoubtedly hidden her lack of education from others for some time. What must her life –have been like? When I worked with the women, they learned very quickly. It was painful to see how embarrassed they were about their situation. I felt that the lack of a decent education was the biggest reason most of these women were in prison. Not only because it would have been hard for them to get jobs but also because they'd likely made bad decisions because they'd never been taught to think things through, another benefit of education. The prison would have a better way of judging which inmates were ready to leave and who wasn't. The current system of a few members of the parole board talking to inmates for fifteen minutes over a TV screen did little more than single out the inmates who were capable of groveling to a degree that would satisfy the board.

The prison did offer reading material, but a majority of it was street lit—books that were basically a glamorization of ghetto life, in which the main characters carried guns, sold drugs for a living, or were pimps or prostitutes. Violence and sexual scenes were frequent, graphic, and exploitive. When I mentioned to teachers at the prison that the material was more corrupting than helpful, they would respond, "At least the prisoners will read this stuff, and it gets them to read."

There was so much to tell the reporter, but how many people were interested in the details of prisoners being deprived of better reading material or offered decent learning opportunities? He was already aware of the sham education effort at the prison. I also told him about the overheated cell and how I was suffering. It turned out that Jeff was the first to expose the death of an inmate from dehydration and heat a few years ago in a Michigan prison, and the article had prompted a subsequent investigation by *60 Minutes* and a lawsuit by the victim's family, who had initially been told their son's death was a result of natural causes. The state paid out a huge settlement, but none of the guards involved lost their jobs.

The *Detroit Free Press* publishes Jeff's article. A few days later despite overwhelming public support calling for my release, the Detroit prosecutor files charges against me for the 33-year-old escape. In addition to the five and a half years I am already facing for the original charge, I am now potential looking at additional time of up to five years for the escape despite the fact that escapes were not prosecuted in the 70's, at least not the ones that occurred from the poorly guarded women's prison.

Chapter 37

In the wake of the *Free Press* article, I receive more letters from friends, acquaintances, and even total strangers that sympathize with my plight. Almost every day a stack of mail arrives, and I read letters from people across the country and all over the world. A letter from Sweden reports a small group has been formed to fight for me until I'm released. A newspaper in Viet Nam writes that I was a fugitive for 33 years and despite having had extensive plastic surgery I was picked up at my high rise apartment because I had been convicted stealing chickens in 1975.

Along with support from my family, the letters I receive from supporters helps me feel more optimistic. I feel overwhelmed and touched that people would take time to write and express such heartfelt empathy. I remember many mornings sitting in my kitchen at home in the months before I was taken by the police. I felt a deep sense of apprehension about the innocent lives being lost in the war in the Middle East. I wondered if people cared any more about others. I asked myself, "If anything ever happened to me, how many people would care?" I questioned which of my friends and family would be there for me. Through these letters I knew the answer was that many did care about what happened to others and my case was simple and clear cut enough for many to voice their opinion that things had gone too far in this country and they wanted to have a voice.

The times that I feel sorry for myself are scarce. I am surrounded by women whose lives are far more tragic than mine. The only "family" many of the women have are aunts, daddies, and grannies they have adopted within the prison. These fragile relationships dissolve easily with the constant transfers and transitions that are part of prison life. I know that no matter what happens to me, I am lucky to know that so many people felt compassionately about my circumstances. In many ways it is a sad statement that there is little stigma for being incarcerated because it is happening to so many people. Paris Hilton, Martha Stewart and singer Lil Kim, have been 'locked up' for miniscule offenses. Who's next?

Meanwhile, I learn that someone is running against the entrenched Saginaw prosecutor in the upcoming primary. Apparently most elections go uncontested since there is at least the perception that there will be retribution against anyone daring to go against the current regime. This is big news. The man running against Duncan is named Tom Frank. He has already given a radio interview saying that he favors treatment over incarceration as a more effective and much less expensive way to treat drug users. He also feels it is a waste of taxpayer money to keep me locked up, and says he would let me go immediately after hearing the bizarre details of my crime and conviction.

Duncan will soon counter, saying that as an attorney who defends criminals, Frank will not be tough on crime. He brags once again that during his 20 years as prosecutor, the city has sent more people to prison every year than much larger cities with the same crime rate.

I've met the large group of women at the prison who are from Saginaw. For a town of its size, true to Duncan's word, Saginaw is well represented at the prison. The women are outspoken about being in prison for unusually small offenses. Stealing a children's video worth $16, having small amounts of drugs in their system while on probation or parole has landed them in prison. The group is almost entirely black except for a white girl who wears her hair tightly braided and chants rap songs almost constantly and calls herself a white nigger. No one seems to question what kind of people are sent to prison when a prosecutor emphasizes the large number of convictions they're responsible for making. They don't seem to realize that when the focus is on the numbers, the harder-to-get real predators are marginalized while the dope heads are herded in like cattle. Despite Saginaw aggressive effort to imprison more people than other cities, the violent crime rate there continues to skyrocket while cities with less aggressive attitudes about prison and stronger rehab efforts have seen a drop in their crime rates. Saginaw has been rated by *Forbes* magazine as the worst city in America to live in, two years in a row yet the same people stay entrenched year after year in elected positions and the public is led to believe that if they just put even more people in prison, things will get better.

The local paper begins its own campaign in support of Duncan, listing details of his accomplishments of church missions and asserting that crime dipped when Duncan was first elected in the 80's.

When I speak to my attorney again, and she tells me she has finished putting together a three-page appeal. She has lined up my former public defender, Joe Amato III who will testify about his role in preventing me from seeing the essential report that would have alerted me to the allegations made against me.

She has also contacted Brady Denton, the man who was prosecutor at the time of my conviction, who is willing to testify about his knowledge of the sentencing pact entered into by the judges of giving everyone with a drug charge the maximum sentence. He would testify that the pact was widely known within the legal community. Denton had already gone public with his opinion that I shouldn't have gone to prison in the first place, and stated that if he were still prosecutor he would release me immediately. In addition, my uncle is willing to admit to the court that he misled me about my ability to appeal the lengthy sentence.

This all sounds good, but I believe that Ebert—the person who worked alongside Greely at the time—and could give his opinion that Greely routinely lied about information to get convictions, would be my best witness to show what Greely was up to. I feel his testimony would make my release compulsory. The fact that I haven't broken the law in 33 years and that I have a nice family had little to do with my appeal. All of the evidence in my case shows that I was wrongly convicted. My goal is to get a hearing date as soon as possible. But the attorney we hired has other plans.

"I'm not going to have Ebert testify." She says. "No one is going to believe him since he went to prison himself, and like I told you...you can't say a cop lied...they'll keep you locked up there forever." She steadfastly refuses to subpoena Ebert's testimony. If he really was set up and sentenced to prison to keep Greeley's activities quiet, it was working.

"We'll have to talk about the issue of Ebert later," I say. "Right now I just want to get the motion filed and get a hearing date."

She pauses and strums her fingers on the desk then says, "I received a call from Barney Duncan, and he has asked me to delay filing your appeal until he's had a chance to review it."

"What are you talking about? Why would I delay filing the appeal any longer? Especially at his request?"

"He said he might stipulate or agree in writing that he won't challenge a favorable ruling from the judge if I give him some time to think it over."

Exasperated, I say, "Cheryl, don't you understand? I've been trying to deal with Duncan for decades. He threatened me against turning myself in, and he'll do everything he can to keep my case buried and me locked away if he has to. He and Greely have been friends for twenty years. This is obviously just a stalling tactic while he and his cronies try to crush me while I'm in custody in the prison."

Cheryl doesn't answer but her face tightens up as I continue.

"Every attorney I talked to said you can't trust Duncan. They say he likes the image that he has no problem keeping innocent people locked up."

"Barney Duncan called me personally. He's never done that before. Maybe he prefers trying your case after the election this fall."

"That is the only reason he's trying to delay it—for his own sake. He's already said he would do whatever he could to keep me locked up. Why else would he keep misleading the press by feeding them a hearsay comment in a secret report about my being a high-level syndicate member? Why do you think he'd suddenly give me a pass when the whole prison industry is watching?"

Still no response.

Then she says, "If Barney agrees to stipulate, we've won."

"But he's not going to do that, trust me. He's just stalling, probably hoping they'll get rid of me in the prison." It bothers me that she calls him by his first name.

"He said he would think about signing off on it."

"Cheryl, Duncan has come right out and said he would do whatever it took to keep me in prison."

"I know what I am doing," Cheryl snaps indignantly. "I've been doing this for twenty years."

"Listen Cheryl, two reporters told me that Duncan has Greely's home number on speed dial."

"I've been doing this for twenty years."

"Duncan is deceiving you. He has no intention of signing off on my appeal. He wants to delay this as long as possible until it's out of the spotlight. He knows I'm innocent and that's what worries him. My case shows how easy it is for an innocent person to go prison. It shows how easy it is to convict people for drug offenses."

"There you go again with you're cosmic idea of right or wrong. Innocence and guilt don't mean anything in this system. It's all about technicalities and knowing the right people. Duncan calls the shots and if you play ball with him you might have a chance; if you don't, he's not someone you want as an enemy. If we can't find a technicality to force his hand, he'll be able to appeal any favorable judgment you might get and he could keep this in the courts for years. The only way to get your release is to get on his good side."

"If I thought groveling would get me out of this hellhole I would do it, but I know Duncan is lying to you. He already has thirty days to review the appeal after you file it. Why is he asking for you to stall filing it? It's a three-page document. How long would it take him to read it?"

"It's a big decision because of the publicity."

"He knows the media will ask me questions about my conviction once I get out and he knows how it will make him and his cronies look. The drug war is the prison industry's bread and butter. They can go after people who are easy to catch and convict instead of the harder to get real criminals. They claim they're being preemptive because a lot of drug users commit crimes but they're just trying to fill prisons and expand the empire."

"You don't know how it works in Michigan—in the real world," she says. "Barney Duncan has asked me to delay this for a little while. I can't just ignore his request."

A "little while" is an eternity because of what the guards are doing to me, and I'm extremely frustrated that my husband and I are paying an attorney who doesn't respect my opinion. I know what I'm saying is right, but I can't convince her. She is adamant that it's all about bowing to the right people.

Finally, I feel I have no choice but to give in, and I agree to allow Duncan one week to review the motion before we file it. Then, as expected, Duncan malingers and asks for another week. Then he goes on vacation for a week. Then Cheryl goes on vacation. The one-week deadline stretches on for a month, then another month, and the attorney still refuses to file it without Duncan's consent. I beg her to file the motion whenever I can get a phone call through, when a guard is on duty who isn't part of the hostile gang. The calls end up adding thousands of dollars to our legal bills, and the issue causes a lot of friction between Alan and me. He doesn't want to get another attorney because he has already sunk so much money into a retainer, plus he doesn't want to make enemies in a town the size of Saginaw. By now he equates Saginaw with the Salem witch trials, and changing attorneys would also mean further delay on my appeal. Finally, I tell Cheryl that if she doesn't submit the motion, the following Monday I will bypass her and my husband and hire an attorney who is not intimidated by the prosecutor. With this, she reluctantly agrees to file it.

Although Duncan has now had several months to render an opinion on the appeal, he takes the full 30 more days to respond to the judge. Then he demands an extension from the judge, saying that one of his employees was transferred. The judge grants him the extension. At the end of that extension Duncan asks for more time. This time the judge gives him another 30 days, warning him it is the last extension he will grant.

When every attempt to stall has been exhausted, Duncan writes the required response as negatively as possible. He states that he will appeal any decision made by the judge that is in my favor.

Both he and Strickland continue contacting the media to initiate articles portraying me in a negative light. Most of what they say is misleading or simply untrue but I have no way to challenge their comments.

Now that I feel I'm getting close to a courtroom, I have to decide on my defense. There is so much at stake. What happens affects not only me but my family. Although I have argued myself hoarse with Cheryl about proclaiming my innocence, I know she has a point about the risk of bucking the system and about innocence being irrelevant. To further convince me, Cheryl has explained my situation to a retired attorney friend. With kind intentions he sends me a long letter with accounts of people he felt had been innocent yet stayed in prison far longer because they refused to admit guilt. The parole board refused to let them out since they weren't showing remorse. In one particularly egregious case, an elderly, terminally ill woman who had been in prison for many years for a crime she steadfastly denied having committed was told she could go home to die with her family if she agreed to admit guilt. She refused and was left to die alone, locked in a prison cell.

I see it is no use arguing any further with the attorney. I decide I am not going to let anyone deter me again from telling the details of what happened to me at 19. I would wait until I got my day in court and I would tell my story. I know the stakes are high if I'm wrong, but I want the details of what happened to me to be exposed. I know I am only one of many hundreds of thousands of people who have been wronged but I am able to speak out where many people can not. I remember the feeling well. Most people who've been behind bars are ignored. No one may listen to me and it won't be easy but I feel I must try. I've waited three decades to tell my story. I have to be patient now to get my day in court. My immediate fight is against Duncan's roadblocks keeping me from getting a hearing.

Alan continues to pay whatever bills the attorneys send him. He thinks that if he pays them promptly, the attorneys will try that much harder. My take is more cynical—that there is little incentive for them to get the case over expediently if he is seen as a bottomless well. When I voice this, he points out that I sound different from my usually optimistic self. I realize he still doesn't fully grasp what I am dealing with. In Ireland the police don't carry guns, and the people aren't sent to prison unless they are hardened criminals or violent. Alan never imagined going through anything like this when he came to America, the land of the free. He tries to be comforting. "We'll get the truth out there soon enough," he writes. "There are thousands of people rooting for you and doing everything they can. They know what kind of person you are."

It is true. In addition to family and friends who offer unflinching support, I learn something about the kindness of strangers. Kathy and Jerry Morse, who live in Wilmington, Michigan, have read about my case and are moved to action. They put a huge lawn sign in their front yard— "Release Susan LeFevre"—and open a website on my behalf; it gets a million hits the first week. Kathy writes to me every few days. I had my family torn away from me as a teenager but I soon feel I have gained another family member in her and others.

I have never met these people, but they soon become an essential part of my life; in fact, they become a psychological rock I can stand on. For one thing, they are people I can call when I need to talk but don't want to make it harder on my family.

The website links to an Internet petition for my release, and Kathy keeps me abreast of its progress. She sends me copies of the comments from petition signers. Childhood friends from Ohio write about having known me long ago. Ann, my best friend from St. Stephen's writes and says she never understood what happened to us and she was rallying for my release. Teachers from my kids' elementary school write to say that they remember me as a volunteer and remember my children in their classrooms, and that they are anxious to tell the judge what a great parent they think I was. Women who had been in prison with me in the 1970s write recalling how scared and young I looked as a teenager facing a 10-to-20-year sentence; one remembers that the prison 30 years ago had backed-up sewers, no heat, spoiled meat, and a law library that consisted of a few old books. People across the country and overseas write to say that I have done nothing they haven't done, and it was absurd that they were keeping me in prison for a minor offense from the 1970s. Some write to say they have cried while reading about my plight and others sign the petition saying they merely don't want their tax dollars spent on keeping me in prison. Others wonder why so many murders go unsolved and why sexual predators remain on the loose while I am hauled all the way back from the other side of the country in the name of "justice." Many professors, politicians, and rights advocates are critical of the aggressiveness of the prison industry and contend that it has become vindictive.

One writes that "keeping Susan LeFevre in prison is not about protecting the public, it feeds only the insatiable appetite of an increasingly gluttonous prison industry."

317

Polls on TV and in newspapers show an overwhelming majority of people support my release—in one poll, 98 percent of those surveyed said I should be released immediately.

Battle lines are drawn in the blogosphere, and as the negative blogs fill up with erroneous information about my case, many of the contributors admit to being members of the guards' union, many don't, but they are greatly outnumbered by the people who rise up to support me. One blogger is so persistent in defending me in cyberspace that my daughter Maureen and I begin to refer to him as CyberKnight. She says that when he answers negative blogs it is apparent that he has put a great deal of research into what he is saying and battles the other side as if he's on a crusade. After awhile, I ask Maureen to contact him to get his address so that I can thank him. We learn that his name is Chris and we begin to correspond frequently. He has learned about the extensive crony system that has a stranglehold on many cities and the state. He tells me about bloggers, mostly people who are no doubt connected to the prison industry who write comments that appear intended to stir up racial tensions. They insinuate that my being white is the only reason my incarceration is being questioned.

While it's undeniable that a disproportionate number of people of color are imprisoned I haven't asked to be released because I lived a law abiding life after I escaped. I was trying to get a hearing based on the bizarre circumstances of my original conviction. As someone who has empathized with all people who are being held unjustly I hate that I am being judged this way. Most of us feel the issue is being exploited by people interested primarily in helping the prison industry conglomerate to continue expanding.

I try not to think about the effort of those fighting to keep me in prison and I focus on my defenders, and I am overwhelmed by their thoughtfulness.

A man in Ava, Michigan named John has printed up bumper stickers and cards saying FREE SUSAN LEFEVRE, and has started a letter-writing campaign with others. A 13-year-old boy in Connecticut writes to say he would be proud if I were his mother.

Our neighbors in California send books along with good wishes, but they do more. They put up street decorations, tie yellow ribbons from trees, and paint signs asking for my release—all in preparation for a rally they plan on my behalf. Then my lawyer tells them the rally is a bad idea; if someone gets out of hand it would look bad for me. She obviously doesn't understand the type of friends and neighbors I have. These are not people who throw rocks or become violent; in fact, the plans for the putative rally feature a prayer vigil. Still, they do as the lawyer asks and cancel the rally.

Some of the letters come from men in prison. I joke to my husband that he now has competition out there. Well, not really *out* there...at least, not yet.

I learn a lot from these letters, and I am grateful for all of them. But it is the letters from my family that keep me going.

My 15-year-old son writes to report that thousands—even millions—of people are screaming for my release. He also says he is sorry for being argumentative the days before I was taken away.

My daughters say they are busy fighting for me. Maureen and Katie assure me that they are taking care of

Dad and Alan Jr. Katie drives her brother to school every morning and helps with cooking meals and keeping the house in order. Maureen encourages me to stay strong, and she says all those endless hours hearing "words of wisdom" from me have paid off. (*Endless* hours?)

In Katie's heartfelt letters, I can see how troubled she is by what has happened to me. Her favorite TV star plays a female detective on *Law and Order*, and she had once thought about being a detective herself. But this isn't like television, and she cannot understand why this is happening.

I miss them all terribly.

I also miss my dog Bailey, who was with me every day, devotedly following me from room to room. Whenever I sat down, Bailey would jump onto my lap—a warm and soft presence. Nothing in the prison is warm and soft. Even the pillows are hard plastic. The one I am given is particularly old and cracked. I see a guard throwing a better pillow into the trash, and I ask her if I can trade it for mine. She looks at me, smiles with half her mouth, and says no.

Chapter 38

Meanwhile, Kathy and others send me copies of articles written about my case. Noted law professors from Michigan, Washington, DC, and California write articles that my case is a good one to show how off track the prison industry has gone. They strongly urge that I be released. While most of the media coverage refers to me as fugitive soccer mom, local articles in Saginaw instigated by Duncan and Strickland embellish their original allegations with statements like, "LeFevre was a known member of a syndicate at a time when many murders were caused by the drug trade," insinuating that as a teenager I was somehow responsible for violence that happened years after I left Michigan.

The attorney contacts the *Saginaw News* to alert them to the faulty information listed on their front page about me. They write the next article using the correct details and then go back to doubling the amount of money involved and other inaccuracies. Saginaw is now home to a major prison; it seems to be an economic engine for the area. I wonder if this has anything to do with the mangling of the facts of my case.

I notice that nearly everyone in power in Michigan in some way or other seems beholden to or petrified of the prison industry. The number of people in Michigan politics who are former prosecutors is astonishing. It is an election year, and most of them run on their record of being tough on crime—the buzz words for being a proponent of the prison industry explosion. If I thought they were putting away the truly dangerous people it wouldn't bother me, but now I know first hand the type of people who are being sucked into this money machine.

The facts have been there for more than a decade. Stories of evidence from violent crime scenes languishing in labs for years because of a shortage of funds to process it, and the apprehension of violent criminals is stalled while million-dollar helicopters search for marijuana patches in the wild or SWAT teams break down doors of teenage parolees who failed to report to a parole officer and give a urine sample. The grim reality is that the frantic rush to fill prisons and look tough to get elected is doing more to allow dangerous felons to stay free.

Inside the prison, the same twisted reality exists as it did 30 years ago. Prisoners with histories as predators become coddled allies with certain guards and in some cases hang out in the office of administrators. Guards not only look the other way while these chronic criminals exploit other prisoners and carry on sordid businesses, but more than a few of the guards share in the profits of drug-dealing and other activities. Prisoners who aren't yet hardened criminals are the inmates most likely targeted with arbitrary violations and other forms of harassment.

The terrifying reality of how prison brutalizes people is crystallized for me in one young inmate—I'll call her Erica—who arrived the same week I did.

Erica is 20 but looks even younger. She is a fresh-faced girl from a small farm town who has written two unauthorized checks on her grandmother's bank account. Grandma didn't press charges, but a prosecutor did, and

Erica will be here for at least two years—an eternity at that age, as I well remember. When she arrives at the prison, her wide-eyed look of terror makes her stand out from the crowd. It is obvious that she is clueless about prison life or about the ghetto fabulous style that is the culture of the prison.

Within days, however, Erica begins wearing her hair in a severe prison style. A small tattoo appears on her neck. Her peaches-and-cream complexion soon turns a sallow prison yellow—whether from the food or stress or maybe just attitude I cannot tell. It takes only a few weeks for Erica to be very nearly transformed into one of the flock. When I talked with her the first week she arrived, she spoke softly and articulately. She was scared, but she enunciated clearly and used no slang or profanity. Now, her speech is more Ghetto than the ghetto, as the expression goes.

Something in me feels broken when I see her in the chow hall surrounded by "bulldaggers"—female pimps—looking like a pack of hungry wolves. Every other word out of her mouth is now *muthafuckin this* and *muthafuckin that*: "You a crazy muthafucka....I ain't messin wit' you, bitch..." She has attached herself to a predator-type veteran inmate who has no doubt convinced Erica that she will protect her against other predators. I know Erica has no idea of the price she will end up paying for this so-called protection. I know that by the time I see her again she will wear that hard, disillusioned look that distinguishes those prisoners who blend right in. She will have crossed the line, and she is unlikely ever to be able to come back. The kind of suffering you do in prison is in no way ennobling. It brutalizes you. It brutalized Erica.

Chapter 39

It's been a couple weeks since the warden mentioned sending me to a second women's prison because of the harassment issues at Scotts. Before sunlight one morning a guard comes to the cell and yells, "Pack up, LeFevre, you're moving out." A short time later several guards take me by prison van to the prison about thirty miles away called Huron Valley. It's known as the ghetto prison by inmates.

Soon after I arrive at Huron my new cellmate informs me that the bunk I am in belonged to a young girl who committed suicide the day before. She says the girl's name was Tamara and she shows me a picture of a pretty African American girl sporting a delicate smile and warm expression. Under her picture is a poem my cellmate wrote about her.

Suicides in prison are not that unusual but Tamara was especially well liked and the details of her death were controversial because of the actions of a guard in the hours prior to her taking her life. The guard was suspended for several days. There is a lot of commotion about Tamara's death because inmates want to hold a simple memorial service for her on the yard and administrators are reluctant to allow it, possibly because Tamara was able to hang herself on hooks in the administration building that were there illegally. By law, hooks in a prison are supposed to be non-weight-bearing in order to prevent suicides, and these weren't.

The next day an article that appears in a Detroit newspaper instigated by Strickland. He doesn't mention

324

Tamara's death. Instead it's an article about me in which he denies the allegations that I was moved because of mistreatment at Scotts by the guards. He says that the reason for my transfer from Scotts was that I was bragging to other inmates that I was in the news and this was bothering them. The headline of the article is; *Advice to Prisoner, Stop bragging*. A sub headline says; *Official says transfer unrelated to her complaints of feeling uncomfortable*.

The worst part is that I hear about the article from my daughter Maureen who has my name on Google alert. She says, "Mom, I can't believe a paper would print something like that. Do they just print anything this guy wants them to? Isn't it obvious he is trying to smear you?"

"He's just trying to cover up the details of the abuse and the death yesterday of a young girl here who killed herself. I've been assigned her bunk,"

"Oh, Mom, don't tell me that." She squeals. Then she tells me about another article Strickland authored. "He says that you let an orange peel fall and told a guard you thought someone else would pick it up."

"What? An orange peel, what are they talking about now?" I respond. For a moment I have no idea what she could be referring to. Then I think about an incident a couple of weeks ago when guards drove me to a hearing and didn't tell me until we were almost back to the prison that a small cooler on the seat next to me was my lunch that day. The guard who spoke said in a gruff manner that I could only eat what I had time for until we got through the gate then the food would be taken away. Since I only had a few minutes I quickly grabbed an orange since fresh fruit was harder to get than drugs in prison and as I tried to peel and eat it while my hands tightly chained to my waist, a tiny piece fell onto the seat. I remember how when the guard opened the door to let me out and saw it, she started screaming, "Who do you think is going to pick that up, me? Do you think we're gonna pick up after you, bitch?"

I don't remember saying anything as I struggled to pick it up but I know I wouldn't have made a remark that was smug to two armed guards who had my fate in their hands as I stood there shackled and defenseless. I didn't think much about it, they're always screaming at me and calling me crack ho, white bitch. I can't believe they put that in the newspaper.

It seemed that with as many troubles as the billion dollar prison industry was dealing with, that whether or not I dropped a piece of orange peel on the seat, it didn't seem to warrant a top prison official make the effort to alert the media. A lot of animosity seemed aimed at me due to the publicity but it was Strickland and the prosecutor who were driving it.

"Don't worry about it sweetheart. I think most people will see through it. How is the rest of the family doing?" I tell Maureen hoping to distract her from thinking about the article anymore than she already had.

"Dad's really sad most of the time and spends a lot of time in his room. It's not the same without you, Mom. The house feels so empty. Alan Junior is at the beach almost every day with his friends and his grades are down. I think it's taking him a while to adjust to all this."

"You and Katie will have to help him with his homework for awhile since Dad has so much to do already. Make sure you do what you can for him. Is someone walking Bailey regularly?"

We chat about events in her life. She has just finished college and is interviewing for a job. At least I have my family behind me. I don't know what I would have done without them.

Just like at Scotts, there are good guards and bad ones at Huron Valley but the articles have the effect of shining a green light for the already tense guards to act aggressively towards me. The day after the articles appear, guards begin clustering on the walk and in the yard and yelling out as I pass, calling me names and threatening to break me down like everyone else in the prison.

After every disparaging article there is a competition amongst guards to write up infractions no matter what I do to avoid them. There is nothing to stop them from fabricating charges as long as they have another guard who backs them.

Senior officers often pressure new officers, the green tags, to sign on as witnesses whether they were present or not. As I guess I should have expected, it isn't long before I learn that Strickland makes a visit to this second prison and again incites the same violence against me as he did with guards over at Scotts. I hear this first from angry guards who are only too happy to tell me what he said wanting to scare me.

Detroit Hearing on Escape Charge

My hearing date for the escape charge arrives. I expect it to go well since the laws in 1975 were more lenient but it is just one more hurdle before I get a hearing in Saginaw on the original charge where I am facing five and a half more years to finish the sentence on the original 10 to 20 year sentence. Any time for the escape would have to be served on top of that time.

I travel to the Detroit jail in the tiny rear metal compartment—something like a sardine can—of a vehicle specially designed for prison transfers. The van looks normal on the outside, but when the guard slides open a side door there is a second door that looks like a metal vault. He spins the handle, and when he pulls the door open I can see that it's 10 inches thick, exposing a small chamber with a metal bench. Once I'm seated, my knees are almost in my face. There are two of us traveling; the other woman is clearly a crack addict and seems incoherent. She had a foul smell that makes being locked in the oppressive box even worse. The only relief is knowing that the Detroit jail is a relatively short distance away, but then I realize the guards are stopping for coffee and doughnuts.

When we finally reach the jail, it looks like an asylum out of an old movie. Many of the guards scratch and nod in the distinctive way of heroin addicts. At Scott and Huron Valley, quite a few of the prison guards came to work drunk or on drugs, but at the Detroit jail some of them are in a total stupor. Once checked into the jail, I sit for more than eight hours crammed into a small cell with forty other women. They scream back and forth to prisoners sitting on the other side of the room the entire time. I noticed that instead of asking other prisoners where they live, they ask, "Where did you stay at?" It is apparent that most of the women rarely had long-term places to live.

The first night, there are not enough beds or bedding. I sleep on the concrete floor without a blanket or pillow. I wake in the night to feel a rat scurrying under my chin, and in the morning I'm told that I should have been glad it was only a rat and not one of the other prisoners on top of me.

The next morning, about 30 of us are herded in a chain-gang formation through a roughly finished, dimly lit underground tunnel with a ceiling that is so low I feel we are like rats traveling through the walls of the building and tunnels not meant for humans. We finally emerge in a cell underneath the courthouse across the street. The cell was built to hold fewer than 10 people, but like cattle we fill the room, bodies touching on all sides. Again, a number of prisoners scream and curse. Over the next eight hours, physical fights are narrowly averted as we await our turn to see a judge. Inmates get about two minutes with an assigned public defender talking through a small Plexiglas window with a hole the size of an apple. Inmates keep asking the public defenders to repeat what they were saying because of the noise. Most of the inmates are back within 15 minutes after seeing the judge. Their fate was decided in 15 minutes. It's an assembly line. Nothing on television is ever like this. It is a secret world.

It reminds me of a movie from the early 1970s called *Soylent Green*, in which people from a seemingly perfect society of the future march in lockstep to a slightly submerged factory, thinking they are reporting to work in a place that makes processed food called soylent green. Charlton Heston sneaks in and discovers the people are actually being processed as food. Horrified, he screams into the camera in the last frame of the movie, "THEY'RE EATING PEOPLE!"

It is my turn at last. When I hear my name, I go to a small window and on the other side is the attorney my husband has hired from the Detroit area to handle the escape charge. It is difficult to hear him or speak, but nonetheless this is my only opportunity to deal with my defense. "Don't you say anything," he says. "I'll do the talking."

I inform him that I may choose to speak and I don't want him to interfere if I do. Soon afterward I am led upstairs to the courtroom. The judge is a distinguished-looking African-American. He gasps when he sees me. "My God!" he blurts out. "What are they doing to this poor woman?"

It's clear that what I've been through has taken its toll. I look thin, pale, sick. The judge says right away that I will get probation as soon as a probation report is finished in two weeks. I suspect that he knows that the actions against me are politically motivated. I burst into tears—whether at relief over his granting probation or out of horror that I will be returned to the rat-infested jail cells for two more weeks, I do not know. Probably both.

The prosecutor pipes up, claiming that I was involved in identity theft. I was not, of course, but again that doesn't matter. My attorney doesn't challenge the allegations and instead gives a prepared statement comparing me to Jean Valjean of the famous novel *Les Misérables*, the story about a poor man in France doggedly pursued for years by a ruthless prosecutor. When the judge asks me a question, I speak up to say that I regret the decision I made years ago and that I hope the way I have lived for the last 30 years showed that I was not the kind of person to normally disrespect the law.

The prosecutor decides to keep me at the Detroit jail for two weeks while I wait for the probation report. Fifty cameras are aimed at me as these rulings are handed down and I feel embarrassed, as if I am a spectacle.

Press coverage is the classic double-edged sword. Although I have been careful not to speak to reporters in

Michigan, the coverage of my case has been widespread and dramatic. Every motion, every court appearance intensifies media interest. I doubt I would have been charged at all for the 30-year-old crime if it weren't for all the press scrutiny. On the other hand, the media interest may also be saving me from the corrupt manipulation of the prosecutor and his cronies.

The prospect of two weeks in such a depraved place is a crushing thought. I feel a terrible anxiety despite my victory in the courtroom. I suspect it may be heightened by withdrawal from Zoloft, which I'd been taking specifically to help me through the court proceedings. Between Huron Valley and the Detroit jail the medication mysteriously disappeared—not uncommon at the jail, where prisoners' possessions and medications are often stolen and sold on the street by staff. It would be days before I could see someone who could write another prescription. Being suddenly deprived of the antidepressant has thrown me into such deep anxiety that I do something I soon regret: I write a letter to Maureen that expresses my fear and despair. That of course alarms her. She has been running the website SaveMyMom, and working like crazy on my behalf. My foolish letter is 14 erratic pages of dread and distress, and it disturbs her greatly. Her earlier letters talk of me being the rock of the family, someone she looks up to. Now I must sound deranged and defeated.

The Detroit jail is so decrepit and in such a bad area I don't want my family to visit, although I desperately need money to buy items like shampoo, pens, paper, a razor. We've already paid the Detroit attorney a generous retainer for representing me on the escape charge, so I ask him to have someone drop off $20. I assure him in my messages that we will reimburse him. I don't hear back and I am forced to wash my hair with an acid solution used for lice, so my hair is burnt and frazzled.

It seems another cruel irony that although the medication I was prescribed has disappeared, the next day I am led to a filthy office where an unkempt woman sits at a desk, holding up a large syringe. She orders me to expose the inside of my arm and ties it off so that she can draw some blood. She stabs the needle into my extended arm and misses, hitting a vein so many times that the inside of my arm has a green and yellow discoloration the size of a grapefruit that looks remarkably like the sign of a chronic drug user. "We're going to be checking your blood every day or two to check for illegal drugs," she says bluntly.

Another prisoner at the jail is Sparkle. She is 19, but so tiny she could pass for an adolescent. She wears her hair in two braids and has childlike features on a frame of what I would guess to be less than 70 pounds. Sparkle is married and has a six-week-old baby. She has just returned from a meeting with the prosecutor. She is younger than my daughters, and she has been told that she is facing 25 years in prison unless she pleads guilty and testifies that she dropped her husband off at a house where a large cache of drugs and weapons was found. If she does as she is told the prosecutor has said he will give her probation. Her husband is facing 110 years if she lies and implicates him.

"I never took my husband there," she tells me. "They want me to lie, and if I don't, I'll go to jail for twenty-five years. No one will be there to raise my baby. My mama's really old and sick."

I was feeling sorry for myself until Sparkle told me about her circumstances. I remember all too well when the same pressure tactics were put on me years ago. All these years later, and little has changed. I think of myself at her age. No one on your side but a defense attorney who is likely more interested in impressing the prosecutor than defending you. Thank God I didn't have a baby to worry about at the time.

"Sparkle, did you get the promise of probation in writing? If you don't get it in writing they may send you to prison anyway. That's what they did to me when I was your age. Once they get a statement from you against your husband, it will be your word against theirs, and they lie all the time to get convictions. I've regretted not getting it in writing for many years."

"They just told me to write down that I dropped him off to the house...they said I would get probation and go home to my baby..." she says. I realize from her slurred speech that she is medicated; almost everyone in the unit is.

"How old is your husband?"

"He's twenty-six."

Wow, a 26-year-old facing 110 years in prison for a controlled substance charge! A story aired the night before about John Wayne Gacy, the serial killer convicted of sodomizing a minor who had been released from prison after serving just two years. After he was released, he raped and murdered a dozen boys. Why hadn't Gacy gotten 110 years the first time he attacked a child?

Since weapons were found at the house, I ask Sparkle about this.

"In our neighborhoods you have to have weapons," she says very seriously.

From the news reports I saw about the violence in Detroit, how could I judge the choices she and her husband made? They lived in a war zone.

Weapons were plentiful in Michigan, along with anti-government militias, and were often a subject mentioned in newspapers. One front-page headline said that residents were angry that there was such a shortage of bullets in the state, people had to go to several stores to shore up their supplies. I couldn't imagine this as a headline in San Diego or Carmel Valley. My family lived in a world that was light years away from here.

I felt bad that this teenage girl had to make the same terrible decision that faced me 30 years ago, and wondered if I couldn't have done more to expose the exploitive system and what it was doing to people who were young and defenseless. I had written articles under pseudonyms and had a few of them published in editorial sections of the news, but I had been so afraid of blowing my cover that I didn't go much further. I read about groups and activists but stayed on the sidelines. People needed to realize that those who were arrested were often badgered into pleading guilty with the threat of long sentences, and promises of leniency if they did what they were told. If those promises weren't kept, who was to know? The attorneys available to poor people got paid the same at the end of the week regardless of the effort they exerted, and it was probably a better career move not to make prosecutors look bad.

Throughout this experience, I feel I am being punished for being remiss in not doing more to expose the abuses that I was witnessing in prisons and the justice system. I know the blur of emotion that Sparkle is feeling, facing life-and-death decisions when she should be deciding on college classes or boys to date. I'm a tall blond lady from a so-called good family and traditional upbringing and Sparkle is a tiny dark-skinned girl from a ghetto neighborhood, but at this moment in time we are kindred spirits.

I also think of how her mother must have felt to name her daughter Sparkle. A daughter that would now have a cross to bear no matter which way she chose to go.

When a cart rolls into the units loaded with cheap candy and snacks, Sparkle buys candy bars like a small child. I ask her to buy me a few pencils and she does. Some of the inmates scream through the night in order to coerce others into giving them something if they'll stop. Since I don't have any money, I am forced to save part of my dinner to give to these inmates to appease them.

Most of the time in this concrete sewer, the day consists of sitting in a room with a TV blasting from its ceiling perch and listening to women who yell to be heard over the booming sound. My bleeding-heart view of the prison situation is challenged when I feel ominous thoughts toward a woman who insists on keeping the TV on all day at top volume. Since everything she watches involves yelping studio audiences, the vulgar sound bounces off the concrete wall from sunup to sundown. The woman claims that she has impaired hearing from years of taking prescription oxycontin. For two weeks, all I hear all day are the Maury Povich shows titled "Who's the Baby Daddy?" in which single mothers get to find out which sexual partner is the father of their children. The father usually screams out in anguish to learn he has a child with the woman. In the evening, the prisoners watch cop shows—as one woman put it, to get ideas. In the jail, just like in the prison, the reading material is paltry or nonexistent, although many of the prisoners spend time trying to find books to read. Skirmishes are often caused by prisoners fighting over a paperback.

I put in several requests to see a doctor to get my prescribed medication, and eventually I am able to see a very kind gentleman who arranges to put me in a medical unit where I will not have to share a cell and worry about being attacked in the night. Since I move, I don't see Sparkle again. I never learn her fate.

In all of the units, the guards sit behind a dark glass partition with a small slit to allow prisoners to communicate with them, although the guards usually stuff it closed with foam and it's impossible to get heard most the time. You can see only their silhouettes passing in front of the computer screen light. Towels are passed out arbitrarily through the slit; most days the guards refuse to pass me a towel.

When I do get a towel and can shower, I find the water is scalding hot and squirts out in strings in a decrepit enclosure the size of a phone booth. In the dim lighting I can see mold on the ceiling.

In my cell is a window that at one time was painted over on the outside to keep prisoners from looking out, but with age, the paint has worn away in some spots, so I can see outside if I stand on my tiptoes. I have a view of skyscrapers in the distance, a fairly pleasant-looking Detroit skyline. At a distance, it looks like a normal Midwestern city. Then one night after dark, I realize I can't see the buildings anymore. The view is completely black. Only then do I realize that all the buildings I see during the day are actually abandoned shells. The only sign of night life I see is from a new casino, which stays busy as people enter and leave on a protected glass second-story walkway. The casino and the jail are the only thriving businesses that seem to exist.

I suspect the jail, like the prison, is purposely degrading—the theory being that if conditions are bad enough, people will quit breaking the law and get a job. Beat 'em long enough and they'll straighten up. It reminds me of my parents' misguided approach when I was a teenager.

I try to rationalize these two weeks as a period of emotional strengthening. I keep reminding myself that people pay big money to go to ashrams for sensory deprivation experiences. My being able to rationalize my circumstances works for a little while—most people who have used drugs have a well-developed ability to delude themselves—but most of the time I think to myself, *Who am I kidding? I'm in an American sewer... a sewer for human souls.*

Every evening I walk in a circle the size of a card table to get exercise and pray over and over again...for me, my family, Sparkle, the other women here, Michigan, and mankind.

When the two weeks are finally up, I again spend a day in a cell packed with bodies waiting for a court appearance. In contrast to the women I met in prison who are serving bizarrely long sentences for nonviolent crimes, many of the prisoners at the jail, many who seem like chronic criminals, tell of having their sentences slashed to a matter of days because of the intense crowding and lack of funding. The jail inmates also mention the election-year theory as the reason they were brought in at all. Inmates have often gone through months of court hearings and dealt with numerous attorneys only to get released after a few days.

When it is my turn to see a judge, he announces that he is bound by the original judge to give me probation for the escape charge but he is tacking on the costs of my being transported from California and I will be on probation for a year. Any time I would have received on the escape charge would have had to have been served consecutive to the time I had to serve on the original charge. There are a lot of cameras in the courtroom, and the judge seems to be very conscious of how he would appear to members of the powerful prison lobby because of the coverage. I never realized that most states charge defendants thousands of dollars to be put on probation and nonpayment can result in prison time. The transportation cost has yet to be determined, but I agree to pay whatever amount they come up with.

The next day I'm again loaded into the cramped compartment of the custom-made paramilitary police vehicle. This time I at least don't have to share the space, but I feel that I am suffocating as I try to see outside through the thick metal grill. I'm filled with anxiety, and when I again feel the vehicle pull off the highway and into a fast-food restaurant my heart drops. I am relieved when the engine starts again and we head back toward the prison.

Chapter 40

Soon after I am back at Huron Valley, I enter the yard and am elated to breathe fresh air for the first time in weeks. The short time I was at Huron before going to the Detroit jail, the guards seemed much less hostile than they were at Scotts. Maybe the worst of the harassment is in the past I think to myself.

The yard is a section of grass enclosed by rows of fence and razor wire, and a craggy old hickory grasps upward in the center like a tree in a Halloween scene. The ground is lumpy, and inmates say the prison was built on a site of a landfill. A rubbish heap. How appropriate.

I'm barely inside the gate and just about to start jogging when several male guards approach me. One of them says, "So you never told your husband all those years?" Before I can answer, another guard says, "I want to know whose identity you stole."

I can tell the questions aren't meant to be friendly, but I feel that maybe if I explain my side they will be less cruel. "I never assumed anyone else's identity. I went by my middle name and a fictitious last name," I respond. "I wanted to make sure I didn't break the law, knowing they would use it against me."

"That's not what the papers say."

"They are just quoting the prosecutor, and he's not telling the truth."

As I am speaking, other guards walk over until there are at least six or seven male guards surrounding me. As the size of the group increases, the questions begin to sound more antagonistic. One of the men says blatantly, "We're pissed, bitch—we can't be letting someone like you show us up." He makes a face and spits on the ground.

"Who turned you in? I heard someone tipped them off."

"No one called in with a tip. An absconder agent, a probation officer in Saginaw, started calling anyone in the country named LeFevre and asking if they knew me and if I was still alive. He kept calling and banging on doors and threatening people for two years, and only found out I was in California after they tapped my family's phone lines when they called to warn me."

"Then why'd the paper say it was a tip?"

"That's what a California detective told the newspapers, but it wasn't true. The absconder agent in Michigan started a website after they picked me up and said the reason he went after me was because he thought it would be quirky. He had no idea if I was still alive or in the country."

"That's bullshit," a guard sneers.

"There were many witnesses and the website was there for months; a family member printed it out. You tell me why I was singled out since I hadn't broken any laws for three decades and I was never violent."

"You still need to do time, LeFevre; it don't look good for us," one of the men mutters, as yet unconvinced.

It feels eerie that they know my name. I realize nothing I can say is going to change their minds.

"The point is, you made us look bad if you got away with escaping like that. They shoulda made an example out of you. It's obvious you don't belong here, but it doesn't look good," says a particularly grizzled-looking guard. Another guard standing farther away also spits—this time on the bench where I'm sitting.

"I've never hurt anyone in my life," I say. "And I wasn't guilty of the crime I was sent to prison for in the first place. I was never a drug dealer. Do you mind if I leave now? I was going to walk the yard if it's all right."

They seem disappointed that I remained so calm. I realize their intent was to provoke an altercation with me. Any officer issuing a violation would be a hero, just like the judge and the drug agent and everyone involved in my conviction had become heroes. In the prison, I'd heard stories about male guards beating up female inmates who were handcuffed and already down on the ground. It was the word of the guards against the inmates. I am glad my confrontation with these guards had been within earshot of other inmates and out in the open. I could easily have become another statistic at the prison.

My friends and family were worried about me being attacked by hostile inmates, but I was finding the mostly amiable inmates were often the only barrier between me and the vindictive guards. The whole industry seems drunk with power and unaccustomed to the thought of losing even a minnow.

I hear again that Strickland has repeated his claim to the guards at Huron Valley, that my escape "made them look bad" implying that they needed to make an example out of me. He tells guards that my three decades of appearing "normal" were all fraudulent, that I'm laughing on the inside at anyone fool enough to believe my story.

There is a hierarchy of three who sets the tone for the abuse. At the top is the supervisor. Her last name is

Jones—I never knew their first names—and she is an exceptionally short, squat white woman who looks like a caricature of a witch. Haggard is the unit manager and reports to Jones. She is a somewhat distant presence; all I really know about her is that the inmates find her brash and repulsive—except for a few, who are serious predators and who hang out in Haggard's office and sit on her desk like gargoyles. The third staff member of the group is named Wacker. She is the one I see most often; the one who torments me one-on-one every day. She is the epitome of what the inmates refer to as "ghetto." She is white, with yellow hair cut severely short on one side and long on the other. She sports two-inch nails with rhinestone designs and a permanent sneer. But these are all just fashion choices; what really defines her is the loud, guttural way she talks. Sentences are littered with "muthafucka" and end with "girlfriend" or "girl." Most words are slurred monosyllables grunted rather than spoken, so that what she says bears only a slight resemblance to the English language. It is evident that she tries desperately to sound as ghetto as possible to fit in, and she's as cruel as she is vulgar.

There is no recourse against this triumvirate—no appeal up the chain of command. As one well-meaning guard says to me, looking me straight in the eye, "People tend to forget what happens in here, and it is best they do. Nobody is going to change what they do to prisoners. No one cares."

Even when a family can prove that the death of a prisoner was due to guard brutality, the result is just a payout by the state to the family—who are never heard from again. These are poor people, and poor people die silently every day.

I wake up before dawn to the sound of Wacker screaming my name and ordering me to move to another cell. This is the eighth time in two weeks that she has made me move. She will not let anyone help me, and since my belongings consist of heavy books, letters, paperwork, all of my toiletries, and my mattress and bedding, I have to make more than one trip. While I am "between cells" moving the stuff, inmates steal things from both the old cell and the new one.

My back begins to spasm after the first move, and I think that is partly the reason Wacker keeps forcing me to move again; it's as if she is trying to injure me. Each move also gains me a worse cellmate—someone who hates whites even more than my previous cellmate, is even crazier, more incontinent, and more violent. All the new cellmates are heavy smokers, and they smoke in the cell, a closed-room environment if ever there was one. It is illegal to smoke in the cells, but the rule is enforced only when a guard wants to target someone. Almost everyone, including the guards, smokes at the prison.

My back is in so much pain I know I have to do something about Wacker, who doesn't show any sign of giving up on singling me out. Tearfully, I approach a sergeant in the chow hall and quietly tell her what Wacker is doing to me. That afternoon the sergeant appears in our wing and checks the computer for the unit, and the data verify that I am being moved almost every day. Her way of handling the issue is to shout out, "We could get a lawsuit if you keep putting her in with smokers!" She leaves the unit, and I realize things aren't going to get better for me now that I have reported the guards to a supervisor.

Chapter 41

The following day, I am pulled out of the shower by Haggard, who is Wacker's supervisor. At the top of her lungs, she orders me to get dressed and summons me to a meeting. She then flings open my cell door as I stand undressed, exposing me to a hallway full of inmates who have come out to see why she is yelling. I end up in a room with the triumvirate—Wacker, Haggard, and the supervisor, Jones. We are in Haggard's office; its walls lined with pictures revolutionaries. The three of them spend the next hour screaming about how I am going to regret snitching out Wacker.

Jones is quiet at first, and this leads me to believe she is possibly more objective, but she finally interrupts the others to have her say. "You're gonna wish you never escaped when we get through with you," Jones says. "You got five more years under us and we're gonna grind you down to the scum you are." She turns the computer monitor around so I can see it. On the screen is my file. Jones points her finger at my name and the out date of 2013. "We've got plenty of time to break you down, bitch. You're scum like everyone else in here. You and your fancy house don't mean nothin' in here. You're scum just like the rest of us." *Scum* seemed to be a popular word.

It is Haggard who raises the threat that I might not live to see my 2013 out date. "The people we're going to put you in a cell with now are probably going to kill you. I don't know what they'll do...." She stretches back in her chair and smiles as if she is daydreaming. "All I know is nobody else wants to be in a cell with the people were gonna put you in with. Something about their being violent and crazy. Like officer Jones says, you're gonna wish you never came back here, LeFevre."

Wacker actually seems a little shaken up by the threats about me being killed, but it doesn't stop her. "And what about the banana peel you left on the floor of your cell." I can feel my mouth drop open as I realize she's trying to start another story about a fruit peel dropping. The guard who initiated the orange peel story no doubt got a great deal of notoriety. Would Strickland be going to the media about an alleged banana peel dropping this time? It's obvious she's making this up and she fails to get any traction so she reverts to another tack. "You been missing anything lately?" she asks. It is not a question but a revelation, or rather a confirmation of what I have suspected—that it is Wacker and Haggard who have repeatedly opened my locker and ransacked it. Over the past few weeks, notes and writings have regularly gone missing. Now I know that these two were primarily responsible, and now their supervisor knows what a good job they have done of harassing me.

"So you think you're gonna write a book, LeFevre? We'll see about that. You ain't writing no book while you're in here—we'll make sure of that. I used to live up in Saginaw too. I read all about you. Why they write about your skanky ass I don't know. So they want to do a cable show on you. That's if you get out, bitch, and you ain't never getting outta here to do nothin'." Jones picks up the newspaper on her desk and I see my picture on the front page.

I am surprised but grateful that our little chat session concludes without any physical harm done to me. The three have acted throughout like rabid animals eager to bite, and I realize that if they had lashed out, nothing I could have said or done would have made a difference. Madness seems epidemic here—mostly among the guards.

These near-zombies are in control in Huron Valley—and possibly throughout the Michigan Gulag. The many decent guards, some of whom I'll never forget for their kindness, have no chance against the crazy ones. Like the rest of us, the good guards lie low and try to stay out of the line of fire. Loud, ugly fights between guards happen frequently. I reflect back on first hearing about the gun fight between the two guards in the parking lot that occurred just weeks before I arrived. The fights are the subject of constant gossip among inmates. (Not long after this show of camaraderie between Haggard and Jones, I hear about a screaming fight between the two of them. Haggard accuses Jones of going through papers on her desk; this, Haggard claims, causes her so much trauma she is forced to take a leave of absence to recover from the mental abuse. Inmates know this claim to be the setup for a lawsuit charging workplace harassment. Lawsuits such as these, thinly veiled extortion by employees, is another dirty secret within the industry.)

Instead of a beating from the triumvirate, I get a new cellmate. Amanda, who is 22, white, and about twice my size, has just been released from segregation. She was put in seg for throwing a chair at someone in the anger management class she was kicked out of. Amanda is a manic-depressive paranoid schizophrenic who has been violent her whole life. Her mother sent her to live with her grandmother in order to protect her other children; she was kicked out of school because she attacked fellow students and she is notorious for trying to beat up inmates at the prison.

Amanda, however, sees things differently. In her eyes, she is the victim, and she has been singled out by others. She threatens me the first day and every day thereafter. When I report the threats, guards ignore me or tell me that Haggard has ordered that I stay in the same cell with her. When Amanda is not in a hostile mood, she walks around the cell without clothes on and asks me to put powder on her back. I soon realize that the reason she is threatening me is that she wants another roommate, preferably one who is closer to her age and probably more apt to want to be sexually active. One day Amanda runs into the cell as I am reading and swings her arms wildly, screaming that I have stolen something of hers. I run into the hallway and report that she is threatening me again.

Haggard orders the guards to take both of us to the segregation cells. The charge against me is that I threatened Amanda. There had been many witnesses present when I ran out of the cell, chased by a frantic Amanda, and everyone knows that it was not I who was threatening anyone. The universal supposition is that Haggard has set me up.

This happens on a night in late November, and it is cold, dark, and blowing. The male guard refuses to let me take my coat, although the dungeon cells are on the other side of the grounds. On the way over there, he pulls harshly on the chains holding my arms behind my back and gropes me several times under my arm. There is nothing I can do.

I am kept in solitary for a week. I am supposed to be able to leave the cell for an hour each day, but that doesn't happen. Nor do the guards give me the pencils, paper, or books I should be allowed to have. Instead, they scream insults into my cell. I get no mail that week, nor does anyone inform me that my attorney has called repeatedly asking that I call her. She wants to tell me that the date for the hearing on my motion has been set; it is soon. Thanks to the guards keeping me from calling my attorney—a basic right of any prisoner in America—I am unable to subpoena several witnesses I want her to track down. Outside the cell one guard in particular tells the other guards about Strickland saying they needed to make an example of me. She works three shifts in a row bragging how she can sleep there and collect overtime pay, and repeats the information to incoming staff and they often react immediately by screaming into my cell or harassing me in other ways. By the end of the week, pubic hair is placed on top of the food the guards slide under my door.

Eight days later I see a hearing officer and the charge against me is dropped due to testimony and written statements from more than half a dozen inmates who were present when I ran from the cell that night. They recall that it was me who was being threatened. The officer is openly upset and writes that she is unable to do anything to me because of the number of statements that contradict Haggard.

When I am out of seg, I involve myself totally in preparing for my court date in Saginaw over the filing of the 6500 motion. The last time I was in a court in Saginaw, my life unraveled. It is difficult to think about this—and impossible not to. I am frightened of what lies ahead, and at the same time, I am eager for the motion to be filed and the proceedings to begin.

The media coverage grows in intensity in the days before the hearing. In statement after statement released to the press, Barney Duncan continues to declare that I was a drug kingpin; he proclaims he will do everything in his power to keep me in prison.

Chapter 42

The Hearing in Saginaw.

The return to my former hometown stirs up mixed emotions. Despite its aggressive record of sending people to prison or probably more because of it, Saginaw's once thriving commercial and industrial base has withered away

The local paper still pumps out article after article, referring to me as "convicted heroin dealer LeFevre." Each one is more inaccurate and damning than the last. Despite complaints from my attorney and family members, the paper again prints completely false information about me. A series of articles tell of my passionate love affair with my co-defendant: "they were inseparable, they lived together, sold drugs together and went to prison together." Of course, I barely knew him. Another article states mockingly that while my high school is holding a reunion on a boat on the Saginaw River I am locked in away in a tiny cell. It seems unnecessarily mean-spirited.

When I was arrested in the 1970s only a single article about the incident ran, and almost everything in it was false or misleading. Thankfully, this time the public has alternative sources for getting information. That is my salvation.

I meet with the attorney that evening. My husband and children have flown in from California and friends have driven from hours away but I won't be able to see them until I am in the court room tomorrow. The first thing the attorney tells me is that Duncan has once again tried to

delay my hearing. She throws a letter at me
from Maryland. "Duncan tried to stop th
yesterday saying he wanted to send
Maryland to question the guy who wrote uᵤₛ ₋
from some guy who says he knew someone who bought
drugs from you. He says he used to live in Detroit; he
doesn't even give the guy's name. It's obvious it's from a
relative of a prison guard or maybe even someone Duncan
knows, but as ridiculous as it sounds Duncan contacted the
judge's office and requested more time to send police
detectives to Maryland to question the guy who wrote it.

The letter was barely legible and nothing in it made
sense. It was obvious Duncan was desperate trying to back
up his kingpin story or probably just trying to stall my
hearing again. There seems to be no end to the amount of
energy and money Duncan and his buddies are willing to
use against me.

For reasons they don't disclose, I am put in a dark
cell by myself in the basement of the jail. Several women
are in adjacent cells and have been held there for months in
solitary confinement. It is hard to hear them but I am able to
make out that they are kept in these dungeonous cells, often
without any clothes when wash day rolls around, and
according to them, they are there for trivial offenses. One
woman says she shook a neighbor child when he threw a
rock at her grandchild and she has been in solitary for
months. In this case I have only her word and no ability to
check documents or collaborate what she is saying but from
what I know of the Saginaw jail I believe her. It's
unbelievable for me that I am back in the Saginaw jail –
three decades later.

The next day as I enter the courtroom I scan the crowd for my family. To ensure that I will not be able to hug my children or husband, they are made to sit near the back of the room while strangers sit in the front row. I ache to have even the briefest moment of physical contact with my family—I haven't seen my children these many months—but orders from the sheriff, a well-known ally of Duncan's, are that I not be allowed any contact. I can only wave to them and blow kisses. Still, seeing my family in a courtroom in Saginaw brings home to me how my two worlds have truly and finally collided. My children glow like angels and are a reminder of a past life that seems a remote dream.

I look around and recognize E. Brady Denton, the prosecutor at the time of my conviction. Amazingly, he is here to testify on my behalf and tell what he knew about the conspiracy between the judges at that time. I look through the crowd to see if my uncle has shown up, but he's not here yet.

My attorney is the first to present her case. She begins by saying that my sentence came as a result of the well-known pact among judges to give everyone arrested on a drug offense, the maximum sentence possible, regardless of the individual circumstances. The argument is shot down minutes afterward when the prosecutor states figures about people who were arrested who didn't get 10 to 20 years. We have no way to prove that people who got less time had no doubt set up other people probably a lot of innocent ones, in order to get leniency.

My witnesses testify next. Denton says that as prosecutor, he knew about the judges' pact to give the maximum sentence in all drug cases without regard to the details of the cases. He declares his opinion that I should never have been sent to jail and that I should be released immediately. He testifies about it being a turbulent period in the criminal justice system in Saginaw at the time of my original conviction.

Other lawyers testify in the same vein. One of them is my former public defender, Joe Amato, who now admits that he kept me from seeing the probation report that detailed the toxic allegations by Greely. It is a bitter irony that Amato, the person paid to defend me, was the key person who prevented my discovering the plans the prosecution had for me. I ask my attorney to probe him further. Specifically, I want him to give answers as to why he went to such lengths to obscure information from me and work along side the prosecution. I want her to ask him if he was enticed into accepting the maximum sentence for me in exchange for a lighter sentence for his father. My attorney refuses. "Not relevant," she insists.

Amazingly the prosecutor does not question my former attorney at all. No one bothers to ask him why he didn't show me the report and kept other information from me.

Next up to the stand is my uncle. He admits to misleading me about my ability to appeal my sentence.

It is now my turn. I take the stand, swear to tell the truth, and sit down. My attorney asks me if I ever brought drugs for friends. I tell her that a few times I did. "But I wasn't what anyone would consider a drug dealer, even a small drug dealer."

I am asked to tell the judge in detail exactly what occurred the night I was arrested. I explain that I was a drug user, not actually an addict, that I was afraid of getting in over my head and using too often. I tell the judge exactly how the drug agent set me up, hoping to get me to later target the man I was dating. I tell him I was a student at the time, and that I had almost no money. The judge seems to listen thoughtfully. I tell him how the drug agent lied about me being involved that night and about him claiming I was a drug dealer.

An assistant district attorney jumps to his feet and asks pointedly, "Are you saying that a drug agent who later became a state police chief lied about evidence in your case?"

My attorney glares at me. I look beyond her in the audience and see my children's faces, and I have no qualms about telling the truth. For three decades I've regretted letting an attorney mislead me when I knew better. This time I state very clearly, "Yes, I am saying that the drug agent lied. I think the evidence shows that clearly."

The assistant prosecutor runs back to the desk in evident disbelief that I would say this about Greely, a longtime friend of Barney Duncan. Seemingly he has no follow-up. He sits down next to Duncan and two other prosecutors. It seems odd that four prosecutors could spend an entire day in a hearing on a small three decades old dope charge.

Cheryl continues to glare at me. She is not happy that I have gone against her repeated warnings about minimizing guilt. She is livid that I have said that I was set up, that I have declared my innocence.

It is the prosecution's turn to question me. I brace for his attacks, but I am not prepared for the distressed look on my children's faces as the relentless badgering intensifies.

My 19-year-old daughter Katie breaks down and sobs. My son watches aghast as the prosecutor spouts outrageous allegations about evidence he says was found at my apartment. He is making things up. He asserts that drugs were found at my apartment; no drugs were found anywhere. He brings out a gun and waves it in the air, letting the assumption grow that it, too, was found in my home.

"Cheryl," I whisper to my lawyer, "how can he get away with lying so blatantly? Nothing was found at my apartment."

Her reply is chilling. "Prosecutors do it all the time," she says. "It's a way to try and throw the defense off guard."

I'm incredulous. "Aren't they under oath?"

"No. Not at all, and they can make up anything they want."

I ask Cheryl to dispute the lies about the drugs and the gun, but she ignores me.

The assistant DA takes over again. He approaches the stand, shows me a piece of paper, and asks if it is my name at the bottom.

I look, see my name, answer yes.

"And isn't that a bank statement that says there is $1500 in a checking account?"

I look more closely. The signature is an obvious forgery—a not very good attempt to duplicate my admittedly slipshod handwriting.

"That is not my handwriting," I say. "My signature has been forged."

Again he runs back to his table. It becomes clear to me that these prosecutors are used to dealing with people they have intimidated. This time I am facing them with a clear head. Thirty years staying away from drugs and alcohol have made me a more challenging target than I was years ago. I remember how scared I was at 19; I would have said anything they told me to say. No more.

My attorney says she has to take a break and leaves the courtroom abruptly. She returns about 40 minutes later. I have no idea why.

By the time the court convenes, the judge announces it is already 4 o'clock. He has decided to put off the controversial decision until after the holidays. He asks the attorneys to give closing arguments in writing for his review.

I feel as if a giant boot has crushed me into the floorboards. Instead of being able to embrace my family for the first time in many months and go home with them, I will instead be going back to the dark basement cell and then back to the brutality of Huron Valley prison. I will be there through Christmas and New Year. My family will fly home without me.

The Saginaw authorities won't allow me to hug my family after the hearing. I see my daughter sobbing again, and my husband looks as crushed as I feel. We have all aged beyond our years. I would have given anything to have been able to hold them for just a few minutes but I am led away, not knowing when I will see them again.

Chapter 43

Back at Huron Valley, the same gang of guards is smugly pleased that I have failed to be released and am back where they can continue to torment me. Haggard is more emboldened than ever, and now unlocks my locker in front of me and takes my belongings and hands them directly to the gargoyle inmates. As she reaches into my locker and pulls out my ear buds, I tell her that I have the receipt showing that I purchased them and she smiles as if to say, so what? She also removes letters that I've received from supporters and chapters of the book I am writing. I report this to another guard who I know is honest, and she tells me to write a complaint. "I have, and it only makes things worse," I tell her. She sympathizes but can only shrug. There is nothing anyone can do.

It's not long before Haggard and the group pull me into her office to taunt me again and warn me against trying to get statements from other inmates about the things they are doing to me. "We'll write them up for interfering with administrative procedure," Haggard says, as if she has been researching how to target interfering inmates. "The inmates who stuck up for you last time didn't fare too well, LeFevre. I think by now they've learned their lesson." It hadn't occurred to me that the inmates that signed statements disputing Haggard's charges that I had threatened an inmate were being targeted now as well.

Haggard again threatens that I better not consider writing a book or talking about things I shouldn't. She continues to steal papers from my locker, while looking for statements from other prisoners about her treatment of me. She has not only confiscated such statements, but also brought the prisoners who wrote them to her office and made threats against them. A couple of inmates give me written statements that they have been threatened against doing so. I figure out that I have to mail the statements out immediately to someone outside the prison that I get from the inmates so that my name isn't on the return address. Haggard can rip my things apart as much as she likes now; she won't find the statements.

One day she glowers with hatred as she tells me she has just assigned me to a cell with four other inmates, three of whom are a trio of the worst prisoners in the place who work together as a gang. Other inmates warn me to keep my eyes open when I sleep; better yet, they say, I should ask to be moved before I get injured. But of course, such a request would never be granted.

Meanwhile, I work at staying balanced, knowing that as long as I survive, I am luckier than many of the other women here. They have lived in danger all their lives. They worry constantly that their children won't remember them. Many are serving bizarre sentences for a single wrong choice. There are inmates who deserve to be locked up, but seeing so many women who are not so different from me and who I know will be staying here for many more years haunts me.

My husband, family and advocates remain a strong support. I continue to get letters every day. My kids send newsy letters about how they are doing and include endearing messages. My husband writes a poem about a place near the ocean where I like to walk. I had taken him there once, but I didn't think he realized what a special place it was for me. As with most husbands, writing me a poem is not something he would have done ordinarily, but these are extraordinary times.

There are visits from Kathy and Jerry Morse, the Michigan couple who are my champions. They tell me that every new development in my case prompts thousand of hits from supporters.

Around this time I hear a story on the news about Jennifer Hudson, the famous singer and movie actress. Three of her family members including her mother and seven year old nephew, have been murdered by a man who was on the same absconder list my name was taken from. He had an outstanding warrant for violating his parole and a violent history. If the agent had chosen his name as someone to spend time looking for and apprehending Miss Hudson's family might still be alive.

On another night I watch a TV documentary narrated by a Detroit Detective Sergeant who tells how in the past, Detroit police were dealing so many drugs that drug dealers were calling the police station to complain because of the unwanted competition.

On a phone call with my son he tells me that my picture and a story about me were featured in a newspaper in Viet Nam. The article tells how after being convicted of stealing chickens, I escaped a re-education camp and stayed on the lam for 33 years until being picked up at my high rise apartment. I can tell my son is disillusioned by what has happened to me but I'm glad he is looking at some of the lighter aspects. His mother has gone from being a king pin/syndicate member to a chicken thief in just a few months.

Along with many of the other inmates I spend time sitting in a common area room the inmates call the crack house mainly because people sit there doing nothing all day the same way they sit in a crack house on the outside. Instead of drugs the women substitute junk food. They line up to use the microwave to heat up items like palm oil laden microwave popcorn. Some of the women become so over weight after coming to the prison they have to pull a chair up to the microwave to wait several minutes for it to pop. The food in the chow hall is often dirty, greasy or as in the case of the white beans, filled with worms. I resort to ordering food from a commissary list inmates are offered. The prison puts a high mark up on the food, most of it junk food that comes from another state, but it helps to supplement on days when the meals are particularly bad. I find that I begin to crave the food the next day and I am hungrier than ever after eating most items, even the noodle soups. I notice that almost everything has palm oil in it and I feel a craving stronger than I ever felt with drugs so I wean myself from eating the food as much as possible. As someone who eats mostly whole foods on the outside, I see how the women have become accustomed to eating junk food that is habit forming.

Another small annoyance at both prisons was that prisoners routinely left water pounding full force out of the faucets. Guards could see the water blasting through out the day and ignored it. When I tried to turn it off, inmates would turn it back on saying they were trying to bankrupt the state so they would have a better chance of going home.

One of the inmates I met while sitting in the crack house/common room was an inmate who said she remembered me from the 70's at The DeHoCo facility. She would be in the prison for six years for shoplifting. She recited poems to me that she had created and memorized that went on for twenty minutes. Every poem made me cry.

I asked her to write them down for me and I would include and credit her in my book but she was reluctant. I realized later she couldn't write. Suddenly one day I realized who she was. Her name was Lisa and she was the inmate who took my ring from me at the prison thirty some years ago. It was obvious she'd had a rough life since then, probably homeless and a chronic substance user, but I felt I could detect in her eyes that she remembered about the ring. I felt that beyond the uniform of a street urchin she was a sensitive and intelligent person.

Day after day I hear stories from inmates that help build my resolve that I have to write a book about what is happening to these women. Most of them, like me, were caught up in an unforgiving system. The difficult part is that I know it is so unnecessary. I receive books from friends that tell of prisons in the past that had rehabilitation programs and boasted a 72% success rate of helping women leave the prison, get employment, and have the ability to support themselves. Today of course, more than 70% of inmates return to prison within three years of leaving it and the prison pushes them out in far worse condition than they went in, in most cases. The women in the system today, appeared to rely on having children as a primary way to survive both emotionally and financially. Women who had many children, sometimes six or seven or more children taken away from them in the past, felt that this time when they had a baby, they would handle things differently. Another common story was how some of the women who already had a brood of children they couldn't take care of, probably because they had substance abuse problems, said they tried to get birth control at a clinic but were discouraged by people holding signs outside the clinic.

They meant to go back another time but didn't get around to it.

Chapter 44

Finally, after the holidays the word comes that the judge has, in effect, kicked a decision down the road, turning it over to the parole board to decide whether or not I should remain in jail. He forwards to the governor the letters of support we presented as testimony, and he tells the governor he is "impressed" that so many people think so highly of me. It seems obvious he is doing whatever he can to try to outmaneuver the prosecutor. Since Duncan, the prosecutor, has vowed to appeal any decision, the situation has become complicated.

As I've come to expect, before every important decision to be made regarding my fate, Strickland or Duncan instigate at least one negative article. Harassment and the issuance of arbitrary tickets continue, and are the basis for a December 24th article in the *Detroit News* headlined "LeFevre's Behavior May Stymie Her Parole." The article quotes Strickland as saying I have had "behavior problems" in prison. He says that I threatened a 22 year old inmate named Amanda. He doesn't feel it necessary to mention that I was found not guilty due to numerous witnesses stepping forward to say that they were there and it was me who was being threatened by an inmate the guards had set me up with. He also mentions that I received a ticket for putting my medication under my pillow. He doesn't mention it was an aspirin and a single pill, a low dosage anti depressant that I had the discretion of taking or not taking. Again, I see that while inmates extort sex and money from other inmates and sell drugs and other contraband almost openly, my having a pill of my prescribed medication under my pillow is an issue Strickland feels is newsworthy.

The prison gets a new warden, and her first move is to change the search procedures for women who have visitors or who work kitchen duty. The new policy is a humiliating one: Anyone who works in the kitchen or has an outside visitor must now sit on the edge of a chair and pull apart the lips of her vagina so a guard can check for food items or drugs stashed there. Many of the inmates are in tears over this. In the chow hall women break down in tears during their meals recounting the new search procedures they've had to endure. When I enter my cell, I find Angel, my cellmate, crying in her bed as she tells me about her experience getting searched in such a way after working a long day in the kitchen. She decides she is going to forfeit the seven cents an hour she is making and quit reporting to work. Within days a major violation is issued against her because she didn't give two weeks notice. She knows the parole board will use the violation against her when deciding her release date. Despite my struggles over the months to add attorneys, family members, and supporters to my visitors' list, I now inform family and friends not to come see me anymore.

But a cousin of mine, the former assistant district attorney who worked for Duncan for several years, is on my attorneys' list, and I can see her without being subjected to the search. She is the only person I will now see. She is the daughter of my infamous uncle, but because she is younger than I am, she and I had hardly gotten to know one another as children. Now we have become friendly. I even tell her a little of the past as I see it. My implication that my father and hers offered little support to me after I was arrested and may have intentionally misled me, causes her to shake her head and say, "Why would they do that?"

I don't know how to answer her......but it's in the past and I have more pressing issues to worry about now. Despite my misgivings about my uncle it is obvious he has raised an impressive family.

It is my cousin who breaks the news to me that Duncan, still working to keep me in prison, has been able to maneuver a close ally onto the parole board to vote against my release. The new board member is a man named Towner, who served as sheriff of Saginaw for some 20 years and through many scandals. I have already heard stories from Chris, my cyber knight, of people who tried to run against Towner or other members of Duncan's group and seemed to have found themselves facing unusual problems—such as a job loss. At least those were the rumors circulating around Saginaw and on the Net. The prison industry lobby is confident, says my cousin, that with Towner on the board, I will remain in prison for many more years.

That would leave only an appeal or a commutation of my sentence by the governor as my remaining options. But Duncan has already said he will appeal any favorable verdict the judge might render, contending that I must stay in prison as long as my co-defendant did. As for the governor, she has been under extreme pressure from the prison industry and has let very few people go—fewer than most of her predecessors.

But there was some good news. The petition organized through the Michigan Chamber of Commerce had more than 40,000 signatures from business owners who over the last couple of years seen their taxes raised through the roof in an already crumbling economy in order to support the ever exploding incarceration industry. The petition demanded that the governor stand up to the MDOC, and order them to reduce the number of people incarcerated.

More than 30% of Michigan's inmates were kept locked up well past their release dates by a parole board handpicked by the industry itself. The prison industry showed no sign of slowing down due to new laws and a parole board that was essentially a stacked deck in favor of the Corrections Department.

My options were narrowing with the appointment of a crony member on the board, but hopefully the petition would make a difference.

Chapter 45

The parole board hearing is held at Huron Valley. Haggard leads me to a chair facing a television monitor. In the foreground of the screen is a white man I guess to be in his mid-60s; in the background, I can see a blurry semicircle of people sitting behind him. The man in front is a former sheriff. I expect him to ask me questions; I expect him to prompt me to say why I feel I won't be a threat to the public.

He begins by screaming at me. It is not what I expected. He seems to be having a nervous breakdown. To this day, I do not recall what he said; all I can remember is the shouting. I wonder briefly if his aim is to throw me off guard, get me to lose my temper, frighten me, pre-empt any defenses I might have.

Then he asks a question. "What do you think of the drug war?" he says. "I suppose you think drugs are a victimless crime?" I hadn't anticipated discussing my political views on the drug war.

I tell him I used drugs as a teenager but assert that "I haven't used them in thirty years." I know it would be bad policy to in any way oppose the sacred "drug war" that is effectively paying all the salaries of the people on the screen and pumping up the prison system to its current place as a superpower in the state.

"Who did you buy drugs from?" he asks. "What was his name?"

"Javier." I give him the answer they wanted 30 years ago. I have nothing to hide anymore. I have no more hard choices to make. I know that I will answer questions to the best of my recollection; that is all I can do, and the knowledge relaxes me.

It is just the opposite of what my attorney has told me. "You can't say you're not guilty," Cheryl has always insisted. "It doesn't matter if you are or not. That's what they want to hear. They want you to show remorse and beg for their mercy. The key word is 'grovel.'" I guess I'm past that now.

I say, "Of course I deeply regret the choice I made in using drugs. It was a bad choice. I hurt my parents, and I know I could have become an addict in time or even possibly have died from drugs. But I was charged with being a drug dealer and that wasn't true. I managed to get off drugs with the help of the tools I learned in the drug program that prisons used to offer; there, I learned a self-control that made my life easier from then on.

"For all of this, I have evidence. Over the course of thirty-three years, I have proved that it is possible to come back from a bad decision. I have pulled myself out of the bad decisions I made as a teenager. By my actions, my behavior, the way I have lived, I have demonstrated that while I cannot undo my earlier mistakes, I can overcome them."

The former sheriff grows angrier and angrier; he appears ready to explode. Then it's over, I am dismissed by the parole board; my hearing is over, and I return to my unit.

Chapter 46

"State Parole Board Didn't Consider Susan LeFevre Truthful, Says Spokesman." That's the headline of an article that appears the next day in the *Detroit News*. Strickland, is the only person quoted in it. He says he personally attended my parole hearing, thus giving himself the authority to speak about it, and he goes on to claim that parole board members found a "discrepancy" in my account of my drug use in the 1970s. He claims there was "no doubt" that I was "minimizing my role in the 70s," that it was "100 percent clear" that I was "a high-level player in the drug trade" when I was 19. As if that tired old lie isn't enough, Strickland goes on to claim that in California, I committed fraud in assuming someone else's name and social security number.

The newspaper prints these allegations, the reporters acting like loyal stenographers instead of asking for facts. They never probe to find out, for example, whose identity I supposedly stole in California or what proof there was that I was a so-called kingpin at the age of 19. It is dispiriting that these lies just keep coming. All I can think of is the Big Lie theory advanced by Joseph Goebbels, propagandist of the Third Reich—that if you repeat a lie often enough, people eventually believe it.

I know that Strickland is peddling these lies to cronies on the parole board. I know that Towner is working against me. Later I will learn that my request for parole is almost automatically denied; as the warden will tell me, she learned on the day of my hearing that "LeFevre isn't going anywhere." But something happens, and the nearly done deal to keep me in prison is undone.

The intervening power that gets it undone—my personal *deus ex machina*—is the then-governor of Michigan, Jennifer Granholm. Whether inspired by common sense or politics or a sense of justice, or all of the above, the intervention by the governor's office, sanctioned by the governor herself, is aimed at influencing the parole board to release me. The opposition to my release—in the form of the powerful prison industry lobby—is fierce. Even with the intervention of the governor's office, Towner is able to cut a deal that postpones my release by four and a half months; the release will coincide with the closing of eight prisons around the state. The delay appeases the prison industry lobby. After all, a lot can happen in four and a half months.

My family and friends are ecstatic at the announcement of my projected release. I am of course also thrilled, but I am not ready to celebrate yet. As if to confirm my caution, Strickland, releases a statement to the press at the same time the parole board's decision is announced; saying I will be released only on condition I don't make any "more" trouble. Once again, he repeats the refrain that "it is clear" I am "one hundred percent guilty of having been a drug dealer in the 70s." So I will be released after four and a half months only if I follow the rules and don't get more tickets.

Despite his statement, I feel a wave of warmth wash through my body: finally, some good news. The door is opening, although I do not know how many landmines are in front of it. I have no illusions about the power of the prison industry—or about their willingness to indulge in brute force; I know that even with the governor and the judge behind me and the public on my side, the good ole' boys and their political allies are formidable foes. I am not going to let my heart celebrate yet.

I say as much to Alan, who is elated by the parole board decision, as is everyone working with us. I tell him it sounds good, but we still have to be careful. I try to impress upon him that it could go either way, and I wonder silently if the guards might step up efforts to harm me, and if this time their efforts might get me killed.

My husband isn't used to me being so skeptical. I had always been the eternal optimist. Had I been dealing with anything but the Michigan prison system I would have been jubilant that the nightmare would soon be behind me, but I just can't manage unqualified jubilation. Alan knows that I am the last person to be paranoid about anything, and while I want him to relax and feel confident, I have to tell him that we can't let our guard down yet.

"Strickland might be trying to buy time to see if things are different in a few months," I tell him. "He probably thinks he can get one of the guards to write up another trumped up ticket against me, and then he'll go to the media and say I'm causing trouble again.

But just as I feared, the other edge of the double-edged media sword now starts slicing away. Strickland and Duncan continue their PR campaign, issuing statement after statement that I am being released even though "it is certain" that I am "100 percent guilty of the original drug charge" against me. As they would know, inmates around me see me as getting preferential treatment, and they aren't happy about it.

The same guards routinely copy the articles quoting Strickland and Duncan and place them near the eating area that all prisoners pass every day. Many inmates are upset to read these articles, and I know they are going to be a threat to me. Those who have to remain in prison will have no sympathy for someone they think is getting out because of media coverage. More and more, I rue the fact that my attorney has not broadcast from day one that I was never guilty and should never have gone to prison in the first place.

Barney Duncan has vowed to do whatever it takes to keep me in prison. I fear the parole board's decision is yet another stalling tactic, the aim being to set me up for another violation so as to revoke my release date. How long can the governor stand up to the relentless drumbeat from the prison industry? I know I cannot exhale until I finally walk out the gates in four and a half months.

Still, a light has been turned on at the end of the tunnel, and I know how long the tunnel is. It changes life in prison.

I am determined to walk on eggshells for these next months more than ever. I ignore the taunts and threats from other inmates. There are many inmates I consider friends, despite my having been moved so frequently that developing relationships is difficult. Shortly after my release date is set, I meet one with whom I feel a particular rapport. Amy and I discuss social issues for hours on end. We're both especially concerned about the many women who are dumped out of prison after they have done their time. I mention casually my concerns about the rising tide of inmate threats against me. Amy is young, with a girlish face; she spends most of the day making greeting cards with rainbows and animal figures. She is also part Native American and as tall and strong-looking as a tree. One day as we are called to the chow unit, she says quietly, "I'll stick near you, and you just let me know who is giving you a hard time. I'll take care of them."

"No," I say, startled that she thought that was what I was suggesting. "I would never want you to do that."

I knew her intentions were good but it was a strange feeling that someone would make such an offer. I knew I had to remember where I was and be careful about what I said. "I believe its best to just ignore troublemakers and not give them any opportunity to do something," I tell her. "Any blow someone could deliver won't be as bad as allowing them to bring us down to their level by getting us to be aggressive."

When I talk to Alan later, I joke about Amy's earnest but misguided offer. "I'll be in a roving gang in here if I don't get out soon," I laugh. The events swirling around us are so strange we have to laugh; the situation is too absurd to take seriously all the time.

It has been a grinding hauntingly horrible experience for me but in many ways I think my family has taken it even harder. They have had support from friends and neighbors as well but not to the extent I have enjoyed. Alan was also raised in a culture where the details of personal life were well hidden. The media trucks parked at the end of our cul-de-sac and the reporters hanging on his every word are tough for him to deal with. I am worried about my husband and kids and the long term effect of this.

I deal with my own concerns by writing them down and mailing them daily to a particular supporter. I keep reminding myself that just as I could never let it leave my mind all those years that I was a fugitive, I now have to remember that I am in a prison, and things can become deadly violent at the drop of a hat.

All I want is to stay out of any kind of trouble and let the clock tick down.

But the threats against me grow every time another article is left out for the inmates. Most of the articles come from the *Saginaw News*, so I suspect that Haggard is bringing them in.

I ignore remarks thrown at me and step as lightly as I can away from fights. These are frequent, occurring several times a week and usually starting with one antagonist spitting at another. But one day in the library, it looks as though I will have no way to escape.

A particularly large group of inmates comprised of a pimp and her entourage try to set me up. The pimp is a large, mannish white woman with a short mullet haircut, the requisite neck tattoo, and a chin that juts out in front of her face. She is a shoplifter serving three years for stealing from a department store. In Michigan, shoplifting is called unarmed robbery, and offenders can serve many years for multiple offenses.

"So you think you're going home, eh, LeFevre?" she says in her artificially lowered voice. "We'll see about that. There's a whole lotta people in here for selling dope. They gotta stay. They say you was a kingpin in Saginaw. You don't seem like no kingpin to me." She pushes her chair toward me.

I put my papers down on the desk and try to ignore her.

"She hit me! LeFevre hit me!" one of the entourage says; it is loud enough for Doc, the librarian, to hear. Doc is a largish black man with, it is said, a master's degree in library science. He is also a decent person. He has been watching the whole thing and knows that the women are setting me up.

What if, instead of Doc, one of the fiendish guards had been on duty? Most of them would like to impress Strickland and the rest of the prison lobby in Lansing. I know I have to do something.

I call my husband. Alan contacts a few of our friends and supporters, who again make calls and write letters reporting the threats. I also write to the prison authorities. My husband and a couple of local attorneys call the governor's office and leave messages.

There is no response, but the activity has clearly done some good, because a few days later, I am summoned to the warden's office and she assures me that I am in a unit with "good" guards and the guards that are outside on the grounds or in the chow hall will not be allowed to write any more invalid tickets. She doesn't say it this bluntly, but it is evident that she is well aware that I was being targeted by the "bad" guards and that they were manufacturing violations against me.

Chapter 47

The night before I am to be released, a unit guard who has always been fair to me, comes into my room and comments that my children are beautiful as she studies their photographs hanging on a bulletin board behind the door.

"Your husband sounds like a good man," she adds. "He's probably a nerd like mine. They're the best kind I always tell the women. Not these fast talking wild kind a guys."

I appreciate her attempt to relax me with small talk on the eve of a day I've waited for more than a year and actually more than half my lifetime.

Angel, my roommate, is sleeping again, probably due to her medication. She's a nice girl and it bothers me that I can't leave her my television. One of the morning guards already warned me that she would check for the television in the unit after I leave and anyone caught with it would get a ticket. I've heard that left-behind televisions or typewriters are taken out and smashed with an axe. Most of the women aren't able to afford either one. They are $150 (on the outside it's only $50) and because inmates are usually paying off court costs and public defender fees that mandate anything in their account over $50 dollars gets confiscated by the state, they can never accumulate enough money for their own TV or typewriter or even correspondence courses. Angel's pay is seven cents an hour and she doesn't have anyone on the outside to help her. Her children are still in grade school. She'll stay in this concrete closet several more years for lighting her empty house on fire one night when she was angry at her husband. She will probably do it without a television.

I decide it's better to donate the television to a charity rather than let it get someone in trouble and then get the axe anyway. The prison has excuses as to why possessions can't be passed on to inmates, but I suspect that the company that makes the see-through televisions and typewriters is probably part of the lobbying force and someone in the prison system is likely benefiting by keeping the rules as they are. Sweet heart deals between contractors and government agencies appear rampant since there seems to be zero accountability.

Thirty years ago, inmates had easier access to unit typewriters than now. The few that are available in the library known within the prison as the gay bar, are mostly dominated by women who use the library as a place to sit with their wives. Finding an opportunity to utilize a typewriter is a hit and miss privilege. Generally it is easier to obtain drugs, sex, or tobacco, than it is to type a letter, take a class or attend a drug rehab course. Thus is life in the Department of Corrections.

The next morning, a guard opens my cell door and screams like a drill sergeant, "LeFevre, get out of your cell. Take your things! You're out of here."

These are the sweetest words I've ever heard. I pile my belongings, mostly books and about twenty-five pounds of letters and legal papers, onto a heavy flat bed cart and push it down the hallway. The clunky old-fashioned television nearly falls from the cart with the first bump. It's upsetting for the inmates left behind to see people leave so I try to do so quietly but to no avail. Many women come out to the hallway to say good bye.

The guard accompanies me to the administration building. Once we're there, they have no idea where to take me. Then someone points out the window to a building across the street. A guard I haven't seen before walks next to me as I push the cart over rugged gravel for about half a mile. The sun is getting uncomfortably hot and I am trying to do my best, but I must stop every few moments to pick up items that fall off the cart, especially the obsolete television. I don't mind the trivial inconveniences; I just can't shake the fear that something will happen and I will have to turn around. While I am jubilant to be leaving, I won't feel secure until I am on the plane flying west.

We reach the second building. As soon as we enter I recognize the room as the same one in which I'd been months ago in a fog of weariness from the bus trip in disbelief that I was back in Michigan. I'd waited next to a long hallway lit like an operating room that extended out to a public waiting area. Such a short distance I'd thought at the time, only a few steps from here to the free world. Just a hallway and a security checkpoint like a metal detector at an airport, and then a world without razor wire, sadistic guards, and wormy food.   Back then the hallway's brightness had seemed like a portal to wonderland and it still does. This time I'll be able to walk through it to the other end.

Haggard has made the effort to appear and gives me a look as if to say, "It was nothing personal. We thought you would be here for awhile and we could get away with terrorizing you. We didn't anticipate you'd actually get released this soon. It's all in the past, right?"

I think, no, it's not in the past. You and some of your co-workers should never have been allowed to torment vulnerable women for so long. I am going to write a book and tell anyone who will listen about what I've experienced and what I've learned. They should know how destructively their money is being spent. If no one is willing to do anything, then so be it, but I will do my part.

I turn from Haggard and Alan is the first person I see. He looks handsome but I can't miss the pain in his eyes. A smile comes to his lips as I embrace him. His skin is warm and the coolness of his leather jacket brushes against me. The touch of him, the familiarity of his smell, it all feels so euphoric. I don't want to let go.

When I do look up, I see that the room is filled with familiar beaming faces. Just the sight of people in multi-colored and textured clothing is strange and welcoming, but more precious is that they are people who I know well, who support me, who I trust. This is the moment I have waited for the last thirty years. This is my return to a normal life, a membership that has evaded me for so long.

My sisters, Kathy and Barbara, pull me into their arms. My brother Dave hugs me as I am hugging them all. Kathy and Jerry Morse begin to hug them and within moments everyone is hugging everyone else. Some of us cry and a few of us laugh. Everyone here has worked hard the past year not knowing if this moment would ever happen. I look around to see a sea of radiant faces and smiles. The moment is magical.

A guard hands me a suitcase that she has just finished inspecting. Alan brought it with him from home. I rush to the restroom, eager to get out of the course blue prison pants and shirt once and for all. The bathroom has a double sink and counter and I set the suitcase over one sink as I mill through, curious as to what they have selected. It occurs to me that I should have advised them but it was one of many details that I hadn't thought to cover. I needn't have worried. The jeans, top, jacket and undergarments they picked are fine. Happily I throw the prison underwear into the trash and kick the blue uniform towards the wall.

My reflection in the large wall mirror stops me for a moment. Just peering into a regular mirror is strange after a year with small aluminum mirrors. My jeans that had always been a tight fit are now loose and the top, one that Alan gave me, has a lace overlay and is in different shades of muted browns. I appear thinner than I want to be and my hair is in serious need of attention but all the same it is refreshing to see my image clearly and even more astounding to see myself as a free person. So many times I had fantasized about what it would be like to see my family and friends again, but I'd never anticipated the small pleasantries like how amazing it would feel to be back in street clothes. I find a pouch with makeup. The kids selected the right shades except for a lipstick that is way too dark for me. I'm still elated to put it on and I do so quickly so that I can get back out and see everyone.

When I rejoin family and friends in the lobby, I notice through the front window that a crowd of reporters and cameras are standing in a roped-off section of the parking lot about a hundred yards from the building. I desperately want to put this behind me and get back to my life and its normal problems of any married person with teenagers. I'm not much of a speaker, and I look drawn and exhausted but it's important to me to thank everyone who supported me through out this and I want to speak out about what a terrible place this is. I want to speak for those who can't speak for themselves about the corruption, the abuse, and the inescapable web.

I loop my arm in Alan's. There's too much going through my head. I want to soak in the love and wallow in the moment of reaching the freedom that lies just outside the door.

I take a moment while walking toward the exit and passing through the heavy double doors to perceive my surroundings in slow motion. The glistening sunlight feels nice and I know it is my imagination but the air smells sweeter.

Alan whispers: "It's over. It's finally over."

I speak briefly to reporters saying something about prisons making people slicker and sicker. I thank everyone who helped me by writing emails and letters and I run to the Morse's waiting car, and we pull out of the parking lot and put the razor wire compound behind us.

Once again as I am leaving a prison, helicopter blades beat loudly overhead, but this time it is very different. Kathy and I laugh and flash back on all the times earlier that we both cried along the way. We look back to see TV news vans following behind. I was surprised they would still follow us. I feel like I've joined the dubious ranks of Octomom or a busted celebrity drug user. I wonder if anyone will take what I said about the justice system seriously. Will my words be of any consequence or am I a mere spectacle because I've endured a bizarre twist of fate in my life?

I will hope for the best but at this moment I'm elated to be free, bolting down a highway surrounded by people I love and trust, heading toward my home and my children. Right now, this is all that matters.

Epilogue

When I return to California I'm officially a parolee and must see a parole officer weekly. Since I don't have a license my daughter, Katie, arranges her schedule in order to drive me. With the usual traffic the drive is more than an hour from our house and Katie waits in the parking lot. It is a waste of a day but I know I'm fortunate as most other parolees don't have cars at all and show up on foot, or come by bus or bicycle, or however they can manage.

On my first meeting, I find myself fighting back tears as I walk into my assigned agent's office. The agent quickly instructs me to return to the waiting room and she'll come out to get me again in fifteen minutes. She has more than 75 people to see that month and no time to get personal. I can understand her point. Visits are primarily to get urine samples to check for controlled substances and collect fees that are charged to parolees for the opportunity of being on parole. The pressure to pay fees is substantial despite the fact that most parolees are destitute.

On one visit I notice a large man in scruffy clothing who has been waiting nearly an hour. He approaches the glass window and is told he must come back again the next day since he arrived ten minutes late for his appointment. Tears well up in his eyes and he leaves the office, head hanging, and walks up the street. He's obviously very depressed. I question how he could possibly maintain a job and still make it in to give a urine sample regularly.

Giving a urine sample involves using the toilet and filling a container with urine while the agent stands in the doorway. People often walk by in the hallway and look in during the process. I think how I give my dog Bailey the respect of looking away when I take him to relieve himself.

For the most part I am doing well in my transition to a normal life. My friends remark that I seem unchanged. I'm able to joke around, sometimes even using the prison experience as new material and I talk easily about issues having nothing to do with prisons or the drug war. Then when I least expect it there are moments that I feel a deep sense of loss or sadness. I am suddenly haunted by abrupt remembrances of dark or sometimes touching moments at the prison. Smells or sounds, or sometimes nothing at all, flood my mind. I feel disoriented and unstable. Little things like deciding what to do, or what to wear, seem like monumental decisions. It's strange that I dealt with the pressures of prison life yet am befuddled by a new television remote or remembering how to unlatch my car's gas tank. I think many times, "How do women or even men who are leaving prison who don't have a family and home waiting for them deal with such an immense transition. Of course they don't and they return back to prison soon afterward as the statistics make clear.

I've been attending my appointments diligently until one month our entire family is sick. Even Alan misses half a day of work, the first time in twenty years. I'm feverish and can't get out of bed. I call my parole officer and leave a message asking her to call me back and let me know she received the message. When I don't hear back I call five more times.

I never hear from her and when I call the next month, visits are monthly now, again no answer. I finally reach her and she screams that she can put me back into prison for a year for missing my last appointment, and that I am put back on weekly visits. The old fear that my fate lies in the hands of a vengeful guard or official comes back and nearly immobilizes me. Will I ever be free of it?

The force that drives me onward is the memory of the inmates I've left behind. Many of them facing decades behind bars for a single infraction or bad choice they made as a young person. Hopefully I can help them in the same way so many people were helpful to me.

A TALE OF TWO LIVES

- The U.S. imprisons people at a rate 5 times higher than any other country in the world.

- State prison population in the US grew 708% from 1972 to 2008. By comparison, the previous five decades saw the population grow by a total of 105%*. Nixon's drug war began in 1971.

- Michigan taxpayers spend $2 billion a year on incarceration and have an incarceration rate 40% higher than its neighbors.

- Michigan is one of several states that spends more on prisons than on higher education.

- There are over 2.3 million persons incarcerated in the American prison and jail system at the current time at a cost to taxpayers of more than $52 billion a year.

* Pew Center Report on Prison Population

Visit our Website: www.susanlefevre.com

Disclaimer

The author has tried to recreate events, locales and conversations from her memories of them. In order to maintain their anonymity in some instances, the names of individuals, places and times have been changed. All statements made are solely the opinions of the author and every effort has been made to ensure that the information in this book was correct at press time.

Made in the USA
Lexington, KY
09 April 2011